READERS
Writing

READERS
Writing

Lessons for Responding to Narrative and Informational Text

ELIZABETH HALE

STENHOUSE PUBLISHERS
PORTLAND, MAINE

Stenhouse Publishers

www.stenhouse.com

Library of Congress Cataloging-in-Publication Data

Hale, Elizabeth, 1971-

  Readers writing : lessons for responding to narrative and informational text / Elizabeth Hale.

    pages cm

  ISBN 978-1-57110-843-2 (paperback) -- ISBN 978-1-62531-030-9 (ebook) 1. English language--Composition and exercises--Study and teaching (Elementary) 2. Language arts (Elementary) 3. Reading comprehension--Study and teaching (Elementary) 4. Exposition (Rhetoric)--Study and teaching (Elementary) I. Title.

LB1576.H2155 2014

  372.62'3--dc23

                                                                                2014017928

PRINTED ON 30% PCW
RECYCLED PAPER

Cover design and interior design by Blue Design, Portland, Maine (www.bluedes.com)

Manufactured in the United States of America

20 19 18 17 16 15 14   9 8 7 6 5 4 3 2 1

This book is dedicated to my parents,
Stanton and Sandra Hale,
and
to my twin sister,
Christine Hale Landino

Your infinite love and support
make me who I am

CONTENTS

Acknowledgments

My first thank-you goes out to my own elementary school, Windham Center School in Windham, Connecticut, whose teachers, classrooms, and library helped to grow my love of school and books. I particularly remember my second-, third-, and fourth-grade years thanks to Mrs. Yanis, Mrs. Matthews, and Mrs. McDermott. Only now do I appreciate all the work you did behind the scenes.

Thank you to George Davison and Meg Duchovny at the Grace Church School in New York City, who gave me my very first teaching job so many years ago. My experiences there cemented my decision to pursue education as a career. I also want to thank John Mathews. Unbeknownst to you, the day you joyfully shared "Antoine's Tulip" by one of your first graders at Grace Church School is what made me take a leap of faith and follow in your footsteps. Thank you also to Linda Dahl, who taught me so much about the intangibles of being a great teacher while at Grace.

Thank you to the professors at the Harvard Graduate School of Education, especially Pamela Mason, Kathy Boudett, Thomas Payzant, John Willett, Nonie Lesaux, and Paola Uccelli for your teaching and support during my doctoral journey. A very special thank-you to my advisor, Professor James Kim, for your support, guidance, and exemplary leadership. Your investment in your advisees' academic and personal growth has made all the difference in my HGSE experience. Thank you also to Helen Kingston and Lisa

Foster of the READS for Summer Learning program. I am grateful for all your advice and support, and it has been such a pleasure to learn from you.

I am grateful to the authors whose work about reading, writing, and teaching has created a foundation for my own learning, thinking, and writing: Isabel Beck, Linda Kucan, Margaret McKeown, Katie Wood Ray, Peter Johnston, Stephanie Harvey, Gay Su Pinnell, Patricia Scharer, and Tony Stead. I also can't imagine writing acknowledgments in which I don't thank Lucy Calkins. Being your student has had such a profound influence on my growth as a teacher and writer.

A big thank-you to my colleagues in Boston Public Schools whose thoughtful support and planning of reading and writing made this work possible, especially Cheryl Watson-Harris, Michelle Decerbo, Maria Cordon, Iris Escoto, Michelle Gulla, Pamela Pitts, Montala Kahn, and Ethan D'Abelmont-Burnes. Thank you also to my colleagues, past and present, in the education department at Emmanuel College for your valued and continued support: Annette Stavros, Sally Dias, Kimberly Sofronos, Diane Bissaro, Fiona McDonnell, and Sister Karen Hokanson.

Thank you to everyone at Stenhouse who contributed to this book becoming a reality. I am so grateful to be part of the Stenhouse family. In particular, thank you to my editor, Bill Varner, for your support and belief in my work from the very start. Thank you also to Terry Thompson. Your feedback was an invaluable contribution in the shaping of this book.

A warm thank-you to my friends Connie Jacquays, Jacquelyn Judge, and Dyan Smiley. Your circle of friendship has become an important part of my life and brings out the best in me, both professionally and personally.

Thank you to the entire Rozas family who are now my family too. In particular, thank you to Michael Rozas, Santiago Rozas, and Eva Dougherty, as well as my own mom, Sandy Hale, who helped with Dexter so I could write and never tired of my saying, "I think I'm almost done with the book."

Finally, thank you to my wonderful husband, Xavier Rozas, for supporting my passions, but mostly for keeping me balanced and making sure we always made time for family walks and coffee on the porch. You and baby Dexter are a dream come true.

CHAPTER 1:

Beyond the Book Report

This book starts out with a confession. When I was in third grade, my school had a reading incentive program called Book Bucks. For every book we read and book report we turned in, we would get a light green dollar bill (with a flying book in the middle instead of George Washington) that we could use every Friday to buy something from the classroom store: a pencil with a wispy top, a marker set, and even a Speak & Spell if you earned enough. Whoever got the most Book Bucks at the end of the month got to choose anything they wanted from the store. I had my eye on an art set with colored pencils, glitters pens, and markers, all in one bright purple box.

Mrs. Matthews recorded the number of Book Bucks everyone earned on a manila poster that hung on the closet door. Every time someone turned in a book report, Mrs. Matthews made a blue or black dollar sign next to their name with a pen. My row was one of the longest, about the same as my two best friends, Valerie Haddad and Michelle Brooks. All three of us loved to read, so reading all those books wasn't much work. Writing a book report, however, wasn't something any of us liked to do. But if that's what it took to get Book Bucks, so be it.

One morning I came into the classroom just as Mrs. Matthews was adding something to the Book Bucks poster. Three blue dollar signs had been added to Michelle's row. Three!? Now she was definitely ahead of me. But I really wanted that marker set. So later that night I took a chapter book off the shelf in my room, read the summary on the back cover, wrote a book report by changing the wording around and then turned it in the next day. One more quick Book Buck for me. I did feel a little guilty turning it in, but that subsided when Mrs. Matthews took out her pen and added a dollar sign next to my name.

Even in fourth and fifth grade, writing about reading usually took the form of a book report. We simply had to explain what happened in the book. This wasn't so much a reflection of my school but of the times. Everyone I know around my age had to write book reports in elementary school. No one was particularly fond of them. Retelling a plot is just not that interesting. Book reports might show that we read and somewhat understand a book (or, in my case, that we read the back of the book), but they don't do much to support our higher-order thinking. Writing about what we *think* about the events and characters in our books was never really an option.

Fortunately, times have changed. In recent years, educators have started to use writing as a vehicle for thinking and learning. Many classrooms now use reader's notebooks, which allow students to explore independently questions and ideas about what they read. This type of reflective writing has allowed written assignments to go beyond assessing literal comprehension to assessing and *developing* inferential comprehension.

One would think that, with this new freedom to write personal reactions, theories, and questions, the reader's notebooks in our classrooms would be full of different types of thinking unique to each student. But quite often, this is not the case. For some students, the direction to "write about your thinking" is enough. But for many students, this kind of direction is not a clear next step for what to do. So even with teachers modeling, talking, and guiding students to make theories, inferences, and connections in lessons and read-alouds, and colorful classroom posters reminding students that "Reading Is Thinking!" many students open their reader's notebooks and write what resembles the traditional book report. The very type of writing I found to be a chore.

One reason for the lack of transfer between whole-class lessons or activities and students' independent entries is that there is a large gap between what students do when they participate in guided instruction or discussions and what they do when they write independently. The skills students need to take part in whole-class and small-group reading lessons or to respond to teacher-generated prompts are just not the same skills they need when they write and think critically about the books they read *on their own*. If we expect students to write quality, independent entries in their reader's notebooks, then their instruction should target the skill of writing about reading.

The lessons presented in this book address this need, providing teachers and students with specific, concrete strategies for thinking critically about texts through writing. These strategies, grounded in language and in specific concepts, support different kinds of comprehension skills but are far more tangible. As a result, these strategy lessons are not only easy to teach but also easy for students of many different ability levels to understand, to do, to remember, and to use when writing independently. Strategy lessons are less about teaching students *about* comprehension strategies and more about teaching students specific ways to verbalize thinking in the context of writing.

Strategy Lessons

There are five main components to the strategy lessons presented in this book (Figure 1.1).

FIGURE 1.1

Components of a Strategy Lesson

NAME IT	Explicitly name the strategy you are teaching.
WHY DO IT?	Explain why this strategy supports thinking and writing about reading.
MODEL IT	The teacher demonstrates the strategy within a paragraph of writing. Students name where you used the strategy.
TRY IT	Students try out the strategy in a designated section of their reader's notebooks.
SHARE IT	Students share entries in pairs followed by a whole-class share.

This lesson format rests on the important idea that, if students are taught one small way of writing about reading, and then have time and space to practice this one small strategy, then they will be able to use it on their own in their independent entries, days after the lesson is over.

The Reader's Notebook

To support this dual emphasis of teaching students specific strategies for writing about reading and giving time for students to write independently, there are two main sections in my reader's notebooks (Figure 1.2).

FIGURE 1.2

Reader's Notebook Layout

Strategy Entries	Independent Entries

The first half of the notebook, called the "strategies" section, is where students try out each of the strategy lessons I teach. The second half of the notebook is for students' independent entries, where students write in response to their own independent reading books. The last few pages in the back of the notebook are for conference notes, where students keep track of strengths and next steps taught in their one-on-one conferences. There are also other sections teachers may want to add such as book logs or places to write book recommendations. During September, students create tabs for each section and decorate a cover, which can be covered with clear contact paper. Even for students in the upper elementary grades and middle school, a colorful cover that reflects each student's personality makes these notebooks more desirable.

Selecting Texts

For both narrative and informational strategy lessons, I use a book we are currently reading or one that has been read recently. These books create a shared context for when I model the strategy and for when students practice the strategy in their notebook. With narrative strategy lessons, for example, I use the same chapter book for many different lessons in a row. Using the same book for many lessons is a very intentional practice because it allows my modeling to match what I am asking students to do in their notebooks.

Using picture books that are "great for predicting" or "great for description" is a common practice and can offer important scaffolding for understanding and developing comprehension skills. But writing about reading well requires students to use a variety of comprehension skills *whether their books lend themselves to certain types of thinking or not.* We don't, for example, want our students to predict only with very suspenseful stories. And we don't want students to be adept at making personal connections only with books that have characters, stories, or settings that are similar to their own lives. In fact, I would argue that it is the subtler, less obvious connections that require and encourage more thoughtful and analytical thinking compared to the more obvious ones that lie at the surface level.

Narrative strategy lessons in this book use *Rules* by Cynthia Lord and the informational strategy lessons use *The Honey Makers* by Gail Gibbons. Although strategy lessons can be used with almost *any* book you use as a read-aloud, Appendixes A and B offer suggestions for narrative and informational read-alouds that work particularly well with strategy lessons. Each book suggestion includes a brief summary and a related chart that explains how that particular book supports each of the five categories of strategy lessons: questioning, connecting, analyzing, synthesizing, and evaluating.

Once in a while I do use a picture book in a strategy lesson, either because my read-aloud is not conducive to a particular strategy or because I am teaching a more advanced strategy and my students would benefit from more scaffolding and a more purposefully aligned text. In this case, I use a picture book students already know or I read the book out loud earlier in the day. Some of the more advanced strategy lessons in this book include suggestions for certain narrative or nonfiction picture books you can use and how you might use them during the lesson.

Differentiated Instruction

I usually teach these writing-about-reading strategies in whole-class lessons. Because strategy lessons are so doable, students at any ability level can be successful. The key is that strategy lessons teach students *one small way* they can bring thinking into their writing at a time. This ability to create conditions of academic success is important for all students, but especially for our students who struggle with reading or writing. As any teacher knows, success is an important aspect of learning because it can have a compounding effect in which engagement, self-perception, and learning reinforce one another (Pinnell and Scharer 2003). I have seen many students who previously disliked anything to do with reading, let alone writing about reading, become engaged in writing strategy entries once they understood they were capable of "doing the lesson." They actually *liked* taking out their reader's notebooks, and their relationship with reading comprehension turned from negative to positive.

Strategy lessons are also particularly beneficial for English language learners (ELLs), for both affective and academic reasons. Research on second-language learners indicates that, even when students are conversationally fluent, they lack academic vocabulary critical to accessing and expressing complex ideas and texts (Lesaux et al. 2010). Strategy lessons not only teach students specific words and phrases that can be used to access different kinds of higher-order thinking, but they do so in a meaningful context. In one lesson, students experience this "thinking language" in multiple ways: direct teaching, modeling, trying it out in writing, sharing it in speech, and finally listening to other students' writing. Through both writing and talking, all students actively process the language taught, which supports ownership of vocabulary taught for *all* students, not just those who raise their hands and want to be called on.

The reader's notebook also offers a place conducive to taking risks with language and where students' points of view are valued, two characteristics of learning that are critical for ELLs' confidence and academic investment (Cappellini 2005). For students whose English is extremely limited, the notebook can provide a context in which students can use both their native language and target language to express critical thinking (Ortiz-Marrero and Sumaryono 2010).

Although the lessons in this book were written for students in the upper elementary and middle school grades, they can also be used for high school students who need support with reading comprehension. Older students in remedial reading often receive ample support in decoding and fluency skills but less support in how to think and write about texts. This over-support in the mechanics of reading is particularly true of adolescent language-minority learners who, despite having a wide range of potential difficulties that could be contributing to reading difficulty, are often seen as one subgroup, all with the same needs (Lesaux and Kieffer 2010). Strategy lessons can offer stepping-stones for thinking about texts and create critical experiences of capability and, even if in small ways, academic success. In addition, because strategy lessons in this book are presented in a developmental order, from the most basic to the more advanced, high school teachers can tailor even whole-class instruction to show students specific, but more complex, ways to write about reading.

While strategy lessons are attainable for below-grade-level students, they are also satisfying, engaging, and beneficial for students who are proficient or advanced in reading, critical thinking, or writing. The strategy entries that students write during the lesson are unique to each student's thinking, experience, and potential. All students practice using the same strategy or phrase, but each student is writing an entry at his or her own ability level. Strategy lessons are also meant to show students one specific way to add variety to the thinking they are already doing. So if a few students are already using the strategies or thinking language I teach, naming the strategy and helping them understand its benefits can help them use these words and phrases more purposefully and call on them strategically.

Connections to the Common Core

The content of this book shares many of the same goals as the Common Core State Standards (CCSS). Both acknowledge the importance of writing in students' ability to process and fully comprehend narrative and expository text. Both also emphasize the importance of investing time and energy in teaching reading comprehension and in supporting students' ability to independently read increasingly complex texts (National Governors Association Center for Best Practices 2010). Appendixes C and D include tables that illustrate which strategy lessons align with each of the ten Career Readiness Anchor Standards for Reading, one for literature and one for informational text. These tables can be used to support strategic lesson planning and curriculum design.

For teachers whose time is highly constricted because of a structured reading program, strategy lessons can be taught for a month or so in the fall, as an investment for the rest of the year, with an occasional follow-up lesson as needed. Although many reading programs require students to write about their reading, few actually *teach* students how to do this kind of writing well. Whatever your reading curriculum, the lessons in this book can help students reach this frequently given, but not often taught, expectation—to independently use writing as a way to think reflectively and critically.

Chapter 2 describes in detail how a strategy lesson looks in the classroom and how one particular lesson might sound. Chapter 3 includes many different strategy lessons that can be taught with narrative text. All lessons are categorized under five general comprehension skills: questioning, making connections, analyzing, synthesizing, and evaluating. The next two chapters focus on informational text. Chapter 4 discusses students' literal comprehension of nonfiction text and offers an instructional strategy called Expert Team reading, which scaffolds students' independent reading of informational texts to their potential. Chapter 5 presents strategy lessons that can be taught with nonfiction texts. These lessons fall under the same comprehension categories used in Chapter 3 and also include lessons that support visualizing, monitoring, and paragraph development.

Chapter 6 looks at the transition from teaching strategy lessons to supporting students as they begin to write independent entries in their reader's notebooks. Chapter 7 describes a process for noticing and identifying comprehension strategies within student writing, which supports effective lesson planning and conferring. Chapter 8 takes a closer look at conferring and shows teachers how the reader's notebook can be used as a powerful vehicle for teaching comprehension in a reading conference. Finally, Chapter 9 describes how homework assignments and notebook rubrics support the strategies students learn in class.

CHAPTER 2:

A Strategy Lesson

Olivia and Joseph, my niece and nephew, have a new favorite bedtime story. It used to be *Curious George*, and for a while it was *Madeline*. But now the most requested story is the one my dad tells about when he was a little boy and all his Halloween candy got stolen while trick-or-treating. The "big kids" from the neighborhood took his bag of candy, and all he got for the rest of the night was an apple, an orange, and a Tootsie Roll. I remember my sister and I loving this same story when we were little. I can recall vicariously experiencing the disappointment of getting an apple for trick-or-treating, especially after having just lost all your candy, as well as the comfort of having your mom put a warm washcloth on your tear-stained face.

The more my dad tells this story to Olivia and Joseph, the more questions and comments they have. One year, when my dad put them to bed after Thanksgiving dinner, he came downstairs smiling and told us their new comments. When he had gotten to the part about getting the apple from the nice lady, Joseph, who had just turned four, sat straight up in bed and exclaimed with wide eyes, "Maybe that's all she had!"

My family, especially my twin sister, loves this comment since it has so much to do with who Joseph is. Because of his naturally compassionate demeanor, he always thinks about situations from other people's perspectives. I also couldn't help but see its connection to the language of thinking and the strategy lessons I taught in my classroom. *Maybe* is one of my favorite words to teach because it is so strongly linked with inferential thinking.

Even at age four, it would be awkward for Joseph to use this word in conjunction with more factual statements such as "Maybe she gave you an apple" or "Maybe you were trick-or-treating." The word *maybe* implies you are making a guess based on the information that you have, in other words, inferring.

The Language of Thinking

Joseph's statement reflects the natural relationship between language and thinking. The thinking often comes first. In Joseph's case, he had an idea about the lady with the apple, and then used language, albeit only a split second later, to express his idea. Usually, our thoughts drive the language we choose, not the other way around. It makes sense then that, when it comes to teaching reading comprehension in schools, most instruction focuses on the first part of this relationship: the thinking.

The strategy lessons presented in this book, however, start with the flip side of the thinking–language relationship. Rather than teach students about the different comprehension strategies, and then hope for language that reflects that thinking in their reader's notebooks, most strategy lessons use particular words and phrases called "sentence stems" that, when used orally or in writing, spark different types of thinking. One strategy lesson, for example, shows students how they can use the word *maybe* after they ask a wonder question. This one word, once written or spoken, naturally encourages students to think inferentially and to theorize. Not all strategy lessons have a sentence stem but they all show students one small, specific way to write about reading.

One of the biggest benefits of teaching strategy lessons is that they give students something concrete to hold on to and are grounded in everyday language. Although using phrases such as "I made an inference when . . ." is certainly a step in the right direction, it is also possible to use these comprehension buzzwords on a surface level without developing any deeper thinking (Buckner 2009). By taking advantage of the more tangible aspect of language and "teaching small," we can support not just students' thinking but also their ownership and independence in using these strategies long after the lesson is over.

Figure 2.1 illustrates the components of a strategy lesson along with general time frames for each component. The rest of the chapter explains each step of a strategy lesson in more detail. Each of the ninety-one lessons in this book includes a description of how each component might sound for that particular strategy.

FIGURE 2.1

Breakdown of a Strategy Lesson

NAME IT	Name the strategy you are teaching and any related sentence stems.	Begin by making a connection to students' ongoing work. Are you introducing a strategy in response to observations of their work? Are you sharing a strategy a classmate displayed? Are your students simply ready to learn a new way of writing about reading?	1 minute
WHY DO IT?	Explain why this lesson supports thinking and writing about reading.	"The why" can be explained by you or you can use a turn and talk to have students think about "the why" first.	2–3 minutes
MODEL IT	Demonstrate the strategy within a paragraph of writing that relates to the current read-aloud.	Ideally this is "live writing" done in real time on a document camera or overhead. A prewritten paragraph on chart paper can also be used if needed.	5 minutes
	Students notice where in your model writing you used the strategy.	Give all students about 15 seconds to turn and talk about where you used the strategy. Then have a brief, whole-class share in which one student offers an answer.	1 minute
TRY IT	Students turn and talk about the strategy they are learning.	Give a prompt that gets students to process the purpose of the lesson, by either naming the strategy they are learning or why this strategy is good for writing about reading.	1 minute
	Students try out the strategy in their reader's notebooks.	Students write the name of the strategy at the top of a page in the strategy section of their reader's notebooks. Give students a prompt related to the read-aloud.	10 minutes
SHARE IT	Students share their entries with a partner followed by a whole-class share.	In pairs, students read their entries to one another.	5–7 minutes
		In the whole-class share, two students share their entries out loud and classmates comment on where they used the strategy.	5 minutes

Like most lesson frameworks, this structure is flexible and can be modified or adapted to best fit the needs of the teacher, the age of students, or a particular lesson.

The rest of this chapter describes one lesson in detail to demonstrate what a strategy lesson looks like. This lesson, called "Writing About Your Thinking" is often one of the first that I teach and introduces students to using the phrase *I think*. This two-word phrase is clearly a very basic one. As simple as it is, this phrase represents the main purpose for reader's notebooks. We don't want students to write us book reports. We want students to use writing to explore and share their thinking. Similar to the "sparking effect" of the word *maybe*, the phrase *I think* gets students to infer because this language is tied to that type of thinking. It would be unnatural or at least awkward to use the words *I think* and then explain a fact in a book, such as "I think Catherine has a brother named David."

This emphasis on writing about thinking, a common expectation for reader's notebooks, is not meant to indicate that any summarizing is undesirable. Explaining a part of the book can provide a context for students' thinking. Writing a few sentences summarizing what they read that day, especially when students first start an entry, can also be a bridge between the blank page and writing that relates to higher-order thinking. There may also be more summarizing when writing about nonfiction text, as will be described in later chapters. Regardless of genre, strategy lessons show students how to use summarizing as a starting point rather than relying on it to fill up pages.

Name It

At the beginning of a typical strategy lesson, I name the strategy I am teaching and any related sentence stems—words or phrases students can use to generate this particular type of higher-order thinking. I also explain why I am teaching this particular strategy, which often has to do with what I have been noticing in their independent entries. Sometimes I want to share a great writing-about-reading strategy I noticed in a student's notebook entry (with his or her permission). Other times I tell students they are ready to learn a new strategy that will elevate their current thinking and writing about books.

For this lesson, I write the phrase "I think" on the document camera (with the light off so students can't yet see it) and then connect what I have been seeing in students' entries with the day's lesson.

> *Everybody's notebooks look so terrific, I'm excited that it's finally time to use them. Today, we're going to have our first strategy lesson. We've already talked about the purpose for these notebooks— they are for sharing your thinking about your books. Soon you will be writing independent entries and making your own decisions about what to write. But first we are going to have a few weeks of just strategy lessons where I will show you some ways to write about reading. Today, I am going to share with you one phrase you can use to help you bring thinking into your writing. It's pretty easy. Are you ready? Okay, it's using the phrase . . . [I turn on the document camera.] "I think."*

Why Do It?

Once I have named the strategy, I explain why I am teaching it. In all mini-lessons, I explain "the why," in both writing workshop and writing about reading, because writing well depends on student ownership. Beyond grammar and punctuation rules, not much about a student's writing can be "correct" or "incorrect" as with a math problem. Rather, the quality of writing is largely based on the choices students make as they write.

In *Crafting Writers* (Hale 2008), I use the example of my car to describe how "the why" affects learning. My sister Chrissy used to tell me to never let my gas tank fall below one-quarter of a tank in the winter. I was sure she was right, but I never wanted to pull into a gas station and pay money when I still had plenty of gas left. Then I took a car mechanics class and learned *why* she advised this: The rise and fall of temperatures in the winter can cause water vapor to freeze, which is not good for your gas tank. After that class, I stopped for gas whenever my tank reached a quarter tank (maybe a little less) because the relationship that influenced my decisions was no longer about me and my sister: it was about me and my car. Giving students "the why" in a lesson supports ownership because it shifts the emphasis from the teacher–student relationship to the relationship between my students and their writing.

> *"I think" is a great phrase to use when you are writing about reading because it helps you move beyond explaining what happened in the book. It's okay to talk about what happened in the book sometimes, but not your whole entry. Starting a sentence with the phrase "I think" gets you to offer your own ideas and interpretations about the book. And it's a very general phrase, which means it can lead to lots of different types of thinking. So if you think you are writing too many sentences about what happened in your book you can use "I think" to get you back to what you are thinking about your book.*

There are two ways to teach "the why." The first is through direct instruction, which is illustrated in the previous example. You simply tell the students why this strategy benefits thinking or writing about reading. Each of the lessons in Chapters 3 and 5 suggests how you might articulate "the why" for that particular strategy. The second way to teach "the why" is to have students think about it first. In this case, after I name the strategy, I would ask my students, "So why might *I think* be a good phrase to use in your reader's notebook entries?" Students then talk in pairs for about thirty seconds followed by a quick share and additional explanations from me as needed. I do not necessarily expect students to always have the right answer. If I have students discuss "the why" first, rather than just explain it myself, it is because I value the thinking my question generates.

Model It

Next, I model using the strategy in my own writing. I write the name of the strategy I am teaching at the top of the document camera (or overhead), if I haven't already. Then,

I write a paragraph, usually about five or six sentences long, about a particular part or character from our current read-aloud that reflects the strategy I am teaching at some point. If there is a sentence stem I've taught, then I make a point to use it once, sometimes twice, in my writing. The model writing for the lesson *I think*, illustrated in Figure 2.2, is about the chapter book *Rules* by Cynthia Lord.

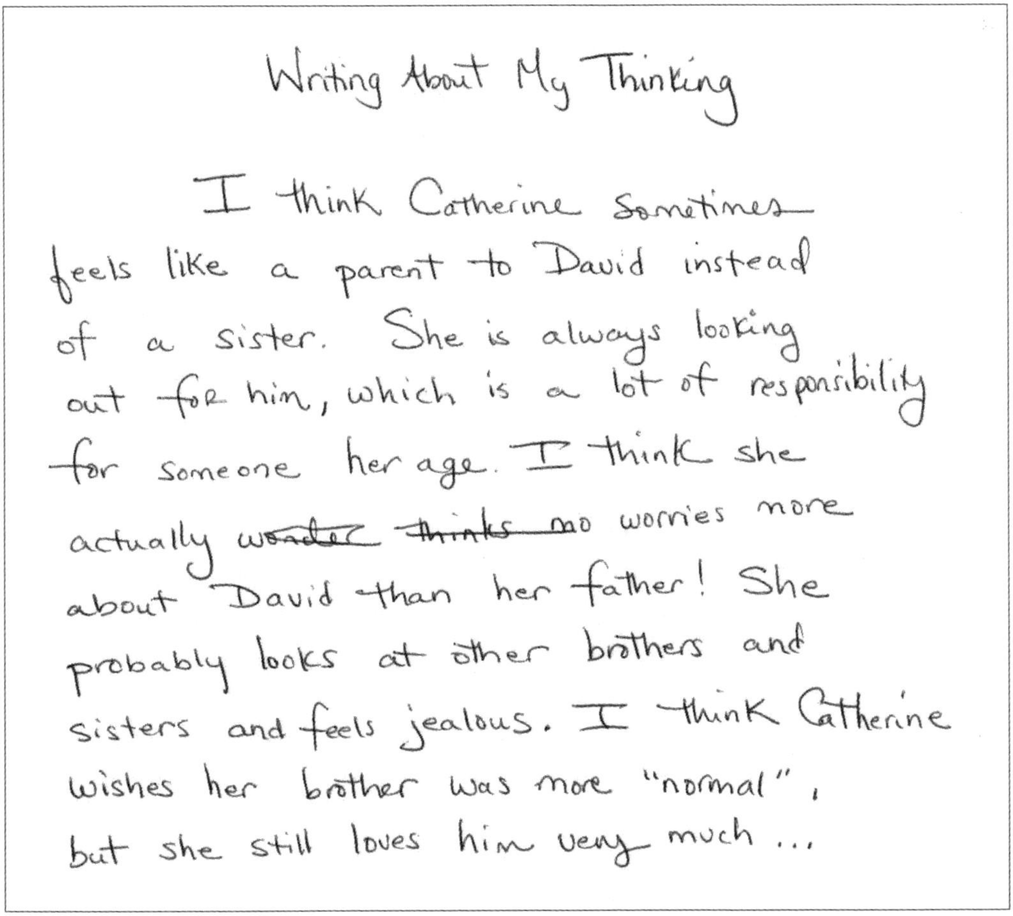

Writing About My Thinking

I think Catherine sometimes feels like a parent to David instead of a sister. She is always looking out for him, which is a lot of responsibility for someone her age. I think she actually ~~wonders~~ ~~thinks~~ worries more about David than her father! She probably looks at other brothers and sisters and feels jealous. I think Catherine wishes her brother was more "normal", but she still loves him very much ...

FIGURE 2.2
Example of Model Writing

One of the most important characteristics of these strategy lessons is that modeling is not composed of a single sentence but a paragraph of writing in which the language or concept I am teaching is *embedded*. The main purpose for writing this way is that it more closely mimics what we want our students to do. We don't ask students to write single sentences in their notebooks, with each one reflecting a different strategy. We encourage them to write developed thoughts that take many sentences to explore. And like our students' writing, model writing is not about writing "an amazing paragraph of thinking." It is about using a certain strategy within a bunch of regular sentences. Some sentences might show related types of thinking, but the focus is on the particular strategy.

While it is certainly possible to prepare this model writing ahead of time, I prefer "live writing" (Hale 2008), in which you think out loud as you write. As Stephanie Harvey and Anne Goudvis point out in their book *Strategies That Work* (2007, 20), "Much of our responsibility when teaching reading is to make what is implicit, explicit." This statement typically applies to think-alouds done during a read-aloud, but the same idea of making thinking transparent can be applied to writing. I want my students to see, not only *what* I write but also the thinking process behind that writing.

One way to help make the thinking process of writing transparent (even if you know exactly what you are going to write) is to pause every now and then and say "Hmmm," or share internal dialogue by asking yourself, "Why *do* I think Catherine is a shy person?" These small gestures demonstrate a kind of stop-and-go thinking, which reinforces that writing does not come out as fluently as it appears on paper (Hale 2008). More important, it shows that bringing thinking into writing takes effort on the part of the reader.

STUDENTS IDENTIFY THE STRATEGY

After I finish my model entry, I read what I wrote out loud in its entirety and then ask my students to identify where I used the strategy. In this case, I simply say, "Turn to someone next to you and tell them where I used the words *I think*." Clearly, this is not a difficult task, especially for this lesson in which the words are so obvious. I include this expectation every time for two reasons. First, it supports active engagement as I am modeling and holds students accountable for processing the lesson. Second, establishing this habit when the strategy is easy to spot creates a foundation for later strategy lessons that are not grounded in specific language. The strategy lesson "analyzing the relationship between two characters," for example, does not have a sentence stem, so no exact phrase is apparent when I am modeling. In this case, when the whole entry may reflect the strategy being taught, I would say, "Tell someone next to you how I used this strategy. What do I think about the relationship between Catherine and David?"

Using a turn and talk during this part of the lesson is crucial for engagement and accountability. I have learned not to rely on students nodding their heads in response to "Do you see where I used 'I think'?" or "Does everyone understand?" These questions are somewhat meaningless because the response is usually a reflexive head nod. In addition, checking for understanding this way does not support learning because no processing is needed. A turn and talk, however, supports understanding what I am teaching because using speech to express an idea is more cognitively demanding than listening (Cazden 2001). Students are more engaged when they play an active role in the lesson. This quick share also influences student engagement *during* the direct instruction part of the lesson: students are just more attentive when they know they will be soon be turning to a peer to express an idea.

Try It

Before students try out the strategy in their notebooks, I have one more turn and talk to support students' memory and understanding of the strategy I am teaching. I ask students to either name the strategy or explain why it benefits writing about reading. Which one I choose depends on the complexity of the strategy and the grade level of students.

For the "I think" lesson, I use one of the following prompts:

- *"Turn to the person next to you and tell him or her what words you can use to bring more thinking into your entries."*

- *"Turn to the person next to you and say why the strategy 'I think' can help you when you are writing independent entries."*

- *"Tell the person next to you why I am teaching the phrase 'I think.'"*

These turn and talks all support student ownership, just in slightly different ways. In the first example, I emphasize the actual language, that is, the sentence stem and its connection to a particular way of thinking. The second example has a stronger emphasis on making an explicit connection between this lesson and students' ability to call on this strategy when they are writing independent entries. The third example focuses more on students' understanding of how this lesson helps them as writers of reading.

Strategy Entries

The second part of the try-it makes a shift from students noticing the strategy in my writing to students trying it out themselves. One of my favorite quotations from *The Art of Teaching Reading* (Calkins 2000, 92) is "the fact that we, as teachers, say something has very little to do with whether our children learn it. Telling is not teaching." Instead of expecting (or hoping) that teaching leads to learning, we can set up structures in lessons that simply get students to process the lesson. Although the turn and talk is helpful in supporting active processing, having students try the strategy in writing creates an even stronger connection between my teaching and students' independent use of that strategy.

First, I ask students to turn to the strategy section of their notebooks and to write the name of the strategy or the sentence stem at the top of the next page. This small step reinforces that they are not just writing an entry about the read-aloud but also learning a particular strategy they can use on their own.

> *All right, everyone turn to the strategies section of your notebook. At the top, write the date and the words "I think."*

I wait about twenty or thirty seconds until everyone is looking up and ready. Then, I give directions for their strategy entry so they know (1) which part of the read-aloud to write about and (2) how many minutes they will have to write.

> *For the next five or six minutes, write about the chapter in* Rules *that we read yesterday when Catherine went to Jason's birthday party. And try to use the words "I think" at least once or twice. Ready? Go ahead.*

As with the model entry, students write a paragraph in which they use the strategy once or twice within a paragraph of writing. If I were to write one sentence that starts with "I think" and then ask students to try it out, most, if not all of them, would probably be successful. Although this kind of modeling can provide scaffolding, if needed, it is an "I do, you do" structure that does not take as much active thinking on the learner's part. When students have to use the strategy within "regular writing," it more closely mimics how they might incorporate that strategy in an independent entry.

Notice that, although I direct students to a particular part of the book, there is a difference between this direction and a typical prompt in which students respond to a teacher-generated question or statement. The try-it prompt guides students to a particular part of the read-aloud or to a certain character conducive for using the strategy being taught. Students may be writing about the same part of the book but they are independent in when they use "I think" and in what context. Giving students the responsibility to decide when and how to use the strategy increases the likelihood they will use it on their own because it is further along the gradual release of responsibility (Pearson and Gallagher 1983). With the strategy lesson "analyze a relationship between two characters," for example, I might scaffold students' entries by designating which two characters they should write about. However, each student decides what they think about the characters and their relationship, what aspects of the relationship to describe, and how they explain their thinking.

Once students begin writing, I walk around to look at their strategy entries, giving quiet comments of positive reinforcement and an occasional nudge if a student has written a lot but not yet tried the strategy. I am also on the lookout for which two students I will invite to read their entries for the whole-class share. Determining who will read their entries out loud ahead of time keeps the lesson running smoothly, but it also allows me to choose which entries other students hear. Strategy entries, unlike independent entries, are part of instruction, and entries read out loud need to reflect the lesson taught. I do use a checklist to keep track of who has not been chosen recently, but the only requirement is that students use the strategy that was taught. However, because students at many different ability levels are able to successfully write a strategy entry, I never rely on my top readers and writers. Figures 2.3–2.6 illustrate how the "I think" strategy can be tried out successfully by students of different ability levels.

Keep in mind that strategy entries are meant to be shorter than independent entries. Trying out a strategy within a paragraph of writing does not usually take more than five or eight minutes, depending on the age of students and the complexity of the strategy. If students write for twenty minutes, just for the sake of a longer writing session, then the point and practice of the strategy lesson is diluted. Once we move into independent entries, expectations for volume and overall quality in using a variety of thinking strategies increase.

Share It

Once time is up, preceded by a one-minute, friendly warning, all students share their entry with a partner. A consistent expectation that every student shares what he or she wrote with someone improves students' attention and engagement *while* they are writing their strategy entry. If you know you will be sharing your writing, you are more likely to invest and engage in your work. In addition, how a peer uses the strategy reinforces the teaching of the strategy.

After three to five minutes of pair sharing, students close their notebooks and shift their seats to face the front of the class. The two students previously chosen come to the front of the room and read their entries out loud. The expectation for the rest of the class is to listen and to identify where or how the student used the strategy.

> *Great, who can tell me where Shauna used the phrase "I think"? What kinds of thinking did she have about her book? Shauna, go ahead and call on someone.*

Listening to how a strategy is applied helps students stay engaged, in an academic way, during the share. In addition, aurally identifying a strategy can strengthen attention to language differently than identifying a strategy in writing with my model entry.

FIGURES 2.3–2.6

Strategy Entries from "I Think" Lesson by Students of Different Ability Levels

I think that Catherine, at the time, is feeling sad, lonley and most of all empty. I think he is feeling empty because he wishes she had Mellissa back. I also think she is scared that Jason will hate her. I think that because she will accidently say that she has many problems and she is lonley. Jason will then feel

I think

I think that KATiN FiLS BAD thAt JASiN CAN't TOK OR WROK ONe SiDE OF KAFiN WORt to BE NORMURL ANd they URDUR SiDE WORS to SAY. I think that DAVine AND JASiN HAVe OveCant CANt DAVite CAN't JUMP AND JASiN CAN't JUMP.

I think...

That Tobias feels unable to love that easily. Marcus abused Tobias, and Evelyn left him alone with Marcus. I think that Tobias has strong hatred towards his father, who repeatedly hurt him, and told him how to live his life. I think that Tobias still loves his Mother, but is angry at her for leaving him with his worst nightmare, Marcus. Tobias is definently obsessive, anxious, and lonely, untill he meets Tris. Tris and Tobias fall deep into love, over time. Tobias's heart is softened up, after dating Tris. Tobias is a interesting, mysterious, and strong character. That is why I chose to write about him.

Writing about my Thinking

I think that Atticus wants to be a good example and teach his children, Scout and Jem, how to genuinly good people. I think he feels that it is important to teach his children that they are not better than anyone just because they have the last name Finch and that what really matters is how you act and treat people. I also think that Atticus sets examples for his children by defending Tom Robinson and actually trying to do a good job and win the case. I think that Atticus is a good single father who wants to do whats best by teaching his kids right from wrong.

Scheduling and Planning

I usually start teaching strategy lessons twice a week in October, primarily focusing on narrative texts. Once students have learned about five or six strategies, they can start writing independent entries, a transition described in Chapter 6. At that point, you might teach one strategy lesson a week, with students writing independent entries two days a week. There is no right way in terms of when to teach narrative versus informational strategy lessons. I prefer to teach informational strategy lessons from Chapter 5 during a concentrated nonfiction unit of study in January and February. For the rest of the year, students write independent entries about nonfiction as part of Expert Team reading, a small-group structure described in Chapter 4 that provides scaffolding for reading nonfiction.

This book is meant to be used as a planning tool for lessons. Most strategy lessons in this book align with the Common Core State Reading Anchor Standards (CCSS), as illustrated in Appendixes C and D, so you can use the charts found there as a guide if you need strategy lessons to support particular CCSS standards for your grade. You can also use the headings in Chapters 3 and 5, which reflect different comprehension skills, to guide your planning. If you know your students need more support synthesizing information when writing about nonfiction text, for example, you can go to that heading in Chapter 5 and then look at the different strategy lessons under "Synthesizing" to find one that best suits you and your students. The next chapter offers forty-eight strategy lessons to support writing and critical thinking about literature.

CHAPTER 3:

Lessons for Narrative Text

When I was twenty years old, my mom gave me a guitar for Christmas. With the help of a small manual that came taped to the guitar case, I learned a few basic chords over the next few weeks. A few months later, I could play two basic songs, which I played over and over. After that, I gave up. I loved the idea of playing guitar, but I was not so committed and passionate about it that I was willing to work through difficult chords on my own. If I was going to get better at playing guitar, I needed someone to teach me.

Enter Sam, my guitar teacher. He had this crazy mop of hair and the funkiest house you have ever seen, complete with a remote-control, life-sized plastic cow that slid out of a closet and mooed with the touch of button. Sam was also a good teacher. After watching me play the two songs I knew, he showed me how to play an F chord on his guitar and then had me try it. After several awkward tries, I could do it. Then, he had me practice moving from a C chord to an F chord, and we worked on a simple song that had the F chord in it. After a few nights of practice, I could play the F chord pretty naturally. With every new chord or technique Sam taught me, my independent skill set grew, and I slowly improved.

Writing, as with guitar playing, is a skill that requires a complex use of a multitude of skills at one time. When students write in their notebooks, they juggle everything from grammar, spelling, and sentence structure to recalling what they read, in addition to the effort it takes to think about your thinking! While inferring, predicting, and synthesizing about what you read are valid expectations for students, they are goals, not next steps in how to get there. Like my guitar lessons, each strategy lesson listed in this chapter offers students a concrete stepping-stone toward the more general expectation of "show thinking in your writing." Because there is a wide range of lessons, from basic to more complex, some lessons have more scaffolding than others. Teachers can, of course, modify scaffolding based on their own students' age and ability level.

Lessons are organized under the broader categories of questioning, making connections, analyzing, giving evidence, synthesizing, and evaluating. The main reason for organizing them this way is so that you can use this book as a planning tool based on your assessments of student writing. Within each category, lessons are presented in a somewhat developmental order so that you can choose lessons that match your students' ability level. A second-grade teacher, for example, may want to teach a more basic way of writing about personal connections, whereas a fourth-grade teacher, whose students have heard the "this book reminds me of . . ." for several years, can look further down the list for a more advanced way to write about connections. Middle school teachers may want to bypass connections altogether and start with lessons that support more advanced higher-order thinking, such as synthesizing and evaluating.

COMPREHENSION SKILL	NARRATIVE STRATEGY LESSONS	NONFICTION STRATEGY LESSONS
Questioning	pp. 23–26	pp. 77–80
Making Connections	pp. 27–33	pp. 81–87
Analyzing	pp. 35–46	pp. 88–91
Giving Evidence	pp. 47–49	pp. 92–94
Synthesizing	pp. 50–54	pp. 95–100
Evaluating	pp. 57–63	pp. 102–108

A second purpose of this chapter is to help teachers become more aware of the variety of "thinking language" that can exist in writing. Knowing and being able to recognize a range of specific ways to show thinking in writing has important implications for one-on-one comprehension conferences, discussed further in Chapters 7 and 8, and for looking at student work when planning lessons.

Lesson Vocabulary

Before teaching a strategy lesson it is important to consider whether you need to review or teach vocabulary that is part of the strategy. For example, when I teach the lesson "analyze a character," my students and I discuss what it means to *analyze* something.

Before I teach the lesson "questioning a character's motive," we spend a few minutes talking about the word *motive*.

Often, I use word study strategies I learned from *Bringing Words to Life* (Beck, McKeown, and Kucan 2002), which emphasizes starting with students' previous knowledge about words. Rather than give my students a definition, students talk about what they think a word means or the contexts in which they have heard that word. For example, when my class discussed the word *analyze*, none of my students could propose an exact definition. However, Kiera said she heard the word associated with test scores, and Shelbbie said she had heard it used in a *CSI* episode when a woman was looking at evidence. After discussing the word *analyze* used in these contexts, we came up with this basic definition related to characters: "to look at a character from different angles."

Components of a Strategy Lesson

Each strategy lesson is broken down into the different components, described in Chapter 2: Name It, Why Do It?, Model It, Try It, and Share It. Some lessons include one or several sentence stems, while others are not anchored by particular language. If there is more than one sentence stem listed, teachers can choose one or use both of them to teach and model in the lesson. A small number of lessons follow with actual strategy entries, which are written by students in a variety of grades, from third to eighth.

All of the examples of model writing in this chapter relate to the chapter book *Rules* by Cynthia Lord, which highlights that strategy lessons are not typically aligned with certain books. The same book can be used to teach many different strategies. I encourage you to read *Rules* (a great book!) to your students so you can use the examples provided in this chapter. Then, once you are comfortable with the structure and practice of strategy lessons, you can model strategies in the context of your other read-alouds. Appendix A also offers suggestions of other read-alouds, both picture books and chapter books, and illustrates how they align with different types of comprehension skills. Many of the lessons in this chapter can also be used with certain types of nonfiction, such as biography and historical narrative, because they have strong story and character elements.

Questioning

Asking questions is a key pathway to higher-order thinking. But the kinds of questions we ask or that students ask themselves when writing greatly dictate the quality of thinking that follows (Duke and Pearson 2002). Sometimes students write questions that are not very thought provoking, such as "Why does she like ice cream so much?" or "Why do they live in a yellow house?" Some students do write interesting or thoughtful questions but then never explore them. Perhaps they think they have "done their questioning" and so move on to another idea. Although including any type of question in writing can be a first step, we don't want students, especially those beyond the primary grades, to think that listing questions is the goal. The benefit of asking questions when writing about reading is not about the questions themselves but the thinking questions generate.

The following lessons show students different types of questions that lead to different kinds of thinking. Although the questions are the focus of these lessons, I still model them within a paragraph of writing to reinforce the idea that questions should lead to thinking. One helpful point to emphasize is that asking good questions sometimes takes effort. "I don't wonder anything" is a valid comment, but students often say this without even trying to wonder. It's as though they are saying, "Nope, no wonder question came barreling over me as I read." While we can do our best to offer students books that match their level and interest so that authentic questioning is more likely to occur, I also set an expectation that, if questions are not just coming to you, then try to wonder!

WONDER QUESTIONS

NAME IT	Writing questions about what you wonder.
	Sentence stem: *I wonder why . . .*
WHY DO IT?	Writing about what you wonder helps you reflect about what you read and can lead to inferential thinking.
MODEL IT	*I wonder why Catherine's dad never gets angry with David? He certainly does a lot of things he is not supposed to do. I know David is autistic and so he has a hard time understanding what he should do. But you would think his dad would still get frustrated sometimes . . .*
	Ask students where you used a wonder question and what you were wondering about Catherine's dad.
TRY IT	**Turn and talk:** Have students tell a partner why it's good to wonder when you read, followed by a brief, whole-class share.
	Strategy entry: Students open the strategy section of their reader's notebooks and write "Asking Wonder Questions" at the top of the next blank page. Ask them to write for a few minutes about the most recent chapter of the read-aloud and try to ask at least one wonder question.
SHARE IT	All students share their entry with a partner. Then two students, previously chosen, read their entries to the class. Classmates comment on where they used the strategy taught.

PREDICTION QUESTIONS

NAME IT	Asking questions about what might happen in the story. **Sentence stem:** *I wonder if . . .*
WHY DO IT?	Asking a predication question helps you synthesize what you already know about the story and characters. These kinds of questions also increase your curiosity about the next part of the story.
MODEL IT	*So now Catherine has to decide whether she will actually ask Jason to the dance. I wonder if she is actually going to ask him? I'll bet she decides she will and then at the last minute backs out. I mean, she cares so much about what other people think . . .* Ask students where you used a prediction question and what you were wondering.
TRY IT	**Turn and talk:** Have students tell a partner what words you can use when you are predicting, followed by a brief, whole-class share. **Strategy entry:** Students open the strategy section of their reader's notebooks and write "Prediction Questions" at the top of the next blank page. Ask them to write about the most recent chapter of the read-aloud and ask at least one prediction question using the words *I wonder if.*
SHARE IT	All students share their entry with a partner. Then two students, previously chosen, read their entry to the class. Classmates comment on where they used the strategy taught.

WONDERING WITHOUT QUESTIONS

NAME IT	Writing about what you wonder (or what confuses you) in other ways besides starting with a question. **Sentence stems:** *I can't figure out why . . . ; One thing I don't get is . . .*
WHY DO IT?	Writing a question as a statement helps you write with more variety: having more choices of how to write about your wondering leads to different types of thinking and different rhythms of words.
MODEL IT	*I can't figure out why Catherine's dad wouldn't just come on time if it makes David so upset. Every single time their dad is just a minute late he freaks out! It's possible that their father keeps meaning to be on time but just runs late. Or maybe he thinks he'd be giving into his son's demands if he made sure he was exactly on time . . .* Ask students what you were wondering even though you didn't ask a question.
TRY IT	**Turn and talk:** Have students tell a partner what two sentence stems you can use to wonder besides writing *I wonder why*, followed by a brief, whole-class share. **Strategy entry:** Students open the strategy section of their reader's notebooks and write "Wondering Without Questions" at the top of the next blank page. Ask them to write about the most recent chapter of the read-aloud and see whether they can write about something they wonder without actually writing a question. Remind students they can use the sentence stems *I can't figure out why . . .* or *One thing I don't get is . . .* if they want.
SHARE IT	All students share their entry with a partner. Then two students, previously chosen, read their entry to the class. Classmates comment on where each student used the strategy taught.

SMALL QUESTIONS

NAME IT	Asking a question about a detail of the story.
WHY DO IT?	Asking different "sizes" of questions leads to different types of thinking about your book. Small questions make you think about the details of a story, which can sometimes stand for larger ideas.
MODEL IT	*I love how Catherine made a card for Jason that says, "stinks a big one!" He seemed to have fun using it right in front of the annoying lady at the office. I wonder if she'll make any more cards like that. I'll bet after only having such boring cards to use it feels good to be able to express negative feelings . . .* Ask students where you asked a small question and what it was about.
TRY IT	**Turn and talk:** Have students tell a partner what it means to ask a "small question," followed by a brief, whole-class share. **Strategy entry:** Students open the strategy section of their reader's notebooks and write "Asking Small Questions" at the top of the next blank page. Ask them to write about the most recent chapter of the read-aloud and try to ask at least one small question. For more scaffolding, have students think of and write down several "small questions" about the read-aloud in their notebook. Students can share their ideas in small groups followed by a whole-class share. Then students write a strategy entry about one of the small questions that was suggested.
SHARE IT	All students share their entry with a partner. Then two students, previously chosen, read their entry to the class. Classmates comment on where each student used the strategy taught.

BIG QUESTIONS

NAME IT	Asking questions that run throughout the whole book and are not particular to any chapter.
WHY DO IT?	Large questions help you think about running themes in the story and are questions you can come back to as your understanding of characters develops.
MODEL IT	*I wonder if David ever thinks about how other people feel? He seems to be focused on himself and his own world. I know he can't help it, but you would think that when other people get upset it would somehow register. Maybe it will take a really big reaction from Catherine or from his dad for him to notice . . .* Ask students what you are wondering about and why it would be labeled a "big question."
TRY IT	**Turn and talk:** Have students tell a partner what it means to ask a "big question" when writing about reading, followed by a brief, whole-class share. **Strategy entry:** Students open the strategy section of their reader's notebooks and write "Asking Big Questions" at the top of the next blank page. Ask them to talk with a partner and to come up with an idea for another "big question" about the book. In a whole-class share, ask for three or four suggestions and write them on the board. Then have students choose one big question to write about in their notebook.
SHARE IT	All students share their entry with a partner. Then two students, previously chosen, read their entry to the class. Classmates comment on where each student used the strategy taught.

QUESTIONING A CHARACTER'S MOTIVE

NAME IT	Questioning the reasons behind a character's actions.
	Sentence stems: *I wonder why . . . ; Why would . . .*
WHY DO IT?	Wondering about a character's motive helps you consider the story from different characters' points of view and to think inferentially about what drives characters to act the way they do.
MODEL IT	*I can't believe Ryan did that thing with the gum. Why would Ryan be so mean to David? It's one thing to be a bully to a younger kid but it seems even worse because David thinks Ryan is his friend! Maybe Ryan gets picked on at school himself and so he picks on someone who is an easy target. It probably, in a warped way, makes him feel better or tougher . . .*
	Ask students where you questioned a character's motive and what you were wondering.
TRY IT	**Turn and talk:** Have students tell a partner what it means to question a character's motive, followed by a brief, whole-class share.
	Strategy entry: Students open the strategy section of their reader's notebooks and write "Questioning a Character's Motive" at the top of the next blank page. Choose a particular scene in the book and have students write about a certain character's motive. In *Rules*, for example, you might ask students to write about why Catherine would take Jason for a ride in the parking lot in his wheelchair even though she knew she wasn't supposed to. Remind students they can use the sentence stems *I wonder why . . .* or *Why would . . .* if they want.
SHARE IT	All students share their entry with a partner. Then two students, previously chosen, read their entry to the class. Classmates comment on where each student used the strategy taught.

Making Connections

The following lessons support students in making different kinds of connections, whether it is between two people, such as the reader and a character, two characters, or two works, such as a text and a movie. Although terms such as *text-to-self* and *text-to-text* can support initial understanding of these concepts, they can be somewhat limiting by the time students reach third grade. Teaching students to use more natural language when writing or talking about connections makes it easier for students to develop this kind of thinking because they are not expressing a thought in a prepackaged way and are more likely to develop their ideas rather than making a statement.

Making connections is not a skill explicitly discussed in the Common Core State Standards (CCSS) for reading since there is a primary focus on textual analysis. But reading is and always will be a personal act, so the connections we make with literature contribute greatly to more advanced processes of analyzing text (Calkins, Ehrenworth, and Lehman 2012). Fortunately, the CCSS indicate that schools and teachers know best how to reach stated goals, which acknowledges our professional understanding of the skills and strategies that lie *underneath* these larger goals. As teachers (and as readers), we know that connecting personally with the characters and story creates an important motivational and personal aspect to reading, which supports close and careful reading as well as a sense of caring about what we read. In addition, making connections between different books and visual media, such as movies, helps students to synthesize understanding based on multiple sources as well as prior knowledge.

One reason making connections may not be more explicitly mentioned in the CCSS is because teaching lessons about this comprehension skill have not always led to writing and talking that reflects higher-order thinking. Sometimes students tend to compare and contrast at a surface level and then move on to the next idea. The following lessons are designed to help students go beyond *observing* obvious connections that already exist between authors, the self, and characters, to encouraging thinking that *builds* connections between these entities.

PERSONAL CONNECTIONS

NAME IT	Comparing a situation or event from the story with something that happened in your life. **Sentence stem:** . . . *reminds me of* . . .
WHY DO IT?	Writing about connections between your life and your book helps you relate more closely to characters you are reading about.
MODEL IT	*Catherine and Kristi's time at the lake reminds me of the lake we swam in at camp. I remember how dark the water was and wishing I could see the bottom. My friend Leah swam to the bottom and came up with this mushy brown muck that smelled a little. She thought it was funny.* Ask students what connection you made between your life and the book.
TRY IT	**Turn and talk:** Have students tell a partner why it's good to make personal connections when you read or when you're writing about reading, followed by a brief, whole-class share. **Strategy entry:** Students open the strategy section of their reader's notebooks and write "Personal Connections" at the top of the next blank page. Ask them to write about the most recent chapter of the read-aloud and see whether they can make at least one personal connection between their life and something or someone in the book. Remind students they can use the sentence stem . . . *reminds me of* . . .
SHARE IT	All students share their entry with a partner. Then two students, previously chosen, read their entry to the class. Classmates comment on where each student used the strategy taught.

BACK TO THE BOOK

NAME IT	Bringing a personal connection back to the book you are reading.
WHY DO IT?	Sometimes a personal connection can turn into a memoir, or a book connection can become a retelling of that book. The purpose of reader's notebooks is to deepen thinking about literature, so you need to find your way back to the focus of this entry: the book.
MODEL IT	This strategy uses "before and after" modeling. You can show the "before" modeling first, before telling students what the lesson is about to see whether they can identify what is "not quite right" with this entry. **Before Modeling** *The way Catherine likes to draw reminds me of when I was that age. I used to love to line up the different colors of my pencils like she did. I loved how calm drawing made me feel too. My favorite thing to draw was flowers. I would draw flowers all the time. Sometimes I went outside and drew ones I saw and other times I just made them up. One time when I was drawing a flower . . .* Ask students to turn and talk about why this might not be the best entry for a reader's notebook followed by a brief, whole-class share. Then introduce the concept of "getting back to the book" when you are writing about a personal connection and why it is important. Erase this version and write another version, with the same first sentence, that connects back to the book: **After Modeling** *The way Catherine likes to draw reminds me of when I was that age. I used to love to line up the different colors of my pencils like she did. I loved how calm drawing made me feel too. My favorite thing to draw was flowers. Even though Catherine likes to draw different things than I did, she seems to get the same kind of peaceful feeling when she does it. Maybe it's her way of forgetting about things that are bothering her . . .* Ask students where you started to get back to the book after making a personal connection.
TRY IT	**Turn and talk:** Have students tell a partner why it's important to connect back to the book when writing about personal connections, followed by a brief, whole-class share. **Strategy entry:** Students open the strategy section of their reader's notebooks and write "Back to the Book" at the top of the next blank page. Ask them to write about the most recent chapter of the read-aloud and see whether they can write about a personal connection and then make a point to connect it back to the text.
SHARE IT	All students share their entry with a partner. Then two students, previously chosen, read their entry to the class. Classmates comment on where each student used the strategy taught.

FEELINGS CONNECTIONS

NAME IT	Making a personal connection that focuses on how a character is feeling.
WHY DO IT?	Gives more options for personal connections; creates more empathy with characters.
MODEL IT	*I totally understand how Catherine's dad is feeling. Wanting to have some quiet time with his garden reminds me of the times I come home after a really busy day and just need some quiet time to check my e-mail and read the news. It's like having that time to myself recharges my batteries . . .* Ask students what kind of feeling connection you made.
TRY IT	**Turn and talk:** Have students tell a partner why it can be good to make a personal connection to how a character feels, followed by a brief, whole-class share. **Strategy entry:** Students open the strategy section of their reader's notebooks and write "Feelings Connections." Ask them to think about the most recent chapter in the read-aloud and suggest how certain characters were feeling at different points and why. Write two or three suggestions, listing the character and the feeling, on the board. Then have students choose one character to write about and make a personal connection about that feeling.
SHARE IT	All students share their entry with a partner. Then two students, previously chosen, read their entry to the class. Classmates comment on where each student used the strategy taught.

SIMILAR AND DIFFERENT

NAME IT	Writing how a character or event in a book is similar to *and* different from your experience.
WHY DO IT?	Even though we might have similar experiences as characters, there are usually still differences. Thinking about both similarities and differences helps you better understand the complexity of personal experiences.
MODEL IT	*This part about the dance reminds me of my school dances from Kramer Middle School. Like Catherine, I was shy about going to any dance. It was less nerve-wracking to just not go at all. But unlike Catherine, I really did like to dance. So once I started dancing with my friends I was more relaxed . . .* Ask students to tell you where you talked about similarities with a character and where you talked about differences.
TRY IT	**Turn and talk:** Have students tell a partner why it's good to write about both similarities *and* differences when you are making personal connections, followed by a brief, whole-class share. **Strategy entry:** Students open the strategy section of their reader's notebooks and write "Similar and Different" at the top of the next blank page. Ask students to choose one character from the read-aloud and see whether they can write about how they are similar to and different from this person. Tell students they can compare themselves to a character in general or they can choose a specific event in the book.
SHARE IT	All students share their entry with a partner. Then two students, previously chosen, read their entry to the class. Classmates comment on where each student used the strategy taught.

CHARACTER DIFFERENCES

NAME IT	Writing about how characters are similar to *and* different from one another. **Sentence stem:** *The difference between them, however, is . . .*
WHY DO IT?	Thinking about how two characters are both similar and different gets you to analyze the details of people's personality and understand them better.
MODEL IT	*Jason and David both have disabilities, and I notice that they both get reactions from strangers. The difference between them, however, is that at first David might appear "normal" from a distance and then people are caught off guard when he is not. Because Jason's disability is so severe people notice right away. But then, kind of the opposite of David, as people get to know Jason and communicate with him, they see that he is more capable and "normal" than he first appears.* Ask students what you said was different about the two characters.
TRY IT	**Turn and talk:** Have students tell a partner why it can be good to think and write about differences when you are comparing two characters, followed by a brief, whole-class share. **Strategy entry:** Have students open the strategy section of their reader's notebooks and write "Character Differences" at the top of the next blank page. Then assign two characters for students to write about and have them try to write about how they are different in addition to how they are similar. With *Rules*, for example, you might have students compare Catherine with her friend Kristi. Remind students they can use the sentence stem *The difference between them, however, is . . .*
SHARE IT	All students share their entry with a partner. Then two students, previously chosen, read their entry to the class. Classmates comment on where each student used the strategy taught.

BOOK CONNECTIONS

NAME IT	Comparing a character or event in your book with one from another text. **Sentence stem:** *. . . reminds me of . . .*
WHY DO IT?	Thinking about the similarities and differences between books gives you perspective about the characters and events in your book.
MODEL IT	*Rules* reminds me of A Prayer for Owen Meany *by John Irving. Both have main characters with disabilities. And like Jason, Owen is also really smart. He doesn't have to use cards to talk, but he still gets reactions from people by the way that he looks . . .* Ask students what book connection you made.
TRY IT	**Turn and talk:** Have students tell a partner why it's good to make connections between different books, followed by a brief, whole-class share. **Strategy entry:** Students open the strategy section of their reader's notebooks and write "Book Connections" at the top of the next blank page. Ask students to write about any part or character from the read-aloud and see whether they make a connection to a previous read-aloud or a book they read independently. Remind students they can use *. . . reminds me of . . .* to start their connection. For more scaffolding, write a list of book titles that your class has read together as a read-aloud or shared text. Have students talk in pairs or small groups about any connection they can make between the current read-aloud and any of the other class texts. Then have students choose one book connection to write about in their notebooks.
SHARE IT	All students share their entry with a partner. Then two students, previously chosen, read their entry to the class. Classmates comment on where each student used the strategy taught.

MOVIE CONNECTIONS

NAME IT	Comparing a person or event in your story with a character or event in a movie (or television show). **Sentence stem:** . . . *reminds me of . . .*
WHY DO IT?	Thinking about the similarities and differences between a book and a movie or television show helps you make connections between different mediums and gives you perspective about the characters and events in your book.
MODEL IT	*Jason kind of reminds me of the main character in the movie* Mask. *The main character wasn't in a wheelchair but he did have a bone disease that made his head bigger and very different from other people. But any time he talked, he sounded like a normal person. And, just like Jason, he had a really good personality and sense of humor . . .* Ask students what movie connection you made with *Rules*.
TRY IT	**Turn and talk:** Have students tell a partner why movies and television shows, and not just books, can be good for making connections when writing about reading, followed by a brief, whole-class share. **Strategy entry:** Students open the strategy section of their reader's notebooks and write "Movie Connections" at the top of the next blank page. Ask them to write about any movie or television show that reminds them of characters or events in the read-aloud and explain that connection. For more scaffolding, have students talk in pairs or small groups, and then have a brief, whole-class discussion to share ideas. On the board or document camera, write the titles of the movies or television shows suggested and a brief sentence about the connection students made to the read-aloud.
SHARE IT	All students share their entry with a partner. Then two students, previously chosen, read their entry to the class. Classmates comment on where each student used the strategy taught.

CONNECTIONS WITHOUT "REMINDS ME OF . . . "

NAME IT	Making a personal or book connection without starting a sentence with the phrase "This reminds me of . . ." **Sentence stems:** *This character is a lot like . . . ; There are similarities between . . .*
WHY DO IT?	Knowing different ways to write about personal connections adds variety to your writing and thinking.
MODEL IT	*There are a lot of similarities between Catherine and my niece Olivia. Not only are they about the same age but they both also love to draw. Olivia enjoys the order and range of colors when she organizes her colored pencils and markers. And just like Kristi, there seems to be something about the act of drawing that she finds soothing or calming . . .* Ask students what kind of connection you made even though you didn't use the words *reminds me of . . .*
TRY IT	**Turn and talk:** Have students tell a partner why it's good to not always use the phrase *reminds me of* when writing about connections, followed by a brief, whole-class share. **Strategy entry:** Students open the strategy section of their reader's notebooks and write "Connections Without 'Reminds Me of . . . '" at the top of the next blank page. Ask them to write about the most recent chapter of the read-aloud and make at least one connection without using the words . . . *reminds me of . . .* Remind students they can use *This character is a lot like . . .* or *There are similarities between . . .*
SHARE IT	All students share their entry with a partner. Then two students, previously chosen, read their entry to the class. Classmates comment on where each student used the strategy taught.

IN A CHARACTER'S SHOES

NAME IT	Writing about how you would feel if you were in a character's situation.
	Sentence stem: *If I were . . .*
WHY DO IT?	Helps you better understand a situation from different characters' perspectives and synthesize what you know about the story so far. Thinking hypothetically also makes you more aware about how similar or different you are from that character.
MODEL IT	*I can't believe Ryan was teasing David! If I were Catherine, I would tell him not to talk to my brother at all. I wouldn't just stand there. Although in reality I suppose I would feel scared to say something even if I know I should. I might think about telling his mother, although that might just make it worse . . .*
	Ask students what you said you would do in Catherine's shoes.
TRY IT	**Turn and talk:** Have students tell a partner what it means to write as if you are in someone else's shoes, followed by a brief, whole-class share.
	Strategy entry: Students open the strategy section of their reader's notebooks and write "In a Character's Shoes" at the top of the next blank page. Ask them to write about the same scene that you wrote about except from a different character's point of view. With *Rules*, for example, you can ask them to write from Ryan's or Kristi's perspective instead of Catherine's. Remind students they can use *If I were . . .* to make this type of connection.
SHARE IT	All students share their entry with a partner. Then two students, previously chosen, read their entry to the class. Classmates comment on where each student used the strategy taught.

FIGURE 3.1

"In a Character's Shoes" Strategy Entry

WORLD CONNECTIONS

NAME IT	Comparing characters and events from your book to current issues and events.
WHY DO IT?	Making connections between your book and current events or issues helps you to understand bigger themes in the book; helps you go beyond your own personal experience to make a more universal connection.
MODEL IT	*I notice there is a lot more awareness about autism these days than when I was in elementary school. There are even support groups for parents of autistic children like David. But it doesn't seem clear if that means there are actually more autistic children. I heard someone say that now there is just more awareness . . .* Ask students what kind of world connection you made.
TRY IT	**Turn and talk:** Have students tell a partner what it means to make a world connection, followed by a brief, whole-class share. **Strategy entry:** Students open the strategy section of their reader's notebooks and write "World Connections" at the top of the next blank page. Have students talk in pairs or small groups about other world connections they can make with the read-aloud, and then write students' suggestions on the board. With *Rules*, topics that might come up include divorce, disabilities, and handicap access. You can also offer your own suggestions if the list is short. Then ask students to choose one of these world connections to write about in their notebooks.
SHARE IT	All students share their entry with a partner. Then two students, previously chosen, read their entry to the class. Classmates comment on where each student used the strategy taught.

THEME CONNECTIONS

NAME IT	Comparing themes in your book with the theme of another book or movie.
WHY DO IT?	Helps you better understand the significance of the story; thinking about similarities and differences between themes of different books also requires more analytical thinking than just a text-to-text connection.
MODEL IT	*I notice that one theme of* Rules *is accepting people's differences. This is kind of the same theme of* Everybody Cooks Rice, *a nonfiction book about how people around the world eat different types of rice in different ways. Even though the books themselves are pretty different, there is a common theme about same and different. In* Everybody Cooks Rice, *there is kind of a celebrating of differences anchored by one thing we have in common. In* Rules, *it is kind of showing us that even though we may all have physical differences, we are all still people with feelings, ideas, and desires. The themes are less about celebrating differences and more about not forgetting the humanity we have in common and accepting that we are all different . . .*
TRY IT	**Turn and talk:** After you finish the model writing, ask students what theme connection you made. Then have students tell a partner what it means to make a theme connection, followed by a brief, whole-class share. **Strategy entry:** As a class, brainstorm ideas for other possible themes for your read-aloud. If "World Connections" was already taught, you can also draw on themes that surfaced in that lesson or, for even more scaffolding, you can suggest themes for students to consider. With *Rules* you can suggest *friendship, forgiveness,* and *escape.* Then have students talk in pairs or small groups about any books or movies they know that have any of these same themes. How are the themes similar and different? Create a three-column chart on the board. Then have a whole-class discussion in which several students describe the theme connections that came up in their conversations. On the chart, write the theme and the two books (or book and movie). Be sure to include at least one read-aloud or shared text in this chart so that all students have at least one theme connection they can personally write about. Then direct students back to their notebooks to write a strategy entry.
SHARE IT	All students share their entry with a partner. Then two students, previously chosen, read their entry to the class. Classmates comment on where each student used the strategy taught.

Analyzing

At first glance, analyzing might be seen as a near synonym with the much-desired skill of inferring. While they certainly overlap, inferential thinking is far more all-encompassing than analytical thinking. We constantly make different levels of inferences as we read and we can also think inferentially after the fact, when discussing or talking about a book (Graesser, Singer, and Trabasso 1994). Analyzing, however, requires space away from text. According to the revised cognitive continuum of Bloom's taxonomy (Bloom 1956; L. W. Anderson and Krathwohl 2001), "analyzing" can be defined as separating a whole into its constituent parts to study the disparate parts, how they relate to one another and to the overall structure (L. W. Anderson and Krathwohl 2001). This kind of relational thinking is difficult to do at the same time as taking in high-level text. Writing, on the other hand, gives students the space needed for the intentional thought and reflection analysis requires.

The relationship between analyzing and questioning is particularly interesting because they are so inextricably linked: If one of the two is in the forefront, whether students are talking or writing, the other is quietly in the background. Analyzing comes out of questions, and questions lead to analytical thinking. When my nephew Joseph sat up in bed and said, "Maybe that's all she had!" for example, his analysis of the nice lady was in reaction to a question. He didn't actually ask a question out loud or even say it to himself. But somewhere in his brain ran the question, "Why would someone give out apples on Halloween?" Such thinking is so quick and unspoken that it's hard to be aware of our minds' constant inferring–questioning dance. Nor would we want to. But being explicit with students about this quiet dance between inferential thinking and questioning can help students become more independent in using questions to drive thinking and in unearthing questions hidden behind theories and analysis.

The following strategy lessons show students specific ways to bring analytical thinking into their writing. Since analysis of text should be grounded in evidence, and not just include sentences about what students think, this section also includes strategy lessons about using text-based evidence to support analyses.

WRITING ABOUT YOUR THINKING

NAME IT	Using *I think* to start a sentence.
	Sentence stem: *I think . . .*
WHY DO IT?	*I think* helps you move beyond explaining what happened in your book to what *you* think about the story and characters.
MODEL IT	*Now that it's time for Jason's birthday party, Catherine is all worried about bringing David. I think Catherine worries too much about what other people think about her brother. Some people just need to get used to David being a little different, but it doesn't mean they won't like him. I think Catherine could be more trusting of other people than she is . . .*
	Ask students what kinds of thinking you wrote about or where you used the phrase *I think . . .*
TRY IT	**Turn and talk:** Have students tell a partner what words you can use in your independent entries to help bring your own thinking into what you write. Follow with a brief, whole-class share.
	Strategy entry: Students open the strategy section of their reader's notebooks and write "Writing About Your Thinking" or "I Think" at the top of the next blank page. Then have them write about the most recent chapter of the read-aloud and use the phrase *I think . . .* once or twice.
SHARE IT	All students share their entry with a partner. Then two students, previously chosen, read their entry to the class. Classmates comment on where each student used the strategy taught.

MAYBE THEORIES

NAME IT	After posing a wonder question or statement, start the next sentence with *Maybe. . .*
	Sentence stem: *Maybe . . .*
WHY DO IT?	*Maybe* gets you to think inferentially and offer theories about the question you asked.
MODEL IT	*I wonder why Catherine's dad never gets angry with David. Maybe he thinks David doesn't understand what he does is wrong. So he thinks it wouldn't be fair to yell at him. Or maybe Catherine's dad is afraid that if he gets upset one time he'll just lose his temper every single time . . .*
	Ask students where you made a *Maybe . . .* theory.
TRY IT	**Turn and talk:** Have students tell a partner what word you can use after writing a question to offer a theory, followed by a brief, whole-class share.
	Strategy entry: Students open the strategy section of their reader's notebooks and write "Maybe Theories" at the top of the next blank page. Then have them write about the most recent chapter of the read-aloud and try to ask at least one wonder question and then start the next sentence with *Maybe . . .*
SHARE IT	All students share their entry with a partner. Then two students, previously chosen, read their entry to the class. Classmates comment on where each student used the strategy taught.

FIGURE 3.2

"Maybe Theories" Strategy Entry

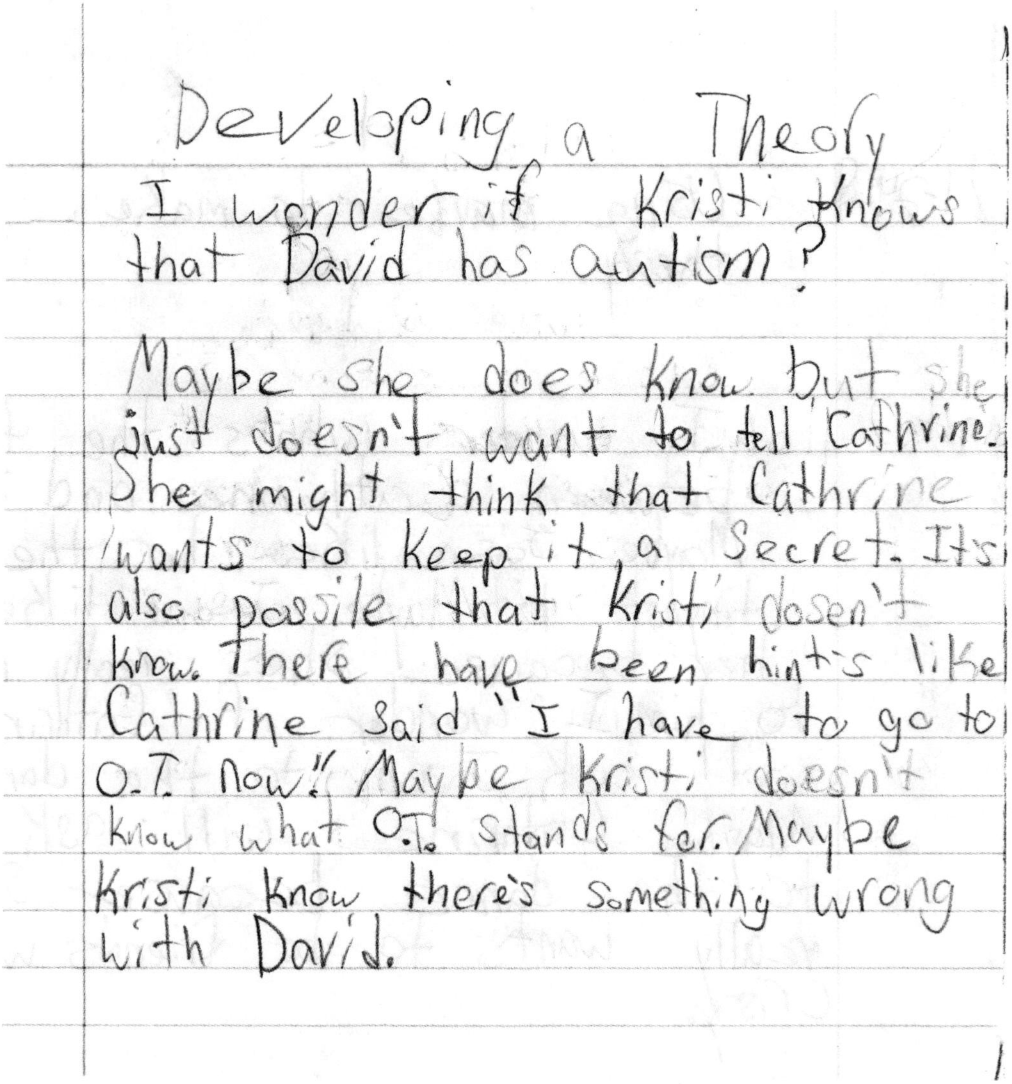

Developing a Theory

I wonder if Kristi knows that David has autism?

Maybe she does know but she just doesn't want to tell Cathrine. She might think that Cathrine wants to keep it a secret. Its also possile that Kristi dosen't know. There have been hint's like Cathrine said "I have to go to O.T. now." Maybe Kristi doesn't know what O.T. stands for. Maybe Kristi know there's something wrong with David.

EXPLAINING YOUR QUESTIONS

NAME IT	After you ask a question, explain your wondering more. What makes you wonder this?
WHY DO IT?	Writing more about your wondering can help you analyze the complexity of a person or situation on a deeper level.
MODEL IT	*I wonder why Catherine's dad never gets angry at David? It's like he is okay yelling at Catherine but not David. Every time David does something he just speaks to him in a calm voice. But the things he does are usually worse than what Catherine does. I can see why Catherine gets so upset with her father. Maybe he doesn't get mad at David because David has less control over his actions . . .* Ask students to describe what you explained about your question.
TRY IT	**Turn and talk:** Have students tell a partner why it can be good to sometimes offer more explanation after you ask a wondering question, followed by a brief, whole-class share. **Strategy entry:** Students open the strategy section of their reader's notebooks and write "Explaining Your Questions" at the top of the next blank page. On the board, write down a wonder question that relates to the story and ask students to copy it down in their notebook. With *Rules*, for example, you could write *I wonder why Jason did not have more word cards before he met Catherine.* Ask students to talk in pairs or small groups about how they could more fully explain this question. Then have students to go back to their entry to add a few more sentences that explain the question before continuing.
SHARE IT	All students share their entry with a partner. Then two students, previously chosen, read their entry to the class. Classmates comment on where each student used the strategy taught.

MAKING A THEORY

NAME IT	Making a theory without asking a question first. **Sentence stems:** *It could be that . . . ; It seems like . . .*
WHY DO IT?	Jumping right into a theory, rather than sparking it with a question, can elevate critical thinking (less question/answer tendencies) and adds variety to analytical writing.
MODEL IT	*It seems like Jason and Catherine might actually become friends. Maybe Catherine is more comfortable with Jason than other twelve-year-olds because her own brother has a disability. She knows there is more to a person than just his or her disability. I also think they will become friends because he has made her laugh with just the few cards that she made . . .* Ask students what theory you made about Jason and Catherine and why you think that.
TRY IT	**Turn and talk:** Have students tell a partner why it can be good to sometimes offer a theory without asking a question first. Follow with a brief, whole-class share. **Strategy entry:** Students open the strategy section of their reader's notebooks and write "Making a Theory" at the top of the next blank page. Then have them write about the most recent chapter of the read-aloud and try to offer a theory about one of the characters without asking a question first. Remind students they can use the sentence stem *It could be that . . .* or *It seems like . . .* to make their theory.
SHARE IT	All students share their entry with a partner. Then two students, previously chosen, read their entry to the class. Classmates comment on where each student used the strategy taught.

ANALYZING A CHARACTER

NAME IT	Thinking about a character from different angles; zooming in on a character and spending time thinking about just that character.
WHY DO IT?	People and characters are complex. Analyzing a character helps you better understand the different sides of a person.
MODEL IT	*Jason really has a great sense of humor. You couldn't tell at first. But he can be funny and sarcastic just like anyone else. He makes Catherine laugh and he doesn't even have that many cards to use! Jason is also very guarded. He doesn't seem to trust people at first, probably from being stared at a lot in his life. He also seems to get angry quickly . . .* Ask students how you analyzed the character of Jason. What were the different things you described about him?
TRY IT	**Turn and talk:** Have students tell a partner what it means to analyze a character, followed by a brief, whole-class share. **Strategy entry:** Students open the strategy section of their reader's notebooks and write "Analyzing a Character" at the top of the next blank page. Then ask them to choose between two suggested characters and write about what this person is like from different angles. With *Rules,* you might have students choose between the character of Catherine or David.
SHARE IT	All students share their entry with a partner. Then two students, previously chosen, read their entry to the class. Classmates comment on where each student used the strategy taught.

OPINIONS OF CHARACTERS

NAME IT	Giving your personal opinion of a character and why you think that. **Sentence stem:** *I think (name) is . . . because . . .*
WHY DO IT?	Helps you to think inferentially about a character and provides evidence for your thinking.
MODEL IT	*I think Ryan is a real bully. He must know David has a disability and yet he makes fun of him right in front of his sister. So not nice. He must be insecure and puts other people down to make himself feel better. He must be pretty insensitive if that is what he does to feel better about himself . . .* Ask students what opinions you had about this character.
TRY IT	**Turn and talk:** Have students tell a partner why it can be good to write about your personal opinions of characters, followed by a brief, whole-class share. **Strategy entry:** Students open the strategy section of their reader's notebooks and write "Opinions of Characters" at the top of the next blank page. Then have students choose between two suggested characters and write about what they personally think of that character and why they think that. With *Rules,* you might have students write about Kristi or Catherine. Remind students they can use *I think (name) is . . . because . . .* to start their entry.
SHARE IT	All students share their entry with a partner. Then two students, previously chosen, read their entry to the class. Classmates comment on where each student used the strategy taught.

FIGURE 3.3
"Opinions of Characters" Strategy Entry

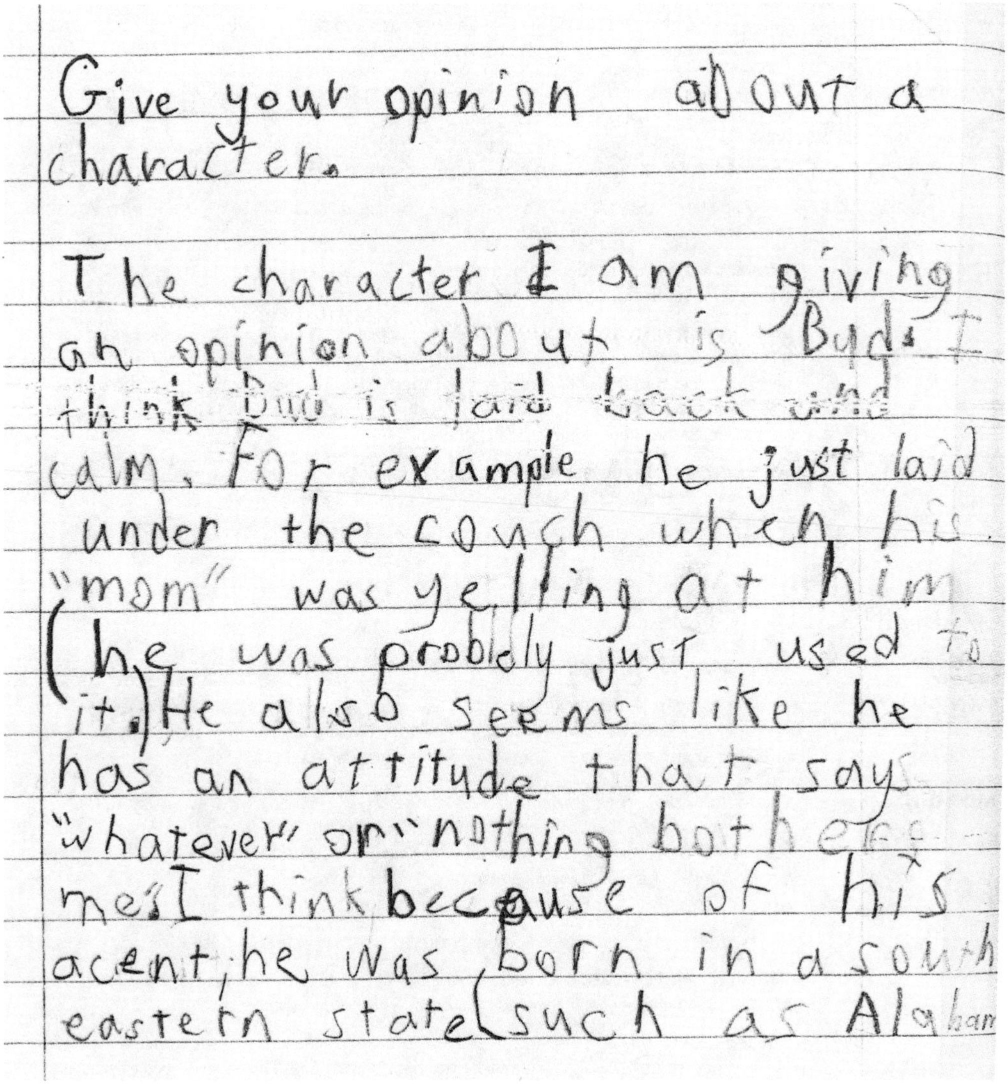

Give your opinion about a
character.

The character I am giving
an opinion about is Bud. I
think Bud is laid back and
calm. For example he just laid
under the couch when his
"mom" was yelling at him
(he was probobly just used to
it.) He also seems like he
has an attitude that says
"whatever" or "nothing bothers
me." I think because of his
acent, he was born in a south
eastern state (such as Alabam

HOW A CHARACTER FEELS

NAME IT	Describing how a character feels and why.
WHY DO IT?	Helps you to think inferentially about a character and provide evidence for your thinking; also strengthens personal connections with characters.
MODEL IT	*Catherine must feel so alone right now. All David is concerned about is getting his tape fixed. He doesn't even notice that she was upset. She was already sad but then having a brother who doesn't notice how you feel must be so lonely. I'll bet Catherine feels like she just gives and gives to David and would just once want him to care how she feels . . .* Ask students to describe what you think about the way Catherine feels and why you think that.
TRY IT	**Turn and talk:** Have students tell a partner why it can be good to write about how a character is feeling, followed by a brief, whole-class share. **Strategy entry:** Students open the strategy section of their reader's notebooks and write "How a Character Feels" at the top of the next blank page. Then direct students to a particular scene in the read-aloud and ask them to write about how one of the characters was feeling. With *Rules*, you might have students write about how Jason was feeling when he invited Catherine to his birthday party.
SHARE IT	All students share their entry with a partner. Then two students, previously chosen, read their entry to the class. Classmates comment on where each student used the strategy taught.

ANALYZING RELATIONSHIPS

NAME IT	Describing the relationship between two characters.
WHY DO IT?	How a character relates to a particular person can show a certain side of his or her personality. Relationships are also complex and thinking about them from several different angles helps you to better understand the characters.
MODEL IT	*The relationship between David and Catherine seems very one way. As his big sister, Catherine is always looking out for David and kind of acts like his mother. She helps take care of him and even makes a book of rules to help him out. David totally loves Catherine but he doesn't seem to think about things from her perspective. But you can also tell that David adores his sister and cares about her very much . . .* Ask students what you observed about the relationship between Catherine and David.
TRY IT	**Turn and talk:** Have students tell a partner what it means to analyze a relationship between two characters, followed by a brief, whole-class share. **Strategy entry:** Students open the strategy section of their reader's notebooks and write "Analyzing Relationships" at the top of the next blank page. Then name two characters and have students analyze this particular relationship. With *Rules*, you might have students write about the relationship between Catherine and her mom or Catherine and her dad.
SHARE IT	All students share their entry with a partner. Then two students, previously chosen, read their entry to the class. Classmates comment on where each student used the strategy taught.

FIGURE 3.4
"Analyzing Relationships" Strategy Entry

Reading workshop!!!
    analyze a relationship
    between two character

Abigail and Mr.caruther
are alike becaus they
are really entrasted in
the "What if" qustions.
Abigail allways is the
first one to raise her
hand. And Mr.caruther
really is calm with her
even though she gets
on his nevors all the time
but he just keeps it in
side hes siston. She
is really wise and he
is too! They can some-
times even sound like
they are brothes and
sister they sometimes be
really really weird!!!!!

ANALYZING A MINOR CHARACTER

NAME IT	Writing about a person who is not a main character from different angles.
WHY DO IT?	Very often we think and write only about the main characters in a story. Minor characters contribute to the story in quiet but important ways and can also tell us more about the main characters.
MODEL IT	*Mrs. Morehouse seems like a nice lady. She seems very patient with Jason and I am sure caring for a child who can't walk or talk is not easy. She never yells at him. I also get the sense that she is not too overprotective of Jason, like when she asked Catherine to see what Jason wanted even though she had just met him. I'll bet she knows that to baby him would not be good and that he is capable of making friends . . .* Ask students to name what aspects of Mrs. Morehouse you described.
TRY IT	**Turn and talk:** Have students tell a partner why it can be good to sometimes write about a minor character instead of just the main characters, followed by a brief, whole-class share. **Strategy entry:** Students open the strategy section of their reader's notebooks and write "Analyzing a Minor Character" at the top of the next blank page. Then name one or two minor characters for them to analyze. With *Rules*, for example, you can have students write about Jason's speech therapist.
SHARE IT	All students share their entry with a partner. Then two students, previously chosen, read their entry to the class. Classmates comment on where each student used the strategy taught.

ANALYZING MINOR RELATIONSHIPS

NAME IT	Writing about the relationship between a main and minor character.
WHY DO IT?	How characters interact with minor characters can say a lot about their personality.
MODEL IT	*Jason clearly can't stand his speech therapist. Even Catherine notices how annoyed he is when she comes out to the waiting area to get him. She talks so loudly and slowly as if he doesn't hear her. Doesn't she know that he is smart? When Jason is in a bad mood, he gets extra annoyed by her. But if he is in a good mood, and jokes about it with Catherine, he doesn't seem to mind it . . .* Ask students what you suggested about the relationship between Jason and his speech therapist.
TRY IT	**Turn and talk:** Have students tell a partner why it can be good to sometimes write about the relationship between a minor and major character. Why not just stick to writing about the main characters all the time? Follow with a brief, whole-class share. **Strategy entry:** Students open the strategy section of their reader's notebooks and write "Analyzing Minor Relationships" at the top of the next blank page. Then have them write about the relationship between a particular character and a more minor one. With *Rules*, you might have students write about the relationship between Catherine and her guinea pigs, Cinnamon and Nutmeg.
SHARE IT	All students share their entry with a partner. Then two students, previously chosen, read their entry to the class. Classmates comment on where each student used the strategy taught.

ANALYZING OBJECTS

NAME IT	Writing about the meaning and significance of an object in a story.
WHY DO IT?	Creates a vehicle for thinking about characters; offers a first step for the concept of symbolism since some objects hold important or meaningful significance to the theme of a story.
MODEL IT	*Catherine's drawing pencils seem to be important to her. She talks a lot about creating lines and shades and turning the page to start a fresh picture. I guess one reason she likes it is because she has total control, something she doesn't really have in her life a lot of times. If she makes a mistake, she can just start over. There is also a connection between drawing and what she thinks of things. I know this because in this chapter she said, "Sometimes I can change how I feel about something by drawing it."* Ask students what you said about Catherine's drawing pencils.
TRY IT	**Turn and talk:** Have students tell a partner why it can be good to sometimes analyze objects from a story, followed by a brief, whole-class share. **Strategy entry:** Students open the strategy section of their reader's notebooks and write "Analyzing Objects" at the top of the next blank page. Then name an object from the read-aloud and have students write about its significance to a particular character or to the story as a whole. With *Rules*, you might have students write about David's *Frog and Toad* video. For more scaffolding, have students talk in pairs or small groups before writing their entries. If your current read-aloud is not conducive to this strategy, you can use the picture book *The Bracelet* by Yoshiko Uchida and have students talk about the meaning of Emi's red sweater or the number tags on the suitcase.
SHARE IT	All students share their entry with a partner. Then two students, previously chosen, read their entry to the class. Classmates comment on where each student used the strategy taught.

SYMBOLISM IN OBJECTS

NAME IT	Writing about possible meaning and significance of certain objects in a story. **Sentence stem:** *In this story, (object) could represent . . .*
WHY DO IT?	Authors sometimes use symbolism to highlight or reinforce themes in a story. Thinking about possible symbolism makes us more reflective about an author's intentions and about the overall meaning of a story.
MODEL IT	*In this story, Catherine's drawing pencils could represent choice. The choices you make when drawing impact how you see something. Catherine says this about her drawing but it could apply to how she sees her own life and her brother. Just like with choosing her pencils, Catherine can choose how she sees or reacts to other people's opinions.* *Catherine's pencils also change Jason's choices because she uses them to create more words for him. They literally add color to his language and his ability to use more "colorful" language. With Catherine's new cards, he starts having fun with words. They let him show his sense of humor by using words to be sarcastic or make fun of his speech therapist.*
TRY IT	**Turn and talk:** Have students tell a partner what symbolism means and what you said Catherine's pencils might represent in this story, followed by a brief, whole-class share. **Strategy entry:** Students open the strategy section of their reader's notebooks and write "Symbolism in Objects" at the top of the next blank page. Name an object from the read-aloud and have students talk in pairs about its significance in the story. With *Rules*, you might have students talk about David's *Frog and Toad* video. Ask students to suggest a word or phrase the object might symbolize. For more scaffolding, have students talk in pairs or small groups before writing their entries. Then direct students back to their reader's notebook to write about the symbolism of this object. Remind students they can use the sentence stem *In this story, I think* (object) *could represent . . .* If your current read-aloud is not conducive to this strategy, you can use *The Bracelet* and have students talk and then write about the symbolism of the bracelet. You can also use *The Other Side* by Jacqueline Woodson and have students talk and then write about the symbolism of the fence.
SHARE IT	All students share their entry with a partner. Then two students, previously chosen, read their entry to the class. Classmates comment on where each student used the strategy taught.

ANALYZING SCENES

NAME IT	Thinking about a particular scene that plays a prominent role in the story and why it is important. **Sentence stems:** *An important part of the story is when . . . ; An important scene is when . . .*
WHY DO IT?	Certain scenes are particularly significant for how a character or a relationship develops or changes. Important scenes may mean one thing on a literal level but hold important meaning about the story on a different level.
MODEL IT	*An important part of Rules is when Catherine finally gets upset at her dad when he takes her to the school dance. This is an important scene because for most of the story she feels sad about not spending any time with him. He is always busy with work or things he has to do for David. Catherine knows David has more needs than her so she doesn't really say anything. In this scene, however, she turns from being sad about all this to mad, which is good! She finally realized that even if David has more needs, she still needs her dad too. And that it's not selfish or being a bad sister if she says that . . .*

TRY IT	**Turn and talk:** Have students tell a partner what it means to analyze a scene from a book, followed by a brief, whole-class share.
	Strategy entry: Students open the strategy section of their reader's notebooks and write "Analyzing Scenes" at the top of the next blank page. Name a recent scene from the read-aloud and have students talk about its significance with a partner. With *Rules*, you might have students write about the scene when David gives Catherine the broken *Frog and Toad* cassette. Why is this scene important or significant? Then direct students back to their reader's notebook to write a strategy entry. Remind students they can use the sentence stems *An important part of the story is when . . .* or *An important scene is when . . .* to begin their analysis of this scene.
	If your current read-aloud is not conducive to this strategy, you can use the picture book *The Other Side* by Jacqueline Woodson. Have students talk and then write about the scene when it rains and Clover watches Annie play outside in the rain.
SHARE IT	All students share their entry with a partner. Then two students, previously chosen, read their entry to the class. Classmates comment on where each student used the strategy taught.

FIGURE 3.5
"Analyzing a Scene" Strategy Entry

Analizing a Scene

One important part of "To Kill a Mockingbird" was when Boo Radly put a blanket on Scout when Ms. Madies house was on fire and Scout was freezing. This was important because Boo Radly had been leaving notes in the tree hole for Scout and Jem like Gems pants and two pieces of Gum. I also believe this was important because Scout thought Boo Radly was a monster before this. Scout thought that Boo was a bad man but from then on wanted to meet with Boo Radly. This is also important because it tells the reader that Boo actually is not a crazy person and that his father was crazy. Finally, this was important because it grew the relationship with Scout and Boo and from that seen anything could have happened.

SYMBOLISM IN CHARACTERS

NAME IT	Thinking about how a character represents a bigger idea or theme in the book.
	Sentence stem: *In this story, I think the character (name) represents . . .*
WHY DO IT?	Sometimes characters represent bigger ideas or themes in a story. Thinking about this symbolism makes us more reflective about an author's intentions and about the overall meaning of a story.
MODEL IT	*In this story, I think the character of Ryan represents Catherine's fears about other people. Most people might show a small reaction when David is acting different but they don't say anything really mean. It seems like what bothers Catherine the most is what people don't say and what they are thinking. But Ryan doesn't hold back. He says mean things and maybe for Catherine, it represents what other people think . . .*
TRY IT	**Turn and talk:** Have students tell a partner what symbolism in characters means, followed by a brief, whole-class share.
	Strategy entry: Students open the strategy section of their reader's notebooks and write "Symbolism in Characters" at the top of the next blank page. Name a character from the read-aloud and have them write about what this person might represent. Remind students there is no right or wrong answer with this kind of thinking, as long as they explain their ideas. With *Rules*, you might have students write about the character of the speech therapist.
	For more scaffolding, have students talk in pairs or small groups before writing their entries or use a picture book that is conducive to this strategy. With *Thank You, Mr. Falker* by Patricia Polacco, for example, students can write about what the grandpa represents, and with *The Bracelet* by Yoshiko Uchida, students can write about what Emi's friend Laurie represents.
SHARE IT	All students share their entry with a partner. Then two students, previously chosen, read their entry to the class. Classmates comment on where each student used the strategy taught.

Giving Evidence to Support Analysis

The following lessons teach students specific ways to give evidence to support their analytical thinking and writing.

I THINK THIS BECAUSE . . .

NAME IT	Explaining your thinking after you offer an idea.
	Sentence stems: *I think this because . . . ; One reason I think this is . . .*
WHY DO IT?	Helps you get beyond just listing ideas to offering evidence that backs up your ideas.
MODEL IT	*I wonder if Catherine is going to ask Jason to the dance? I think she will get too nervous. I think this because she already gets sensitive to what other people think about her little brother. But this is about a school dance! I am sure just about everybody will be there so she will be even more sensitive than usual . . .*
	Ask students where you used *I think this because . . .* to give evidence to support your ideas.
TRY IT	**Turn and talk:** Have students tell a partner what words you can use to offer evidence for an idea, followed by a brief, whole-class share.
	Strategy entry: Students open the strategy section of their reader's notebooks and write "I Think This Because . . ." or "One Reason I Think This Is . . ." at the top of the next blank page. Then give a prompt that directs students to write about a particular part of the read-aloud. With *Rules*, for example, you can have students write about why they think Catherine likes to draw so much and see whether they can use either *I think this because . . .* or *One reason I think this is . . .* to offer evidence for their ideas.
	For more scaffolding, have students talk out their ideas and why they think this before they start their strategy entry.
SHARE IT	All students share their entry with a partner. Then two students, previously chosen, read their entry to the class. Classmates comment on where each student used the strategy taught.

ONE TIME

NAME IT	Giving an example from the story to back up an idea or theory using the words *One time*.
	Sentence stem: *One time . . .*
WHY DO IT?	The words *One time . . .* get you to write about a particular scene from the book and offer evidence for what you think. Rather than just explain an idea, examples from the book help you show it.
MODEL IT	*I think Catherine wants to keep her friendship with Jason a secret. One time Kristi saw the picture she drew of him and when she asked about him Catherine practically lied! She said he was some boy she doesn't know very well and then went on to talk about something else . . .*
	Ask students what scene from the book you described to give evidence for your thinking using *One time . . .*
TRY IT	**Turn and talk:** Have students tell a partner why the words *One time* can help you give evidence for your thinking, followed by a brief, whole-class share.
	Strategy entry: Students open the strategy section of their reader's notebooks and write "One Time. . ." at the top of the next blank page. Then give a prompt that directs students to write about a particular part of the read-aloud. With *Rules*, you can have students write about Kristi and see whether they can use the words *One time . . .* to give an example from the story.
SHARE IT	All students share their entry with a partner. Then two students, previously chosen, read their entry to the class. Classmates comment on where each student used the strategy taught.

FOR EXAMPLE

NAME IT	Giving an example from the story to back up an idea or theory using the words *For example*.
	Sentence stem: *For example . . .*
WHY DO IT?	Giving an example from the book helps you show your idea and helps you go from being general to being specific.
MODEL IT	*Catherine is a great sister. Even though she can get frustrated with David, she is always looking out for him. For example, whenever he gets upset she says his favorite lines from* Frog and Toad *to calm him down and wipes his tears . . .*
TRY IT	**Turn and talk:** Have students tell a partner why the words *For example . . .* can help you give evidence for an idea or description.
	Strategy entry: Students open the strategy section of their reader's notebooks and write "For Example . . ." at the top of the next blank page. Have students choose one character to write about and try to go from a general description of that person to a specific part of the book that demonstrates that description, using the phrase *For example . . .*
	For more scaffolding, choose one character to talk about as a class. Ask for a few sentences that generally describe this person and write them on the board. Ask students to suggest specific examples of this characteristic from the book that show this characteristic and write down their suggestions in bullet form. Then direct students back to their reader's notebooks and have them write a strategy entry in which they use *For example . . .* to describe this character.
SHARE IT	All students share their entry with a partner. Then two students, previously chosen, read their entry to the class. Classmates comment on where each student used the strategy taught.

QUOTING DIALOGUE

NAME IT	Quoting what a character says in your book.
WHY DO IT?	Using the actual words of a character offers concrete evidence to back up your ideas.
MODEL IT	*I think Catherine is starting to see similarities between Jason and her brother. In this chapter she says, "I want to show Jason I'm sorry for not-looking at him the same embarrassed way I hate people not-looking at David." She even uses the same word not-looking to describe the same thing that happens to both of them . . .* Ask students where you quoted dialogue and how it provided evidence for your thinking.
TRY IT	**Turn and talk:** Have students tell a partner why quoting dialogue can sometimes be a good way to offer evidence for theories. Follow with a brief, whole-class share. **Strategy entry:** Students open the strategy section of their reader's notebooks and at the top write "Quoting Dialogue." Choose one chapter to focus on for this lesson. Pass out copies of two to four pages from this chapter. Have students write about what they think of one of the characters and use part of what a character actually says to give evidence for their thinking. For more scaffolding, have students work in pairs to choose a character to write about, and look for quotations that would support their argument, before writing their strategy entries.
SHARE IT	All students share their entry with a partner. Then two students, previously chosen, read their entry to the class. Classmates comment on where each student used the strategy taught.

Synthesizing

Synthesizing, like analyzing, consists of a multistep, higher-order thinking process, except it reflects an almost opposite movement of thought from analyzing. Instead of examining parts of a whole and breaking them down, synthesizing considers the constituent parts and how they relate as a whole (Bloom 1956). Like all the other comprehension strategies, synthesizing occurs continuously as we read, whether or not we are aware of it. But it is not until we pause to write or talk about our thinking that we can activate this type of thinking to its potential. When readers synthesize information or comprehension of a story, they pull back from the individual pages of the text and compile overall meaning with a kind of bird's-eye view of the text.

The following strategy lessons offer students specific ways to synthesize their understanding of a story and its characters by drawing on different sources of information, either within the book or between the book and their own background knowledge. When teaching these lessons, students should understand that synthesizing benefits the reading process by doing it at different points throughout a book and not just at the end.

POINTS OF VIEW

NAME IT	Thinking about a situation from more than one character's perspective.
	Sentence stems: *But if I think about it from (name)'s perspective . . . When I think about it from (name)'s perspective, however, . . .*
WHY DO IT?	Helps you synthesize what you know about each character so far; helps you better understand how people have different experiences and interpretations of the same event.
MODEL IT	*Catherine was pretty disappointed that her dad didn't want to make plans with just her. All he seemed to care about was that he had time to work on his tomatoes. I know I'd be annoyed if that happened to me. Thinking about it from the dad's perspective, however, he has to deal with people all day at the pharmacy. He probably never gets quiet time and just wants a little of it. It's not that he doesn't care about Catherine . . .*
	Ask students what two perspectives you drew on to synthesize your understanding of what was happening in the story.
TRY IT	**Turn and talk:** Have students tell a partner why it can be good to write about the same event from different points of view, followed by a brief, whole-class share.
	Strategy entry: Students open the strategy section of their reader's notebooks and write "Points of View" at the top of the next blank page. On the board, write two events from the last few chapters of the read-aloud. With *Rules*, for example, you might put down "drawing Jason in the office" and "dad arriving late for the video store." For each event, ask students to list the two or three characters who might see this event from different perspectives. Have students choose one of the scenes to write about, first from one character's perspective then the other. Remind students they can use the phrase *When I think about it from (name's) perspective . . .* to help make that transition.
	For more scaffolding, have students talk in pairs about two different points of view from a scene in the read-aloud before they write a strategy entry.
SHARE IT	All students share their entry with a partner. Then two students, previously chosen, read their entry to the class. Classmates comment on where each student used the strategy taught.

PRIOR KNOWLEDGE CONNECTIONS

NAME IT	Making a connection between the story and information you know.
	Sentence stem: *I know about (topic) because . . .*
WHY DO IT?	Writing about connections between what you read and your background knowledge makes you more aware of what you are contributing to your own understanding of the story.
MODEL IT	*I wonder if Jason doesn't like going to occupational therapy just because of the speech lady. I know a little bit about OT because we had an OT specialist at our school. She would work with kids on their motor skills by using balls and playing games. For the most part it seemed really fun. Maybe he's just been to it so many times, it's not fun anymore . . .*
	Ask students what prior knowledge connection you made and how that knowledge affected your understanding of the story.

TRY IT	**Turn and talk:** Have students tell a partner what it means to make a prior knowledge connection and what phrase you can use to help you do that. Follow with a brief, whole-class share. **Strategy entry:** Have students talk in pairs or small groups about anything in the story they thought they understood a little bit better because of previous experience or prior knowledge. Remind them they can use the phrase *I know about* (topic) *because . . .* to start their conversation. For more scaffolding, you can offer a few things in the book that people might have varying amounts of experience with, such as *guinea pigs, autism, wheelchairs,* or *drawing.*
SHARE IT	Follow this small-group activity with a whole-class share in which students describe the prior knowledge connections that came up in their conversation. Write a model strategy entry in which you write or type what one student says as he or she describes a prior knowledge connection. Then have all students copy this entry in their reader's notebooks after writing "Example of Prior Knowledge Connection" and the contributing student's name at the top of the page.

ARGUING YOUR OWN THEORY

NAME IT	Writing about a theory you have and then arguing against it. **Sentence stem:** *On the other hand . . .*
WHY DO IT?	Thinking about a theory from two different sides acknowledges the complexity of relationships and people, and even helps you process the story through more than one lens.
MODEL IT	*I am thinking Catherine is more comfortable with Jason than other kids her age because her own brother has a disability. She probably knows that just because someone seems different or is not like everyone else, doesn't mean they don't want to have friends too. On the other hand, maybe she has become friends with him because she got a chance to interact with him in the waiting room. In which case, any other kid her age may have done the same thing. It kind of reminds me of inclusion classrooms where kids of all ability levels get to know each other because they are in the same environment . . .* Ask students to describe the two theories you wrote about and how they are different.
TRY IT	**Turn and talk:** Have students tell a partner why it can be good to sometimes argue against your own theory, followed by a brief, whole-class share. **Strategy entry:** Students open the strategy section of their reader's notebooks and write "Arguing Your Own Theory." Have students write a theory about one of the characters in the read-aloud for a few sentences and then see whether they can argue against that theory using the phrase *On the other hand . . .* For more scaffolding, first create a T-chart on the board under a general statement about a character. With *Rules,* for example, you can write the sentence *Catherine seems like a patient sister.* Ask students to talk in pairs or small groups about examples that support this idea and then write down their suggestions. Label the right side of the T-chart "On the other hand . . ." Ask students to suggest examples to argue why Catherine *may not* always seem like a patient sister. Then direct students back to their reader's notebooks to write their strategy entries.
SHARE IT	All students share their entry with a partner. Then two students, previously chosen, read their entry to the class. Classmates comment on where each student used the strategy taught.

CHARACTER DEVELOPMENT

NAME IT	Writing about how a character has changed and why.
WHY DO IT?	Characters often evolve in some way by the end of a story, but they usually make smaller changes throughout the book. Thinking about how and why characters develop helps you synthesize your understanding of a character and the overall themes of the story.
MODEL IT	*Catherine is finally telling her dad how she really feels. This time she just yelled at him and said, "Maybe he does need you more than me, But that doesn't mean I don't need anything at all!" She had gotten frustrated before but all those other times she kept it inside. Maybe seeing Jason stand up for how he is treated had an impact on her. She seems to now understand that even if she does not have unusual needs, like David, just being someone's daughter means her needs are important too.* Ask students to name how you think Catherine has changed and why.
TRY IT	**Turn and talk:** Have students tell a partner why it can be good to write about how a character changes, followed by a brief, whole-class share. **Strategy entry:** Students open the strategy section of their reader's notebooks and write "Character Development" at the top of the next blank page. On the board, write the names of two or three characters from the read-aloud. Have students choose one character and write about how this character has changed so far in the book and why they think he or she has changed. Remind students that they don't have to be big changes: even small changes can help you synthesize what you know about a character so far.
SHARE IT	All students share their entry with a partner. Then two students, previously chosen, read their entry to the class. Classmates comment on where each student used the strategy taught.

FIGURE 3.6

"Character Development" Strategy Entry

Character Development

Jem has changed from a child to a teenager.
He is finally understanding more things about
the trial (racism) One example, from the book
that shows his development is when he no longer
really wants to play with Scout, who is
younger, he is more mature and doesn't enjoy
playing the games he used to. Another example
that shows his development is when he
tells Atticus about Dill hiding under Scouts
bed, instead of hiding him because he knows
that it is the mature dicision and he
knows that an adult will know what
to do. I really feel that Jem has
matured a lot and has changed the
most.

BOOK THEMES

NAME IT	Thinking about the book as a whole. What are the themes and lessons in the story so far? What is the book about?
	Sentence stem: *Right now I am thinking the book is about . . .*
WHY DO IT?	Pausing to think about the theme of a book every now and then (and not just at the end) helps you synthesize your understanding of the book along the way, which creates an awareness of themes for subsequent chapters.
MODEL IT	*Right now I am thinking the book is about the judgments people can make about other people when they are different. It might be more obvious with someone like Jason who looks very different from your average person. But people do this all the time. They make judgments about who someone is on the inside based on their clothes, the color of their skin, or the way they talk. The theme of judging people also comes up with Catherine's awareness of how people perceive her brother . . .*
	Ask students to describe what themes you are seeing in the book so far.
TRY IT	**Turn and talk:** Have students tell a partner why it can be good to think about the theme of a book every now and then and not just at the end of the story? What words can you use to help you think about book themes? Follow with a brief, whole-class share.
	Strategy entry: Students open the strategy section of their reader's notebooks and write "Book Themes" at the top of the next blank page. Have students talk in pairs about what themes seem to be surfacing in the read-aloud so far. Encourage students not to simply think about the chapter that was read recently but to pull back and think about the book as a whole. Remind students they can use the phrase *Right now I am thinking the book is about . . .* to start their conversation.
	For additional scaffolding, have a whole-class discussion about theme ideas before students begin their strategy entries.
	You can also use a picture book students haven't heard before so they can practice thinking about themes in the middle of the book and not just at the end.
SHARE IT	All students share their entry with a partner. Then two students, previously chosen, read their entry to the class. Classmates comment on where each student used the strategy taught.

FIGURE 3.7
"Book Themes" Strategy Entry

Book Themes

I think the theme of the book is to walk in somebody else's shoes before judging them. For example Scout judges Boo Radley before she knows ~~the~~ him. She goes by word of mouth not what she really knows. She learns at the end of the book that Boo Radley was actually a good person. A quote from the book that really proves my point is "One time he said you never really know a man until you stand in his shoes and walk around in them. Just standing on the Radley porch was enough." This quote took place at the end of the book after Scout had walked Boo home. She finally realized that Boo's shoes were hard to fill and he had a lot on his plate. ~~so the~~ The book's main theme ~~is~~ is to know somebody before you pass judgements and that you should know somebody's story, before you set judgements

Evaluating

Evaluation is deemed the most cognitively demanding comprehension skill in the hierarchy of Bloom's taxonomy (Bloom 1956) because it encompasses the use of the other categories in addition to one's assessment and value judgment of texts. Evaluating, then, depends first on students' awareness of certain aspects of text and then their ability to incorporate their background knowledge and personal set of standards on which to make a comparison. Therefore, some strategy lessons in this section include scaffolding that gets students to practice noticing certain aspects of a text. In these foundational strategy entries, students write about their opinions from a more personal perspective.

The next day, or several days later, you can teach the next tier of evaluating strategy lessons, which focuses on a more objective evaluation of text features and author choices. Instead of describing their own personal opinions or reactions, students practice assessing or judging the effectiveness or shortcomings from a more judgmental and less personal standpoint. I point out to students that one difference they should notice in these two different types of strategy entries is that they will use the words *I* or *me* when writing about their opinions, but when writing is evaluative they will not be using these personal pronouns.

Because evaluating lessons requires students to look closely at the way an author writes, it is helpful if students have their own copies of the text. Usually I just copy two or three pages from the chapter book and staple them together. Students can keep these "author pages" in a folder and use them several times for different lessons.

NOTICING BIG TEXT FEATURES

NAME IT	Writing what you notice about the more substantial text features of a book, such as chapter titles, dedication pages, maps, and any other additional pages besides the text. **Sentence stem:** *I notice how the author . . .*
WHY DO IT?	Helps you think about choices an author makes and how they affect your experience or understanding of what you read.
MODEL IT	*I notice how the author starts each chapter with one of David's rules. I just love how Catherine comes up with these rules for how to live an everyday life. But I also like how Cynthia Lord uses them as chapter starters and gives a hint of what the chapter might be about. It makes me curious about what will happen and then, when I am done with the chapter, I understand why she gave it that name.* Ask students to name what text feature you noticed in *Rules* and why you liked it.
TRY IT	**Turn and talk:** Have students tell a partner what text features you might find in picture and chapter books that you could write about. Follow with a brief, whole-class share and write their suggestions on the board. If needed, offer additional text features with explanations so there is a complete list on the board. **Strategy entry:** Students open the strategy section of their reader's notebooks and write "Noticing Big Text Features" at the top of the next blank page. On the overhead or document camera, show students a different text feature from the read-aloud. With *Rules*, for example, you can show them the "Rules For David" page at the front of the book. What is their opinion about it? If they like it, why? After students talk in pairs, you can have a brief, whole-class conversation about their opinions of this text feature. Direct students back to their notebooks and have them write about their opinion of this text feature. Remind students they can use the sentence stem *I notice how the author . . .* If your read-aloud is not conducive to this strategy, choose a previous read-aloud, either a picture book or a chapter book, that has text features students can notice. Two suggestions are *Thunder Cake* by Patricia Polacco, which includes a dedication page and a recipe, and *Thank You, Mr. Falker* by Patricia Polacco, which includes an illustrated dedication page, a prologue, and an epilogue. Give students copies of the text feature pages or show them on a document camera.
SHARE IT	All students share their entry with a partner. Then two students, previously chosen, read their entry to the class. Classmates comment on where each student used the strategy taught.

NOTICING SMALL TEXT FEATURES

NAME IT	Writing what you notice about way the actual text is written, which can include layout, font style, size of text, and use of bold or italics, and what you think of it. **Sentence stem:** *I notice how the author . . .*
WHY DO IT?	Helps you think about choices an author makes and how they affect your experience or understanding of what you read.
MODEL IT	*I notice how Cynthia Lord sometimes puts words in italics when she writes dialogue. It makes you say the word with extra emphasis in your mind, like when Catherine says to David, ". . . and that is the last time I'm saying it!" So I can really hear Catherine say that word really loud and I can tell that Catherine is really getting annoyed.* Ask students to name what characteristic of text you noticed in *Rules* and why you liked it.
TRY IT	**Turn and talk:** Have students tell a partner what it means to notice small text features. **Strategy entry:** Students open the strategy section of their reader's notebooks and write "Noticing Small Text Features" at the top of the next blank page. Then ask them to take out their author pages and see if there are any small text features they notice. After a few minutes, students can talk in pairs about what they noticed. For *Rules*, students will likely notice how Cynthia Lord has David's rules in a handwriting font or how words on Jason's cards are in a different font. Direct students back to their notebooks and have them write a strategy entry about this author's use of small text features. Remind students they can use the sentence stem *I notice how the author . . .*
SHARE IT	All students share their entry with a partner. Then two students, previously chosen, read their entry to the class. Classmates comment on where each student used the strategy taught.

EVALUATING TEXT FEATURES

NAME IT	Assessing the value of text features and the effectiveness of author choices. **Sentence stems:** *The author does a good job . . . ; This is effective because . . . ; The author might have considered . . .*
WHY DO IT?	Helps you think beyond your own personal reactions; requires you to draw on your background knowledge of text structure and author choices to make a comparative assessment.
MODEL IT	If you have taught one of the lessons about opinions of text features, it is particularly effective to write about the same text feature but now from a more objective view. *Cynthia Lord does a good job creating titles for her chapters. Each one starts off with one of the many rules Catherine makes up for David on how to live an everyday life. This is effective because each rule hints at what the chapter might be about, which can spark interest for the reader. But it is also effective because it reminds us of David's frame of mind. One thing Cynthia Lord might have considered was putting David's whole list of rules in the front of the book like a table of contents. Then she could have put David's actual list of rules later in the book . . .* Ask students what you said was effective about Cynthia Lord's use of chapter titles and what she could have also considered doing.

TRY IT	**Turn and talk:** Have students tell a partner what the difference is between stating your opinion about a text feature and evaluating a text feature. Follow with a brief, whole-class share.
	Strategy entry: Students open the strategy section of their reader's notebooks and write "Evaluating Text Features" at the top of the next blank page. Use the author pages or copies of the text used in one of the "Noticing Text Features" lessons. Ask students to talk in pairs about a text feature they already wrote about, but this time to think about it from a more evaluative standpoint. What is effective about it? What could the author have done differently? Then direct students back to their notebooks and have them write an entry in which they evaluate a text feature. Remind students they can use some of the sentence stems you shared: *The author does a good job . . . , This is effective because . . . ,* or *The author might have considered . . .*
SHARE IT	All students share their entry with a partner. Then two students, previously chosen, read their entry to the class. Classmates comment on where each student used the strategy taught.

FIGURE 3.8

"Evaluating Text Features" Strategy Entry

Evaluating Text features

The faction Manifestos are a good idea for readers to look at. Veronica Roth had a good idea when adding these to the text feature section. The manifestos cleary state the rules of each faction, in a way that even further expresses their qualities. Ex: Amity's manifesto is written like a play. One thing Veronica Roth may want to do, is put the faction symbols somewhere in the section, just to add something to look at, make it more interesting. Overall, I greatly appreciate the faction Manifestos.

NOTICING AUTHOR'S CRAFT

NAME IT	Writing what you notice about the way the author writes.
	Sentence stems: *I like how the author . . . ; I notice how the author . . .*
WHY DO IT?	Helps you become more aware of a particular author's writing style; creates reading-writing connections.
MODEL IT	*I notice how Cynthia Lord uses a lot of short sentences in her writing. It's funny because her writing is very powerful and full of feelings, but when I look closely there are a lot of simple sentences. Sometimes she even just has three- or four-word sentences like "They look broken" or "I close my sketchbook."*
	Ask students to name what you noticed about the way Cynthia Lord writes.
TRY IT	**Turn and talk:** Have students tell a partner what it means to write about author's craft in your reader's notebook.
	Strategy entry: Students open the strategy section of their reader's notebooks and write "Noticing Author's Craft" at the top of the next blank page. Write a list on the board of aspects of writing to consider, such as imagery, descriptions, sentence variety, and dialogue. You can also ask students to offer suggestions first, particularly if they have learned about these aspects in writing lessons. Then ask students to take out their author pages and have them talk in pairs about anything they notice or like about the way this author writes.
	Follow partner discussions with a whole-class share in which you write their ideas on the board or chart paper. Encourage students to be as specific as possible about what they notice and give examples from the text. Keep this list on the board (or create a poster) so it can be used with the next lesson. Then direct students back to their reader's notebooks to write a strategy entry.
	For more scaffolding, you can direct students' attention to a particular aspect of writing. With *Rules,* for example, you might ask students to talk in pairs about what they notice about how Cynthia Lord writes dialogue, how she shows emotions, or the different ways she uses dashes.
SHARE IT	All students share their entry with a partner. Then two students, previously chosen, read their entry to the class. Classmates comment on where each student used the strategy taught.

EVALUATING AUTHOR'S CRAFT

NAME IT	Judging what is effective about the way an author writes.
	Sentence stems: *This is effective because . . . ; The author might have considered . . .*
WHY DO IT?	A more objective way of assessing the way an author writes based on general knowledge of writers' craft; helps us think beyond our own personal reactions.
MODEL IT	If you taught the lesson "Noticing Author's Craft," write about the same topic but with a more evaluative tone and point of view.
	I notice how Cynthia Lord uses a lot of short sentences in her writing. This is effective for two reasons. First, it adds variety to the rhythm of her sentences and her writing. A lot of times these short sentences come after long sentences like this: "In my sketchbook I try to draw my ankles distorted by pond water, but they don't look warped and interesting. They look broken." There is something about writing a long sentence first that makes the short sentence stand out and be more powerful. It's kind of like Cynthia Lord is making you really pay attention to those few words . . .

TRY IT	**Turn and talk:** Have students tell a partner what it means to evaluate an author's craft as opposed to just saying what you like about it.
	Strategy entry: Students open the strategy section of their reader's notebooks and write "Evaluating Author's Craft" at the top of the next blank page. Have students take out the same text that was used in "Noticing Author's Craft" and direct their attention to the list they created. They can write about the same author's craft, but now from an evaluative point of view, or they can choose another aspect of craft from the list.
	Have students reread the text again on their own, this time with a more evaluative eye. What is particularly effective, and why? Is there anything the author might have done differently or in addition? Remind students they can use the sentence stems *The author does a good job . . .*, *This is effective because . . .*, or *The author might have considered. . . .*
SHARE IT	All students share their entry with a partner. Then two students, previously chosen, read their entry to the class. Classmates comment on where each student used the strategy taught.

EVALUATING WORD CHOICE

NAME IT	Evaluating a particular sentence and how it affects the reader.
	Sentence stem: *This sentence is effective because . . .*
WHY DO IT?	Narrowing down our analysis of writing to just one sentence supports critical thinking about writing and word choice in general.
MODEL IT	*"Dad smiles, but it's a worn-out smile that doesn't light his eyes." This sentence is so effective because in only a few words it shows how your body language can give away how you really feel. He is smiling at Catherine's request to spend time with her but his eyes show that his heart is not quite in it. And the worn-out smile hints that he's tired, maybe tired from David and his job, and he just doesn't have the energy to give Catherine a real smile. So he fakes it. But his eyes give it away. So it's kind of like showing a complicated feeling instead of telling it . . .*
TRY IT	**Turn and talk:** Have students tell a partner you thought was effective about this sentence.
	Strategy entry: Students open the strategy section of their reader's notebooks and write "Evaluating Word Choice" at the top of the next blank page. Have students take out their author pages and look for one or two sentences they think are particularly interesting or effective. Then have them share with a partner and talk about why these sentences are interesting or effective. After a few minutes, ask students to choose one sentence to write about and then copy that sentence at the top of their strategy entry.
	Once they have their sentences written, have students write an entry in which they analyze and evaluate the sentence and how it affects the reader. Remind students they can start with the sentence stem *This sentence is effective because . . .*
SHARE IT	All students share their entry with a partner. Then two students, previously chosen, read their entry to the class. Classmates comment on where each student used the strategy taught.

EVALUATING TOPIC PRESENTATION

NAME IT	Judging how well an author portrays a particular issue through a story. **Sentence stems:** *The author writes effectively about this topic because . . . ; The author might have considered . . .*
WHY DO IT?	Encourages us to draw on previous knowledge about a topic and to think critically about how an author handles a particular topic.
MODEL IT	*The author writes effectively about the topic of autism. Cynthia Lord seems have a personal understanding of what an autistic child is like because David seems like a very real character. She also brings in an interesting comparison by having another character, Jason, with a different disability. Having both characters makes the reader think about what it means to be "disabled" and how different disabilities are perceived by people . . .* Ask students to describe what you said was effective about the way Cynthia Lord handles the topic of autism.
TRY IT	**Turn and talk:** Have students tell a partner what it means to evaluate an author's treatment of a topic, followed by a brief, whole-class share. **Strategy entry:** Have students turn to the next blank page in their notebook and at the top write "Evaluating Topic Presentation." On the board write the names of topics that come up in the read-aloud. You can also have students offer suggestions first. Other topics from *Rules* include bullying, divorce, and siblings. Have students talk in pairs about how the read-aloud handles one of these topics. Then direct students back to their reader's notebooks to write a strategy entry. Remind them to offer evidence to support their ideas, and also that they can begin their entry with *The author writes effectively about (topic) because . . .* For more scaffolding, you can use a read-aloud that is particularly conducive to this strategy, such as *Thank You, Mr. Falker* by Patricia Polacco, which explicitly addresses bullying and dyslexia, or *The Other Side* by Jacqueline Woodson, which explicitly addresses racism, innocence, and friendship.
SHARE IT	All students share their entry with a partner. Then two students, previously chosen, read their entry to the class. Classmates comment on where each student used the strategy taught.

EVALUATING CHARACTER DEVELOPMENT

NAME IT	Assessing how an author develops a particular character.
	Sentence stem: *One way the author develops the character of (name) is . . .*
WHY DO IT?	Cultivates an ability to evaluate and think critically about *how* an author develops a particular character over time.
MODEL IT	*One way Cynthia Lord develops the character of Catherine is that she shows her having a greater awareness of her own feelings as the book progresses. In the beginning, she mostly describes how she tries to be a good sister by making the world easier for David with all her rules. Catherine also is more aware of what other people think about David. In later chapters, she becomes more reflective about herself and starts letting out emotions . . .*
	Ask students to describe your evaluation of the way Cynthia Lord develops the character of Catherine.
TRY IT	**Turn and talk:** Have students tell a partner what it means to evaluate how an author develops a character as opposed to just writing about or analyzing a character. Follow with a brief, whole-class share.
	Strategy entry: Have students turn to the next blank page in their notebook and at the top write "Evaluating Character Development." Ask students to work in pairs and choose a different character from the read-aloud and discuss how the author develops that character. With *Rules*, you might have students evaluate how Cynthia Lord develops the character of Jason. How does she introduce readers to this character? How does she show how this character changes from the start of the book? Does she do these things effectively? Follow pair discussion with a whole-class share. Direct students back to their reader's notebooks to write a strategy entry, and remind them they can use the sentence stem *One way the author develops the character of (name) is . . .*
SHARE IT	All students share their entry with a partner. Then two students, previously chosen, read their entry to the class. Classmates comment on where each student used the strategy taught.

The lessons provided in this chapter are, of course, not exhaustive. You can develop your own strategy lessons based on observations of your students' writing. The key is to start out by just noticing sentences that show an interesting kind of thinking and then try to name what it is. This kind of planning is best done (and more fun) with fellow teachers so you can have a dialogue about what to name the strategy, how to verbalize why it's good, and how you might model it with one of your read-alouds. Then you can teach your own strategy lessons using the structure of "name it, why do it, model it, notice it, try it, share it."

CHAPTER 4:

Comprehension of Nonfiction Text

In third grade, the same year I was introduced to Book Bucks, I wrote my first official research report. My favorite part was stapling green construction paper together and drawing a picture of the state of Indiana, my assigned state. It looked very official. I found a book on Indiana from the school library and used the "I" encyclopedia. Looking back, I can't really say I *read* either book: it was more like picking out information from the text. Most of the work I remember doing was reading sentences about what crops and resources Indiana produced and then trying to figure out how I was going to write it "in my own words."

Today, the nonfiction books in classrooms are, fortunately, much more child friendly, designed to engage students of different reading ability levels in all sorts of topics. The expectations of reading have also changed since my elementary school years. There is a much bigger focus on teaching reading comprehension, which the RAND Reading Study Group defines as "the process of simultaneously extracting and constructing meaning through inter-action and involvement with written language" (Snow 2002). Unlike my Indiana book report days, there is also an expectation that, even though the processes may differ between reading narrative and informational text, students should be actively reading and comprehending the pages they read, regardless of the genre.

Despite a greater emphasis on nonfiction reading and the availability of high-interest texts, there still seems to be a discrepancy between how well students comprehend fiction books they read versus nonfiction books of the same level. On occasion, a student becomes engrossed in nonfiction (especially when the subject *is* gross), but generally most students have a harder time reading nonfiction text fluently. I've worked with many students who do what I call "sort of reading," where they mostly study the colorful pictures and diagrams or they "read" the sentences in the pages of their nonfiction book, but in a passive way rather than actively making and monitoring meaning.

Connections to the Reader's Notebook

This "sort of" reading not surprisingly leads to "sort of" comprehending, and the domino effect continues into the reader's notebook. Without a strong literal understanding of a text, students stand on a shaky foundation when asked to write about what they learned *and* think critically about what they read. When that happens, the book, rather than the student, becomes the primary source of information. As a result, students resort to overrelying on the text and picking out information, just like I did when I wrote my Indiana report.

"Sort of reading" occurs more frequently with expository texts because of the more challenging and content-specific vocabulary. We can, and should, teach and model "in-the-head actions" readers take when comprehension breaks down, such as going back to the beginning of the sentence or using context clues to figure out an unfamiliar word (Fountas and Pinnell 2001). But using these strategies first requires consistent engagement of text. After all, to be aware when you're not understanding something, you have to be engaged and understanding in the first place! In simple terms, reading nonfiction well simply requires more effort on the part of the reader: more effort to monitor understanding, more effort in using word-solving strategies, and more effort in using provided text features. An added challenge is that students can look at the pages of a nonfiction book, with all their colorful pictures and diagrams, and garner information without actually reading much. We can and should teach students how to get the most information out of the diagrams and pictures often found in this type of text (Allen 2008), but such strategies are meant to be used in addition to students fluently reading the text.

Though the challenges in reading nonfiction text well may be understandable, it is critical to still have expectations that students read informational text as fluently as possible and to find ways to support this expectation. Reading and writing about information is arguably one of the most important skills our students will learn. Most of the reading and writing students do in middle school, high school, and any kind of postsecondary education is expository. And it doesn't end there. Nonfiction reading accounts for nearly

90 percent of all adult reading, including reading related to work (Zinsser 1998). So students' interactions with nonfiction texts in elementary and middle school grades create a critical foundation for the rest of their lives.

Before presenting strategy lessons for informational text, this chapter addresses this critical first step of students independently reading expository text *to their potential* so that they can comprehend and then write about it to the best of their ability. Although there are many ways to support quality independent reading, this chapter describes one particular strategy called Expert Teams. This reading structure that uses student-facilitated reading groups creates a social context for reading and provides scaffolding for attending to and processing expository text.

One of the key features of Expert Team reading is that it gives students the opportunity to talk and process information in small increments. Students read a few pages at a time, and then discuss what they learned, which makes reading with a high degree of attention easier. And when students more thoroughly process information along the way, both through attentive reading and time to process orally with peers, they are better able to use themselves as the main resource for writing; the book can be a secondary tool, as it should be, to use in a supportive fashion. In addition, because students tend to have a stronger literal comprehension of what they read, there is more cognitive room to incorporate higher-order thinking while writing. As students become more accustomed to reading this way, and also experience the learning benefits of attending fully to texts, these habits can transfer to the way they read nonfiction books independently.

Getting Teams Ready

I usually start Expert Team reading as part of a nonfiction unit of study. Teams are made up of three or four students who are somewhat on the same reading level and meet several times a week. Similar-ability grouping, as opposed to mixed-ability groups, offers the important aspect of accountability: a group of students who have read the same pages can clear up misconceptions for one another, ask clarifying questions, and compare the similarities or differences in their reactions to a particular fact.

The books students read in Expert Teams will depend on availability of texts in your school and classroom. Nonfiction guided reading books work the best because they often come in sets at different reading levels, and the topics and text features are of high interest. Understandably, not every classroom has this option. Short texts and articles can also be used or even nonfiction chapters in basal reading books. What matters most is that each student in a team has his or her own copy of a text and that the book is on or at least near that team's reading level. In my classroom, I used *National Geographic* books that come in groups of five and cover a variety of topics, such as Egyptian pyramids, the moon, and rain forests. I also supplemented what I had with guided reading sets borrowed from a second-grade teacher for one group of my below-grade-level readers.

Sets of books are kept in bins labeled by content topic, such as "Plants," "Weather," or "Biographies." The books in each set have either a yellow, green, blue, or red sticker on the front cover to indicate a general order of reading level, ranging from a second- to fifth-grade level. Each team is assigned a color so they can autonomously choose books on their level.

Introducing Expert Team Reading

The anchor chart in Figure 4.1 illustrates the steps of Expert Team reading.

FIGURE 4.1

Expert Team Anchor Chart

EXPERT TEAM READING
- Record book information
- What do you already know?
- Word quiz
- Read and share*

Repeat until it's time for reader's notebooks.

Each Expert Team is assigned a particular area of the classroom to meet in. Using the whole classroom spreads students out, which helps with noise level when teams are discussing text with one another. Meeting in different spots besides their desks also adds variety to the school day. In my classroom, two teams sat on the rug, one team got the comfortable blue chairs, one team sat at my desk, and one team sat on pillows in the hallway. Every month, teams rotated their meeting spot so everyone got to be in each place.

Recording Books

Once we have established the where of Expert Teams, and practiced the transition, I share the book log students will fill out each time they choose a new book (Figure 4.2). Each person in a team records the title, author, and topic in his or her own book log, which is kept in a folder. Beyond the typical reasons for documenting reading, students can also use this sheet to help them decide which book they might read next. The bird's-eye view of their choices helps teams to monitor a balance between science and social studies and to consider specific topics they have not yet chosen. Students like the formalness of the checklist, and when it comes time to choose the next book, a team can see at a glance which topics they have yet to cover. This component of independence is particularly important as students move into the middle school grades, because it aligns developmentally with students' desire for autonomy (Eccles et al. 1993).

FIGURE 4.2

Expert Team Reading Book Log

EXPERT TEAM READING BOOK LOG									

Team Name _____

Team Members _____ | _____

		Science				Social Studies		
Title of Book	Date	Earth Science	Plants & Animals	Astronomy & Space	Human Body	American History	Countries & Cultures	Biography	Geography

For the first day of Expert Teams, you can teach and model this process of choosing and recording and then take students through it step by step in their actual teams. They will also need to see and practice what to do when they finish a book and need to choose a new one. By the end of that first day, each team should have their first book chosen, recorded, and ready to go for the next day. You can also use this first day to go over any group norms and expectations.

What Do You Already Know?

The next day students learn and practice the "What Do You Already Know?" step in which they look at the book cover and talk with one another about what they already know about this topic. Talking about what you already know, or what you think you already know about a topic (Stead 2006), is a common practice in whole-class read-alouds and guided reading. It stimulates background knowledge and creates interest. But how often students talk or think about what they already know on their own when they choose a new book is questionable. Having students talk in small, student-facilitated groups, however, provides that important middle step in the gradual release of responsibility (Pearson and Gallagher 1983) so that there is scaffolding between guided teacher instruction and independence.

To introduce and model this step, show students the cover of a nonfiction book, offer a few comments about what you already know about the topic, and then ask several students to offer their own comments. Remind students that they can share any background knowledge, no matter how small or commonly known it may seem. Students then meet in their own Expert Teams to try out "What Do You Already Know?" with their new books. On this first day, after the teams try this step, follow up with a whole-class share to talk about how this step went and what came up in their discussions.

Word Quiz

Either that same day or on another day, you can model and have teams practice the "word quiz" step in which students talk about the key vocabulary words in their books. It's not really a quiz in the conventional sense, but calling it a quiz solidifies it as an expected step, and students embrace the activity as more than a "Look at the key vocabulary and see if you know them." Creating this space to talk about content-specific words not only stimulates group knowledge about word meanings but also provides a strong basis for vocabulary acquisition because these words will be in contextually relevant sentences once they start reading independently (McKeown et al. 1985).

Because books differ according to how and whether they highlight key vocabulary, there are several ways students can do the word quiz. If all the books in the Expert Team bins have the same format, you only have to teach one of the options. You can easily model all three options, but, if this is needed, you may want to make a small anchor chart or a handout (see Figure 4.3), that they can keep in their folder or binder to remind them of which option goes with a certain type of book.

FIGURE 4.3
Word Quiz Choices

WORD QUIZ	
A glossary and a word list	Start with the word list, then look at the glossary.
Just a glossary	One person is the word quizzer.
No glossary	Choose two words to quiz your team.

The first option is for books that have both a glossary and a list of the highlighted vocabulary words on the first page. In this case, teams start with the word list and, using a piece of paper or large index card, reveal one word at a time and discuss what they think this word means or in what context they have heard it used. Once they finish with all the words, they can turn to the glossary to check their understanding. One student can read the definitions out loud and pause to see whether anyone has a comment or question before moving on to the next definition.

If students' books only have a glossary, then the team can designate one person to be the "word quizzer" and quiz their teammates. In this case, the word quizzer reads the word and then the team talks about what they think the word means. The word quizzer can use the "reveal one word at a time" method with an index card so that he or she can also be part of the conversation. After each word is discussed, the word quizzer moves the index card and reads the definition aloud.

Finally, if students are reading books that have neither a word list nor a glossary, then all students skim the text for a few minutes and choose one or two content-related words to ask one another. Some books may have boldfaced or italicized vocabulary words while others may not. Students then take turns quizzing one another on the words they chose. Similar to the other two word-quiz protocols, students talk about the possible meaning of each word or where they have heard it used.

Regardless of which option students use, the point of the word quiz is not to recite or to guess the exact definition but to build meaning through dialogue. By quizzing one another, students have to actively think about their understanding of words. Just reading definitions from a glossary, on the other hand, is a more passive way to process word meaning. Even in the third option, when students can't check their understanding of words against a correct definition in a glossary, there is still value in students' actively thinking and talking to create a shared understanding of words they will encounter.

Read and Share

For most of Expert Team time, students alternate between independent reading and discussing text. It's important to emphasize that this "read and share" step is not a time for students to read out loud as a group. Students read a few pages of text *on their own* and then share one fact they have learned. Once Expert Teams get going, you can also raise the expectations of what students talk about in this discussion space. Eventually, I encourage students to use fact sharing as a springboard for conversation in which they share what they think about the information they just read. But first, I focus on the primary purpose of Expert Teams, which is supporting quality literal comprehension and attention to text.

Ideally, each independent reading session takes about three or four minutes, although this will depend on the age and ability of your students. The amount of text students choose each time should be long enough so that they learn new information but not so long that attention to text might dissipate. Since nonfiction books differ in font size and amount of text on a page, each team decides how many pages to read after they talk. One group might decide to read up to the next chapter, while another team agrees to read from page 12 to page 16. The boldfaced headings, a common text feature in nonfiction books, can also serve as good markers for where to read up to next.

This read and share pattern continues for about ten or fifteen minutes, at which point the students take out their reader's notebooks and write independent entries about what they just read. Because teams are somewhat on the same reading level and students independently read only a few pages at a time, they tend to read at about the same pace. That said, I suggest that anyone waiting for their teammates can examine related diagrams, photographs, or illustrations. I also point out early in the year the common error of equating good reading with fast reading, and that being done first does not mean a student is a "better" reader. If a team finishes a book before it's time to move on to writing, they can either have a longer share time to talk about their book or they can simply take out their reader's notebooks and get an early start.

The Benefits of Talk

Giving students opportunities to talk about what they learned at different points throughout a single text, as opposed to just waiting until the end of the book, creates several unique and important benefits. First, readers are better able to construct meaning when they have time to digest and synthesize information (Harvey and Goudvis 2007), a concept that is particularly true with nonfiction text. Talking allows students to synthesize understanding because students have to actively process ideas in order to talk about them (Cazden 2001). Second, purposeful talking creates opportunities for students to develop expressive and receptive vocabulary (Vasilyeva and Waterfall 2011).

This read and share process also supports monitoring of comprehension, both because students can check or clarify understanding with a peer and because it reinforces the idea that "building meaning from text is an iterative process in which one takes in text and considers the ideas it offers" (Beck and McKeown 2001, 231). Using a social context for learning can also positively impact student engagement, motivation to read, and experiences of self-efficacy (Ruddell and Unrau 2004). In addition, interest-driven social reading builds content knowledge in an authentic way, especially compared to textbook reading, since it more closely resembles how real readers, both children and adults, learn about the world.

Including times in the school day when all students talk, as opposed to only calling on students who raise their hands, is critical because it determines who reaps the benefits of talking. Students who are less likely to raise their hand during whole-class discussions— either because of a lack of confidence in their ideas or English language limitations—are more likely to be passive learners, only listening to and relying on the ideas of their peers.

One of the most important benefits of giving students time to talk during reading, however, is not about the talk itself but about how talking can influence the way students process text *as they read independently*. If I know I will be turning to another ten-year-old once I finish reading a few pages, I will more likely read the text with a higher degree of attention. A short-term goal of the read and share structure is that it helps students process sections of text more carefully so that they have a stronger foundation on which to understand subsequent sections of text, which in turn creates a solid foundation for writing in their reader's notebooks. The long-term goal, then, of the read and share structure is that it scaffolds independent reading and creates the habit of reading informational text with attention, effort, and reflection.

Content Connections

An additional benefit of Expert Team reading is that it increases students' exposure to a wide variety of content topics. The books I use reflect the science and social studies standards, not just for my grade but for many grades. Creating space for wide reading of nonfiction books has been shown to be an effective, indirect way to build background knowledge and has even led to increases in content-area achievement (Fisher, Ross, and Grant 2010). Given the increasing gaps in students' background knowledge of content topics, which tends to vary greatly along socioeconomic lines, finding ways to expose students to a wide variety of content topics, particularly in the early years, is critical (Neuman 2006). Expert Teams contribute to students' background knowledge in a unique way because they strengthen students' ability to build their own background knowledge through independent reading and to talk about what they learn in a social setting.

Bringing in the Reader's Notebook

During the first few weeks of Expert Team reading, the focus is on getting students familiar and comfortable with these new routines and expectations. I wait until teams can independently go through each step and then I reintroduce the reader's notebooks. Each Expert Team reading session is then followed by ten to fifteen minutes of students writing independent entries in their reader's notebooks. After the writing session, teams get back together to share their entries with one another. Then we end the period with a whole-class share in which members of one team share their entries with the whole class.

When students write these independent entries, there are no prompts or guidelines. Supported by independence lessons described in Chapter 6, students understand they can write about what they learned that day and what they think about that information. This is where the connection to informational strategy lessons occurs. Through informational strategy lessons, taught on different days from Expert Team reading, students learn specific ways to ask questions, make connections, analyze, synthesize, and evaluate information when writing about their books. The next chapter presents forty-three strategy lessons for thinking critically and reflectively with informational texts as well as lessons that support visualizing and monitoring comprehension.

Expert Team reading is not an end unto itself. The ideal, of course, is that students read nonfiction text to the best of their ability without the support of a group. The goals of Expert Team reading are to engage students with this genre and to create the habits of mind for reading informational text well. Once students become used to reading nonfiction with focus and intention, and experience the positive benefits from connecting with text and learning new information in a social setting, they are more likely to sustain this habit when they read on their own.

Even when our formal unit of study on nonfiction is over, I still keep Expert Teams going. Without reinforcement or practice, the habit of reading nonfiction with a high level of attention and accountability is more likely to diminish over time, especially for our more reluctant readers. Continuing Expert Team reading beyond a nonfiction unit of study also demonstrates that nonfiction is not something we read because it's the genre of the month but because learning new information is a way of life, something we do as lifelong readers.

CHAPTER 5:

Lessons for Nonfiction Text

everal years ago I took my niece Olivia to see a special showing of *March of the Penguins*. The theater was packed, full of squirming and giggling kids, many whose heads barely peeked over the seats. The adults, looking quite tall in their seats, alternated between shushing their kids and watching trivia facts about Tom Cruise and Melanie Griffith that flashed on the screen. Soon the lights dimmed, the squirming died down, and all heads stared straight ahead as the frozen world of Antarctica came to life.

Just as the female penguins were about to return to their mates who had been carefully guarding the eggs, a high-pitched fire alarm filled the air, the lights came on, the movie shut off, and an usher calmly shouted, "Please file to the exit doors on the right and left of the movie screen!" For about ten minutes Olivia and I, along with everyone else, stood outside on the sidewalk while we waited to see what the firefighters would say. Naturally, we started talking about the movie.

Liz: *So, Olivia, what do you think? Do you like it so far?*

Olivia: *Yeah. The penguins are so cute.*

Liz: *I know. I love the way they waddle.*

Olivia: *But why, why . . . how come they live in such a cold place? I mean, if it's so hard, why don't they live somewhere else?*

Liz: *Hmmm. That's a good question. You know I am not really sure.*

Olivia: *Maybe they only know how to live in snow and cold. Kind of like how flamingos only know how to live where it's warm . . .*

Then a fire marshal announced that we could return to the movie theater and that it had been a false alarm. We shuffled back to our seats, and in a few minutes, the movie picked up where it had left off.

The good part about that unexpected, ten-minute break (besides the fact that it was not winter) was that I got to hear some of Olivia's thoughts about the movie. Not that we hadn't been thinking during the movie. Even though our thinking was internal and lightning fast, we were making personal connections and predictions that kept us engaged and wanting to know what would happen next. We just weren't really aware of those thoughts. What we were most aware of was . . . watching the movie! Analyzing a movie on a deeper level is difficult when, at the same time, your mind is still trying to *take in* more information.

The same thing can be said about reading. We think when we read. But it's hard to be aware of our thoughts until we are no longer taking in the words on the page. This is especially true with informational texts because students are taking in so many new facts as they read. It's when we are *not* reading or, in the case of Olivia, *not* watching the movie, that we can think thoughtfully about our reactions, questions, and analysis about the information we read.

One of the benefits of teaching comprehension lessons using informational texts, besides that fact that students are reading nonfiction, is that the concreteness of information can create a higher awareness of the different comprehension strategies. Learning specific ways to write and think about this genre of text is extremely important because there are differences in how we think critically about information than we do about characters. *Reality Checks* author Tony Stead (2006) also points out that the inferential thinking students learn and practice with nonfiction texts can be transferred to fiction texts, but not the other way around.

The lessons in this chapter can be taught within a nonfiction unit of study, or, for teachers who prefer to emphasize a variety of genres throughout the school year, these lessons can be taught alongside their narrative counterparts. Some lessons in this chapter parallel the strategy lessons presented in Chapter 3 and some are specific to nonfiction. Also included in this chapter are strategy lessons to support writing about visualizing and monitoring. Although these comprehension skills apply just as much to the reading of narrative text, students tend to need more support in using them with expository texts and so benefit from active reflection about using these skills.

For the lessons in this chapter, I use the book *The Honey Makers* by Gail Gibbons to model the strategy and as the basis for students' strategy entries. Similar to Chapter 3, some lessons are followed by actual strategies written by students in grades three through eight. Because thinking and writing analytically and critically about nonfiction text can be more challenging for students, many lessons have a higher degree of scaffolding than a narrative strategy lesson. I encourage you to use *The Honey Makers* as a read-aloud in your classroom so you can take advantage of these lessons. Appendix B offers a list of other nonfiction picture books you might also consider using with strategy lessons.

One particular supportive strategy that is described in the following informational strategy lessons is the use of a shared text, either actual copies of the read-aloud you use in the lessons or paper copies. In my classroom, for example, I had enough soft cover copies of *The Honey Makers* that pairs of students could share the book during a lesson. When students have visual access to the text they can focus on using the strategy being taught rather than spending energy trying to remember parts of the book. Recalling information is simply more challenging compared to remembering scenes of a story or characters that recur throughout many chapters.

Another advantage of having these shared texts is that, after you finish this book as a read-aloud, you can use it for weeks or months of strategy lessons. The more familiar students become with a certain book, the more they can focus on their thinking about that book. Using the same text also reinforces that there are numerous ways to think and write about the same information.

For additional scaffolding you can read aloud the page or pages you will be asking students to write about that day while they follow along. Whether you do this depends on your students' ages and the complexity of the text. Since the point of strategy lessons is thinking and writing *about* reading, and not the actual comprehension of text, it's important that all students have the access they need to the information they will write about.

Questioning

The kinds of questions we ask about information are often different from questions we ask about characters. Not that asking questions about information is a new concept to students! Even before they get to kindergarten children ask question after question that begins with *Why?* They just simply want to know "how this big, wide, wonderful world works" (Stead 2002, 11). An important aspect of this kind of wondering is that it is often part of a dialogue with adults. We do our best to answer their *why* questions, both to share information and to encourage curiosity (although even my sister has admitted to, after the fifteenth *why* question, finally saying, "Why is the wall blue? Because it is! That's why!").

So when it comes to asking questions about our big, wide, wonderful world, children are often used to saying their questions out loud to someone and, more important, are used to getting answers in return or, at the very least, a response. In reader's notebooks, we're asking students to write a question to—nobody! We certainly don't express it this way. But writing about your thinking, even if you know the teacher will read your entry, holds a strange middle ground between writing for yourself and writing for an outside audience.

Another difference about wondering with information is that questions about bees or the solar system or China usually have definitive answers unlike, say, the motive of a character in a story. So it makes sense that with nonfiction texts students are even more apt to write down a question and leave it at that. With strategy lessons, we can show students that, similar to writing about narrative text, the benefit of asking questions is not so much the questions themselves, or whether you can find out the exact answer, but where those questions can take you.

WONDER QUESTIONS

NAME IT	Asking a question about something you wonder.
	Sentence stem: *I wonder why . . .*
WHY DO IT?	Helps you to be reflective about what you read and can lead to inferential thinking.
MODEL IT	*I wonder how a beekeeper can tell which one is the queen bee? I know she looks a little different but there are so many bees! How would they possibly tell them apart? I mean, don't they need to know which one is the queen if they want to start a new hive?. . .*
	Ask students to say what you are wondering about bees.
TRY IT	**Turn and talk:** Have students tell a partner why it can be good to wonder about information you learn. Follow with a brief, whole-class share.
	Strategy entry: In the strategy section of their reader's notebook, students write "Wonder Questions" at the top of the page. Ask students to take out their shared text and turn to one particular page of the read-aloud. As you read one or two pages aloud, ask students to keep in mind what they might wonder. Then ask students to write a strategy entry in which they ask a least one wonder question and explain their wondering.
SHARE IT	All students share their entry with a partner. Then two students, previously chosen, read their entries to the class. Classmates comment on where each student used the strategy taught.

CONFUSION QUESTIONS

NAME IT	Questioning a fact or part of the book that does not make sense to you.
	Sentence stem: *I don't understand the part about . . .*
WHY DO IT?	Helps you identify exactly which part or concept does not make sense, which makes subsequent thinking more specific; also supports monitoring your understanding of the text.
MODEL IT	*I don't understand the part about how the larva turns into a pupa. How can the larva possibly spin something around itself? It doesn't even have any legs yet! In fact, the illustration shows the larva being nothing but a gray blob. So how can a blob spin something? Maybe it spins the silky stuff but just not in the way a spider does, which is the way I'm picturing it.*
	Ask students to name what part of *The Honey Makers* confused you and why it confused you.
TRY IT	**Turn and talk:** Have students tell a partner why it can be good to write about a part that is confusing to you. Follow with a brief, whole-class share.
	Strategy entry: Have students take out their shared text and turn to a part that you think might produce some confusion questions. With *The Honey Makers*, for example, you might have them turn to the "Dances of the Honeybee" section, which describes how bees communicate. Ask students to reread the three pages about how bees communicate and think about any fact, even if it is a detail, that they don't quite understand. Then have students write a strategy entry, reminding them they can use the phrase *I don't understand that part about . . .* For additional scaffolding have students talk in pairs before they write.
SHARE IT	All students share their entry with a partner. Then two students, previously chosen, read their entries to the class. Classmates comment on where each student used the strategy taught.

SMALL QUESTIONS

NAME IT	Asking a question about a detail on a particular page, either in the text or the illustration.
WHY DO IT?	Asking different "sizes" of questions leads to different types of thinking about your book. Small questions help you look at and wonder about information you might not have considered.
MODEL IT	*I wonder what a bee sees with her compound eyes? It says that each eye is made up of many lenses. But does that mean the bees see different things in one eyeball? On the one hand, that could be helpful for seeing flowers. But wouldn't it also get confusing? Maybe her eyes do see one thing at a time like we do but the different lenses do something else, like let in different amounts of light . . .*
	Ask students to say why your wonder question is an example of a small question.
TRY IT	**Turn and talk:** Have students tell a partner why it can be good to sometimes ask small questions, followed by a brief, whole-class share.
	Strategy entry: In the strategy section of their reader's notebook, students write "Small Questions" at the top of the page. Direct students to a particular page in their shared text, and, if needed, read aloud as students follow along. Have students talk in pairs or small groups, and see whether they can come up with one or two small questions they could ask from those pages. After a few minutes, ask for several suggestions and write those small questions on the board. Direct students back to their reader's notebooks to write a strategy entry in which they ask at least one small question. Students can choose either a question they talked about or one from the list on the board.

SHARE IT	All students share their entry with a partner. Then two students, previously chosen, read their entries to the class. Classmates comment on where each student used the strategy taught.

BIG QUESTIONS

NAME IT	Asking global questions that run throughout the whole book and are not particular to any page.
WHY DO IT?	Asking different "sizes" of questions leads to different types of thinking about your book. Big questions help you think about themes that run throughout a book.
MODEL IT	*I wonder if the bees understand that all the honey they make is being taken? I mean originally they make it for their own survival and for their offspring. Although, a lot of the bees, since their life is so short, don't know any other way I guess. Maybe the first few generations have to adjust, but not after that. So maybe it's all part of the process. I still wonder if they would make honey a different way if they were in a real hive and not making honey for people . . .* Ask students to say why your wonder question is an example of a big question.
TRY IT	**Turn and talk:** Have students tell a partner why it can be good to sometimes ask big questions about what you learn, followed by a brief, whole-class share. **Strategy entry:** In the strategy section of their reader's notebook, students write "Big Questions" at the top of the page. Have students talk in pairs or small groups, and see if they can come up with two or three big questions about the topic of the read-aloud, in this case about bees and beekeepers. Since these are global questions, it is better to have students skim through all of the shared text pages for one minute rather than direct them to particular pages. After a few minutes of partner talk, ask for several suggestions of big questions and write them on the board. Have students write a strategy entry in which they ask at least one big question. Students can either choose a question they talked about or one from the list on the board.
SHARE IT	All students share their entry with a partner. Then two students, previously chosen, read their entries to the class. Classmates comment on where each student used the strategy taught.

PERSONAL QUESTIONS

NAME IT	Asking a question or wondering about the personal experience of a person, animal, or living thing in your book. **Sentence stem:** *I wonder . . .*
WHY DO IT?	Makes you think beyond facts to how the people and living things you are reading about experience life; helps you more personally connect with the information.
MODEL IT	*I wonder if the bees get confused when they keep getting their honey taken away? They have been working so hard to get the honey there in the first place. And to them it must look like this great big hand coming in and taking what they made! The book says that the honey collectors use a smoker to calm the bees before they open their hive. So maybe they don't really know what's going on. But when the smoke wears off, I wonder if they actually realize the honey is gone . . .* Ask students to say why the first sentence is an example of a personal question.
TRY IT	**Turn and talk:** Have students tell a partner how personal questions benefit your experience with information you learn, followed by a brief, whole-class share. **Strategy entry:** In the strategy section of their reader's notebook, students write "Personal Questions" at the top of the page. Give students several minutes to skim their shared text and look for a particular person or type of bee they could ask a personal question about. Then have students write a strategy entry in which they ask a personal question and write more about that idea. For more scaffolding, have a pair share or whole-class share in which students can share ideas for personal questions.
SHARE IT	All students share their entry with a partner. Then two students, previously chosen, read their entries to the class. Classmates comment on where each student used the strategy taught.

KNOWLEDGE QUESTIONS

NAME IT	Wondering how people know certain information that is presented in your book. **Sentence stem:** *I wonder how . . .*
WHY DO IT?	Helps you go beyond learning facts to think about how people learn and the discovery process of information.
MODEL IT	*I wonder how people know that the color white makes bees calm? Maybe they did a test with different colors years ago when they first came up with the beekeeping outfits. Or it could be that they noticed certain people kept getting stung but anyone who happened to be wearing white was not getting stung as much . . .* Ask students to say what knowledge question you asked about bees.
TRY IT	**Turn and talk:** Have students tell a partner what it means to ask a knowledge question, followed by a brief, whole-class share. **Strategy entry:** In the strategy section of their reader's notebook, students write "Knowledge Questions" at the top of the page. Have students talk in pairs or small groups to come up with two or three questions about the topic of the read-aloud, in this case about bees and beekeepers. They can skim through the shared text for ideas if they want. After a few minutes, have a whole-class share and write three or four of students' suggestions for knowledge questions that start with *I wonder how . . .* Then have students choose one of the knowledge questions to write about in a strategy entry. For more scaffolding, write one or two of your own knowledge questions on the board that relate to a particular page in their shared text. For *The Honey Makers* you might have students turn to "Dances of the Honey Bees" and then give students the question *I wonder how people figured out what the different movements of bees meant?* to begin their entry.

SHARE IT	All students share their entry with a partner. Then two students, previously chosen, read their entries to the class. Classmates comment on where each student used the strategy taught.

Making Connections

Making personal, text, and world connections are fairly common agenda items in the world of reading comprehension instruction. Most curricula seem to encourage this type of thinking throughout many different grade levels, particularly with narrative texts. Less emphasis is placed on making these same types of connections with nonfiction texts. And yet the connections can be just as rich. Of course, the more exposure students have to different cultures, books, museums, and discussions with adults, the more background knowledge they have with which to make many of these connections. But connections to information can be made on many different levels and through many different mediums. Similar to strategy lessons with narrative texts, the following lessons aim to go beyond noticing similarities that lie at the surface to using connections as a starting place for comparative and critical thinking.

PERSONAL CONNECTIONS

NAME IT	Making a connection between something in the book and an event or experience in your life.
	Sentence stem: *When I read the part about . . . it reminded me of . . .*
WHY DO IT?	Creates additional meaning to the information you are reading and stimulates background knowledge.
MODEL IT	*When I read the part about using the wax from honeycombs to make candles it reminded me of the time when I was ten years old and we stopped at a store in Block Island that made their own honey. We ended up buying several off-white beeswax candles. I remember they seemed so smooth and really did smell a little like honey . . .*
	Ask students to say what personal connection you made with *The Honey Makers*.
TRY IT	**Turn and talk:** Have students tell a partner why it can be good to make a personal connection when you are writing about nonfiction, followed by a brief, whole-class share.
	Strategy entry: In the strategy section of their reader's notebook, students write "Personal Connections" at the top of the page. Have students skim the shared text and look for any place they can make a personal connection (or where they remember making one) and have them describe this connection to a partner. Then have students write their strategy entry, reminding them they can start their connection with the phrase *When I read the part about . . . it reminded me of . . .*
SHARE IT	All students share their entry with a partner. Then two students, previously chosen, read their entries to the class. Classmates comment on where each student used the strategy taught.

FIGURE 5.1

"Personal Connections" Strategy Entry

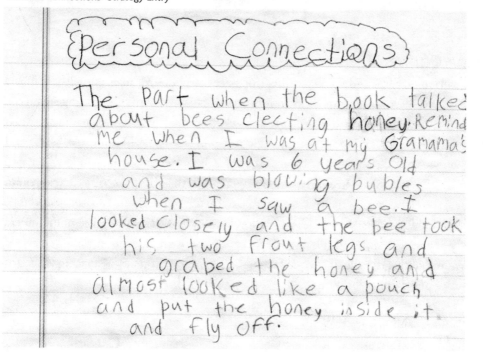

BOOK CONNECTIONS

NAME IT	Making a comparison between your book and another book.
	Sentence stem: *This book reminds me of . . .*
WHY DO IT?	Makes us aware of choices different authors make about how to present the same information; develops our ability to be evaluative of the books we read.
MODEL IT	The Honey Makers *reminds me of* The Magic School Bus *book about bees. I remember Ms. Frizzle took the kids to see what a bee's work was like. The illustrations in the two books are similar because they are both very colorful and they have lots of little pictures and diagrams on the sides of the page (although* The Magic School Bus *book has so much going on in one page, it's more like reading a comic strip). That book also talked about other types of bees, not just honey bees . . .*
	Ask students to say what similarities and differences you noticed between *The Honey Makers* and *The Magic School Bus* book about bees.
TRY IT	**Turn and talk:** Have students tell a partner why it can be good to write about book connections. How does that help you as a reader? Follow with a brief, whole-class share.
	Strategy entry: This lesson works best if you read the first four or five pages of another nonfiction book that covers the same topic as your shared text. Before you read, remind students to look and listen for similarities and differences between this book and your read-aloud. You can also remind them that a book connection can relate to anything about a book: the way an author writes, the text features, the topic and message, or the illustrations.
SHARE IT	All students share their entry with a partner. Then two students, previously chosen, read their entries to the class. Classmates comment on where each student used the strategy taught.

MOVIE CONNECTIONS

NAME IT	Making a comparison between a book and a movie (or television show). **Sentence stem:** *This book reminds me of . . .*
WHY DO IT?	Helps us see how similar information can be presented in different ways through other types of media; stimulates background knowledge we might not have thought about yet.
MODEL IT	The Honey Makers *reminds me of* Bee Movie *with Jerry Seinfeld. Even though the movie is a cartoon story, and not really nonfiction, it still explains a lot about how bees work together and how important bees are to our world.* Bee Movie *was a lot funnier than* The Honey Makers *and it also made a bigger impression on me about what a critical role the bee plays in our environment . . .* Ask students to name what similarities or differences you saw between *The Honey Makers* and *Bee Movie.*
TRY IT	**Turn and talk:** Have students tell a partner why it can be good to make a movie connection, followed by a brief, whole-class share. **Strategy entry:** In the strategy section of their reader's notebook, students write "Movie Connections" at the top of the page. Have students skim the shared text and look for any place that makes them think of something from a movie or television show. Give students several minutes to talk in partners and then have one or two students describe their connection in a whole-class share. Remind them to explain their connections, not just state them, and talk about differences as well as similarities. If not all students seem able to make a book or movie connection, you can choose one person to share and explain his or her connection, which you write or type on a document camera or overhead. Other students can write down this model strategy entry in their reader's notebook and put the name of the student sharing at the top.
SHARE IT	If all students wrote their own entry, have them share their entry with a partner. Then two students, previously chosen, read their entries to the class. Classmates comment on where each student used the strategy taught. If you chose to do a model strategy entry, have classmates describe what similarities and differences each student mentioned in his or her entry.

AUTHOR CONNECTIONS

NAME IT	Noticing similarities and differences between books by the same author.
WHY DO IT?	Develops our awareness of author style and our background knowledge about authors.
MODEL IT	The Honey Makers *reminds me of another Gail Gibbons book I read called* From Seed to Plant. *I notice that in both books the illustrations are all very bright and bold. Both books are about flowers and have close-up pictures of flowers parts like stamen and pistil labeled. One difference is that, in the plant book, when she wrote about pollination she explained how birds are a part of the process. She wrote about it, and there are pictures of birds. The* Honey Makers *didn't mention anything about birds helping with pollination . . .* Ask students to say what similarities and differences you noticed between Gail Gibbons's two books *The Honey Makers* and *From Seed to Plant.*
TRY IT	**Turn and talk:** Have students tell a partner what the difference is between a book connection and an author connection, followed by a brief, whole-class share. **Strategy entry:** In the strategy section of their reader's notebook, students write "Author Connections" at the top of the page. Have students take out their shared text and also pass out copies of several pages from a book by the same author (or show it on the document camera). With *The Honey Makers,* for example, you can read aloud three or four pages from *The Milk Makers,* or any other Gail Gibbons book. Then have students talk in pairs about what the author does that is similar or different in the two books in terms of the way they present information. After several minutes, direct students back to their reader's notebooks to write a strategy entry. For more scaffolding, choose a book by the same author for a read-aloud before this strategy lesson. Stop several times during the read-aloud and ask students to name any similarities or differences they notice about how the author writes and/or illustrates these two books.
SHARE IT	In pairs or in small groups, students share what they wrote. Then two students, previously chosen, read their entries in a whole-class share.

WORLD CONNECTIONS

NAME IT	Thinking about connections between information in a book and issues and events that are happening in the world. **Sentence stem:** *Makes me think about . . .*
WHY DO IT?	Helps us better understand themes in a book as well as events that are going on in the world; helps us understand why learning information makes us more informed citizens.
MODEL IT	*When I was reading the part about how the forager bees pollinate flowers it made me think about concerns people have about the bee population. There seems to be a growing awareness about their importance in the pollination process. For example, I once saw on a container of honey and granola Häagen-Dazs frozen yogurt that the company was donating a portion of the proceeds to a foundation that helps the bee population. I thought this was a great way to raise awareness about bees . . .* Ask students to describe why your connection is an example of a world connection.

TRY IT	**Turn and talk:** Have students tell a partner what it means to make a world connection, followed by a brief, whole-class share.
	Strategy entry: Hold up the last two or three of the most recent nonfiction read-alouds, including your current one. Ask students to see if they can make a connection between one of these books and any issues or events in the world, whether it is an issue that concerns their country, another country, or even their city or town.
	For more scaffolding, you can, earlier in the day, read aloud a book that is particularly conducive to this strategy such as *Pink and Say* by Patricia Polacco or *The Other Side* by Jacqueline Woodson. On the board write a T-chart with one side labeled "Text" and the other side labeled "Event/Issue," and then write "World Connections" under the book connections that are already there. Ask a few students to share their connection with the class, writing down their suggestion on the T-chart.
SHARE IT	In pairs or small groups, students share what they wrote. Then two students, previously chosen, read their entries in a whole-class share.

SIMILAR AND DIFFERENT

NAME IT	Writing about differences as well as similarities when making any kind of connection.
	Sentence stem: *One way they are different, however, . . .*
WHY DO IT?	Since no two books or no two experiences are alike, thinking about differences in addition to similarities helps us go beyond initial surface connections to think more analytically when making comparisons.
MODEL IT	*Reading about the metamorphosis that happens when bees are just babies reminds me of the metamorphosis that happens with butterflies. They both go through a lot of changes. Both butterflies and bees go through a cocoon phase and change into something else. One way they are different, however, is that the butterfly is first a living creature—a caterpillar. But the bee cocoon happens before the bee is actually born . . .*
	Ask students to name a difference you described between the life cycle of a bee and a butterfly. What similarities did you describe?
TRY IT	**Turn and talk:** Have students tell a partner why it's good to write about differences in addition to similarities when making connections, followed by a brief, whole-class share.
	Strategy entry: In the strategy section of their reader's notebook, students write "Similar and Different" at the top of the page. Direct students to particular pages of the shared text and have them write about any kind of connection you have talked about (personal, book, movie, or world), but to be aware of describing differences as well as similarities. Remind students they can use the phrase *One way they are different, however, . . .* to make that transition. For more scaffolding, have students look independently at the shared text for a few minutes and then tell a partner what connection they will write about.
SHARE IT	In pairs or small groups, students share what they wrote. Then two students, previously chosen, read their entries in a whole-class share.

VOCABULARY CONNECTIONS

NAME IT	Making a connection between a vocabulary term in the book and how it relates to other uses of the same language. **Sentence stem:** *I have also heard this word used . . .*
WHY DO IT?	Develops awareness of vocabulary and how the same language can be used in different contexts.
MODEL IT	*One vocabulary word I thought about was* barbs. *It is a term for the hooks on the worker bee's stingers. These are what get in your skin and hurt when you get stung by a bee. I have also heard this word used when someone insults another person. If a person says a bunch of mean things to a friend, you might say "she was throwing barbs at her friend." When I think about it, I guess this word is used when it is a bunch of little comments but ones that are really hurtful, just like the barbs on a bee—little but painful.* Ask students to explain what language connections you made.
TRY IT	**Turn and talk:** Have students tell a partner what it means to make a vocabulary connection, followed by a brief, whole-class share. **Strategy entry:** On the board (or chart paper) draw a T-chart labeled "Vocabulary Connections" and have students copy the T-chart in their reader's notebooks. Direct students to a particular page of the shared text that would be conducive to this strategy. With *The Honey Makers*, for example, you can have them study the first few pages of the book and look for vocabulary words (either in italics or in the pictures) they have heard in other contexts. How is the meaning the same or different? Students can keep track of their connections by writing the word in the left column of their T-chart and the connection in the right-hand column. After students work in partners for a few minutes, have a whole-class share in which students explain the language connections they made. For more scaffolding, tell students two or three vocabulary words they can write in their T-chart. With *The Honey Makers*, for example, you could suggest they write the words *social, colonies,* and *cell.* For more advanced vocabulary, you can use words such as *transfer, moisture, regurgitate, forager,* or *evaporate* from the two pages about bringing the nectar back to the hive. As a class, read aloud the paragraphs that have the words you chose.
SHARE IT	In pairs or small groups, students share what they wrote. Then two students, previously chosen, read their entries in a whole-class share.

LANGUAGE CONNECTIONS

NAME IT	Making a connection between the book's topic and expressions in our language (common idioms, similes, metaphors). **Sentence stem:** *This comparison makes sense because . . .*
WHY DO IT?	Develops awareness of how the same language can be used in different contexts and why a certain topic offers an effective comparison or description.
MODEL IT	*I remember once a high school teacher describing her classroom and saying "it was like a beehive." Instead of having actual walls they had these dividers between each classroom. You could hear everything and people would come in and out because there were no doors! This comparison makes sense because the activity in a beehive is insane! It is so crowded, and there is no privacy at all. There are so many bees squished into one space. So calling a classroom a beehive is definitely not a compliment!* Ask students to explain what language connection you made.
TRY IT	**Turn and talk:** Have students tell a partner what it means to make a language connection, followed by a brief, whole-class share. **Strategy entry:** Ask students to talk in pairs about any idioms, similes, or expressions they have heard in relation to the topic of the read-aloud. For *The Honey Makers* ask students to talk in pairs about any expressions that have to do with bees or honey. For more scaffolding, you can write on the board several expressions for students to discuss. With *The Honey Makers* you can write on the board *busy as a bee, sweet as honey, like a bee to honey,* and *she acts like a queen bee.* After students have a few minutes to talk in pairs, have a brief, whole-class discussion to share ideas. Why are these effective comparisons or descriptions? A more advanced option is to write a less-well-known quotation that relates to the topic of your read-aloud (which can be found with an online search). With bees, for example, you can offer the following quotations: "Everything takes time. Bees have to move very fast to stay still." — David Foster Wallace "One can no more approach people without love than one can approach bees without care. Such is the quality of bees." — Leo Tolstoy Have students talk in pairs and then write a strategy entry about what the quote means, reminding them they can use the sentence stem *This comparison makes sense because . . .*
SHARE IT	In pairs or small groups, students share what they wrote. Then two students, previously chosen, read their entries in a whole-class share.

Analyzing

Some strategy lessons that support analytical thinking with narrative text have obvious translations with expository text, while some are not so obvious. The type of nonfiction text also matters. Analyzing people and their relationships in a biography, for example, is not much of a stretch from analyzing characters in a fiction book. Books and articles about animals and sea life also lend themselves to analysis of relationships. Applying the same concept to a book about the moon is also possible but with more creative thinking on the part of the reader. As a result, there is much more flexibility in how children choose to interpret the concept of "relationship." One student might write about the relationship between the moon and the ocean waves, while another student might choose to write about the relationship between and the moon and Earth. Both ideas lead to analytical thinking about information so there is no one right interpretation.

As mentioned in Chapter 3, quality analytical writing depends on the ability to think analytically as well as to develop those ideas with evidence. This section also offers several lessons for grounding one's theories with evidence in addition to particular ways students can analyze informational texts. In addition, because writing about nonfiction texts is particularly conducive to writing ideas in paragraph form, there is also a lesson and brief discussion related to this writing skill.

WRITING ABOUT YOUR THINKING

NAME IT	Describing what you think about nonfiction text. **Sentence stem:** *I think . . .*
WHY DO IT?	Shifts the purpose of writing from describing what you learned to describing your thinking about that information.
MODEL IT	*Bees can make different kinds of honey depending on what type of flower they visit. In the small illustration, they show a picture of a jar of clover honey that is light colored and a jar of buckwheat honey. I think beekeepers must purposefully plant certain kinds of flowers near the beehives. That way they can determine what kind of honey they want to make!* Ask students what kinds of thinking you shared using *I think . . .*
TRY IT	**Turn and talk:** Have students tell a partner why it can be good to use *I think . . .* when writing about nonfiction. How does it help you? Follow with a brief, whole-class share. **Strategy entry:** In the strategy section of their reader's notebooks, students write "Writing About Your Thinking" or "I Think" at the top of the next blank page. Direct students to a particular section of the shared text. If needed, read aloud the selected page or pages as students follow along. Have students write a few sentences about what they learned from these pages and then use the phrase *I think . . .* to make a shift from describing what they learned to writing about what they think about that information.
SHARE IT	All students share their entry with a partner. Then two students, previously chosen, read their entries to the class. Classmates comment on where each student used the strategy taught.

MAYBE THEORIES

NAME IT	After asking a wonder question, start the next sentence with *Maybe . . .* **Sentence stem:** *Maybe . . .*
WHY DO IT?	*Maybe* gets you to infer possible answers using information you know; helps to slow down your thinking.
MODEL IT	*I wonder how bees know they have to change jobs. Maybe they just have an internal signal that tells them. I know that some animals are born just knowing how to do something. Or maybe their bodies actually change and make them more fit to do a different job like making wax for the cells. So maybe it's their physical bodies that let them know it's time to change jobs...* Ask students what theory you made after you asked a question.
TRY IT	**Turn and talk:** Have students tell a partner what it means to make a theory about something, followed by a brief, whole-class share. **Strategy entry:** In the strategy section of their reader's notebooks, students write "*Maybe* Theories" at the top of the next blank page. Direct students to a particular part of the shared text and have them write a strategy entry in which they start by wondering something and then use the word *maybe* to make a shift to offering a theory about that question. For more scaffolding, have students brainstorm ideas for wonder questions in pairs or small groups before starting their strategy entry.
SHARE IT	All students share their entry with a partner. Then two students, previously chosen, read their entries to the class. Classmates comment on where each student used the strategy taught.

EXPLAINING YOUR QUESTIONS

NAME IT	Explaining your wondering in more detail before moving on to offer a theory.
WHY DO IT?	Helps you narrow down and analyze what you are asking; makes you more aware of what exactly you wonder, which helps subsequent thinking.
MODEL IT	*I wonder how bees know they have to change jobs. First, they are house bees and are in charge of cleaning the hive. Then after only three days they somehow know they are supposed to change roles and become nurse bees. Then ten days later they change roles again. Maybe . . .* Ask students how you explained your question in more detail.
TRY IT	**Turn and talk:** Have students tell a partner why it's good to take some extra time to explain your wondering, followed by a brief, whole-class share. **Strategy entry:** In the strategy section of their reader's notebooks, students write "Explaining Your Questions" at the top of the next blank page. Direct students to a particular part of the shared text and have them think about a wonder question they could ask. Then have them write a strategy entry in which they ask a wonder question and explain this question in more detail. Why are they wondering this? For more scaffolding, have students talk about their wonder question with a partner before writing their strategy entry. After each student shares a question, partners should ask each other, "Why do you wonder that?"
SHARE IT	All students share their entry with a partner. Then two students, previously chosen, read their entries to the class. Classmates comment on where each student used the strategy taught.

FIGURE 5.2

"Explaining Your Questions" Strategy Entry

> Explain my Question
> I wonder how the bees
> comunicare. First howdo they
> know what the other
> person is trying to say.
> What if there is a
> emergency. How would everyone
> know, are there signals?

ANALYZING FEELINGS

NAME IT	Thinking about information from a person's (or animal's) perspective on an emotional level.
	Sentence stem: *I am guessing that . . .*
WHY DO IT?	Makes you think about information from a particular point of view; helps you to connect personally to the experiences of people or animals you are reading about.
MODEL IT	*I am guessing that the beekeepers feel nervous the first few times they go to collect honey. Even though they are covered from head to toe in their coveralls it just would be weird to walk into an area where hundreds and hundreds of bees are flying around you and landing on you! But maybe after a few minutes of not getting stung, they start to feel safe and it is probably kind of fun.*
	Ask students how you thought the beekeepers felt and why you thought that.
TRY IT	**Turn and talk:** Have students tell a partner what it means to analyze feelings when writing about nonfiction, followed by a brief, whole-class share.
	Strategy entry: In the strategy section of their reader's notebooks, students write "Analyzing Feelings" at the top of the next blank page. Direct students to the same part of the shared text you used for modeling and have them write a strategy entry about how a different person, animal, or living thing might feel. With *The Honey Makers*, for example, you can have students write from the perspective of the bees. How might the bees feel when the beekeepers come to get the honey? Remind students that they can use the sentence stem *I am guessing that . . .*
SHARE IT	All students share their entry with a partner. Then two students, previously chosen, read their entries to the class. Classmates comment on where each student used the strategy taught.

DESCRIBING YOUR REACTIONS

NAME IT	Describing a reaction you had to a fact you read and why you think you had that reaction.
WHY DO IT?	Helps us become more aware of the different reactions we have as we read; helps us better understand how our background knowledge and our personality affects the way we read.
MODEL IT	*I couldn't believe it when I read that a queen bee can lay up to 2,000 eggs a day! That's just crazy! I know there are a lot of bees in a hive. But if all those eggs become bees, that's about 14,000 new bees a week! How could they have room for all those new bees? I know they are small and don't live very long but that is just a crazy number . . .* Ask students to name what reaction you had while reading and why you had that reaction.
TRY IT	**Turn and talk:** Have students tell a partner why it can be good to write about your reactions to what you read, followed by a brief, whole-class share. **Strategy entry:** In the strategy section of their reader's notebooks, students write "Describing Your Reactions" at the top of the next blank page. Direct students to a particular part of the shared text that would be conducive to having strong reactions of surprise, amazement, tenderness, disgust, or any other feeling. With *The Honey Makers*, have students turn to the "Dances of the Bee" or "Forager Bee" section. As you read the excerpt out loud, ask students to be aware of any kind of reaction they have. Students then write a strategy entry in which they describe one or two reactions they had and why.
SHARE IT	All students share their entry with a partner. Then two students, previously chosen, read their entries to the class. Classmates comment on where each student used the strategy taught.

FIGURE 5.3
"Describe Your Reactions" Strategy Entry

Giving Evidence to Support Analysis

The following lessons teach students specific ways to give evidence to support their analytical thinking and writing.

I THINK THIS BECAUSE . . .

NAME IT	Giving a reason for an idea or theory you have. **Sentence stems:** *I think this because . . . ; One reason I think this is . . .*
WHY DO IT?	Helps you offer evidence to back up your ideas.
MODEL IT	*Bees must be smarter than most other insects. I think this because they are able to actually communicate with one another. They do different dances to tell each other where the flowers are and how far away the flowers are. I know lots of other insects like ants work together to get a job done, but I don't know any other insects that can actually communicate by dancing!* Ask students to name what evidence you gave for your theory about bees being smarter than most other insects.
TRY IT	**Turn and talk:** Have students tell a partner what phrase or phrases they could use to help them provide evidence for their thinking. Follow with a brief, whole-class share. **Strategy entry:** In the strategy section of their reader's notebooks, students write "I think this because" at the top of the next blank page. Ask students to write a strategy entry in which they first describe something they think about a particular topic in the shared text and then follow it with evidence about that idea. With *The Honey Makers*, for example, have students describe what they think about the job of being a beekeeper. Remind students they can use *I think this because . . .* or *One reason I think is because . . .* to shift from what they think to giving evidence for their thinking.
SHARE IT	All students share their entry with a partner. Then two students, previously chosen, read their entries to the class. Classmates comment on where each student used the strategy taught.

FOR EXAMPLE

NAME IT	Giving an example from the text to support an idea or theory. **Sentence stem:** *For example . . .*
WHY DO IT?	Helps you give concrete evidence for an idea; helps you go from being general to be being specific.
MODEL IT	*Bees seem to be extremely efficient at working together. For example, they always have a job such as taking care of the queen, or guarding the hive or foraging for nectar from flowers. And they seem to be doing their job constantly. Bees also do dances to explain where to find more flowers so they can all benefit from one bee's discovery . . .* Ask students what kinds of evidence you gave using *For example . . .*
TRY IT	**Turn and talk:** Have students tell a partner why *for example* can be a good phrase to use for giving evidence, followed by a brief, whole-class share. **Strategy entry:** In the strategy section of their reader's notebooks, students write "For example" at the top of the next blank page. On the board, write a general fact pertaining to the read-aloud, such as "Bees are very busy creatures" or "Being a beekeeper is a lot of work," and have students copy down that sentence in their notebooks. Then have them to work in pairs looking through their shared text for examples that support one of these ideas. After several minutes, have students continue with their strategy entry and use the phrase *For example . . .* to go from a general statement to offering specific examples.
SHARE IT	All students share their entry with a partner. Then two students, previously chosen, read their entries to the class. Classmates comment on where each student used the strategy taught.

Developing Paragraphs

One of the best ways to help students develop the writing they do in reader's notebooks is to have an expectation that they write in paragraphs. While it may be tempting to teach formulas for writing paragraphs, they often hamper students' ability to write *well-developed* paragraphs and to do so independently. The "hamburger" structure, for example, which has an introductory sentence, three sentences in the middle, and concluding sentence, is an example of this kind of scaffolding. A benefit of teaching this formula is that directions are clear: Students know what to do, and teachers know how to grade it. In addition, it produces a type of organized paragraph.

What you gain in uniform expectations you lose in quality of writing, student decision making, and, often, student engagement. You also create a ceiling of sorts for students to be able to develop much richer, longer, and thoughtful paragraphs. These kinds of formulas also have little in common with real nonfiction writing. Open up any nonfiction book, for children or adults, and you'll rarely see paragraphs that are all the same size with the same structure.

One way we can support students' understanding of paragraphs is to have them notice the differences between paragraphs in the informational texts they read. What changes in content between different paragraphs? Not every paragraph seems unique in its subject matter, particularly with longer texts. A book about caterpillars, for example, might have two or three paragraphs on how a butterfly eats. But look closely. Is there a difference between what each paragraph is talking about? Is one paragraph about *how* a caterpillar eats and the next one about what kinds of plants different species prefer?

In addition to helping students understand how paragraphs are used through the lens of a reader, we can also teach students how writing in paragraphs benefits them as writers. What is most effective is staying true to the two common criteria of a paragraph, at least in expository text, which are (1) it is more than two sentences long and (2) all the sentences are about one idea. This may seem rather general, but in reality, there are few criteria for what makes a paragraph because their form is so specific to the ideas you are writing about at that time.

Rather than focus on the outcome of what a paragraph should look like, I focus on the thought process of developing paragraphs. As demonstrated in the lesson below, students can take advantage of the physical boundaries of a paragraph to think about the development of their ideas. If I have only written two sentences about an idea, for example, I can see that it doesn't really *look* like a developed paragraph. So we can teach students, when they *think* they have written a paragraph, to first pause and think about what else they could say before moving on to the next paragraph. Since we want students to use reader's notebooks for both writing about what they learn from nonfiction texts *and* writing about their thinking, I suggest they can ask either "What else did I learn about this particular topic?" or "What else do I think about this information?"

DEVELOPING PARAGRAPHS ON YOUR OWN

NAME IT	Pausing to think about what else you could write before moving on to the next paragraph. **Thinking stem:** *"What else did I learn about this?"* or *"What else do I think about this?"*
WHY DO IT?	Taking time to think about what else we can write about a particular topic helps us independently develop paragraphs, and our ideas, to our potential.
MODEL IT	Write a few sentences about the shared text on the document camera or on chart paper. Then pause to do a think-aloud such as, "Hmmm, what else can I say about this? Oh yeah, I could write about. . . ." Write a few more sentences, and then pause to do the other kind of think-aloud, "Hmmm, what do I think about this?" Write a few more sentences about what you think.
TRY IT	**Turn and talk:** Have students tell a partner what two phrases you can ask yourself when you *think* you have finished a paragraph, followed by a brief, whole-class share. **Strategy entry:** In the strategy section of their reader's notebooks, students write "Developing Paragraphs on My Own" at the top of the next blank page. Ask them to also write down the two questions you can ask yourself: *What else did I learn about this? What else do I think about this?* Direct students' attention to a particular part of the shared text and have them write two or three paragraphs about this section. Let them know you will be giving them extra time for this strategy entry since it will be longer than usual. Tell students that, before they make a paragraph space, they need to ask themselves one of the two questions for developing paragraphs at least once and see what more they can add to develop their paragraphs. Let students know that, after writing for seven or eight minutes, they will have to put down their pencils and tell a partner which question they asked themselves and what they added. Then have students continue their paragraphs.
SHARE IT	All students share their entry with a partner. Then two students, previously chosen, read their entries to the class and share at what point they asked themselves a "developing paragraphs" question.

Synthesizing

Nonfiction provides a terrific backdrop for teaching and supporting the skill of synthesizing. Children tend to have a clearer idea of how their own understanding shifts and changes as they learn new information. The following lessons help students fuse information learned and reflect on what they now understand or how their thinking and knowledge has changed.

PUTTING IT ALL TOGETHER

NAME IT	Describing what you have concluded so far about a particular topic in the book.
	Sentence stem: *So I guess . . .*
WHY DO IT?	Helps us use different facts we have learned from the book so far, in combination with our own background knowledge, to verbalize our understanding of a certain idea.
MODEL IT	*So I guess bees do all their jobs to make honey for their own use. They are programmed to do all those jobs so that they can keep living! It's how they feed their babies. I never really thought about the fact that the honey was originally for the bees themselves. But because humans keep collecting it for their use, the bees have to keep starting over.*
	Ask students to name what you have concluded about bees so far and why you think that.
TRY IT	**Turn and talk:** Have students tell a partner what words you can use to synthesize information, to put your learning all together, followed by a brief, whole-class share.
	Strategy entry: In the strategy section of their reader's notebooks, students write "Putting It All Together" at the top of the next blank page. Ask students to think about some conclusions they have made about the different topics of the shared text. With *The Honey Makers*, for example, what have they learned about bees and making honey? Have students write a strategy entry in which they try out the phrase *So I guess . . .* and then continue with their own ideas.
SHARE IT	All students share their entry with a partner. Then two students, previously chosen, read their entries to the class. Classmates comment on where each student used the strategy taught.

BEFORE AND AFTER

NAME IT	Assessing how our understanding of a topic has changed.
	Sentence stems: *I used to think . . . but now I understand . . .*
WHY DO IT?	Makes us aware of the prior knowledge we bring to books and how we combine it with new information.
MODEL IT	*I used to think that honey came from the pollen they collected and it just turned into honey once it was put in the honeycomb. But now I understand that the honey is actually from the nectar they drink from flowers that they store in their "honey stomach." Then when they get to the hive they throw up the honey (eww!) and then pass it around to other bees until it loses moisture. Even when they first put the nectar in the cells it still is not as thick as honey.*
	Ask students to name how your understanding of honey has changed from reading *The Honey Makers.*
TRY IT	**Turn and talk:** Have students tell a partner what it means to synthesize information using the before and after strategy. What words can you use to do this? Follow with a brief, whole-class share.
	Strategy entry: Create a T-chart on the board or on chart paper with one column labeled "I used to think . . ." and the other column labeled "Now I understand . . ." Have students copy the same T-chart in the strategy section of their reader's notebook, and write "Before and After" at the top of the page.
	Ask students to think about what they have learned from the read-aloud and how it compares to what they used to think about this information. With *The Honey Makers*, for example, ask students to think about what they learned about how people keep bees and make honey or what bees do all day and how this compares to what they used to think. Give students a few minutes to write down a few "before and after" ideas in their T-charts, using the shared text to get ideas if needed. Then have students share what they wrote in partners or small groups, reminding them they can use the phrase *I used to think . . . but now I understand . . .* to structure their ideas.
	For more scaffolding, have a brief, whole-class conversation in which several students share their "before and after" ideas. Then direct students back to their reader's notebooks to write a strategy entry.
SHARE IT	All students share their entry with a partner. Then two students, previously chosen, read their entries to the class. Classmates comment on where each student used the strategy taught.

FIGURE 5.4

"Before and After" Strategy Entry

Before and After

I used to think that there were only 2 types of bees, worker bees and the queen, but now I know that there are actually 3. There is a queen bee, whos job is to make sure that the hive never runs out of bees. The queen be lays up to 2,000 eggs a day. Another tupe of bee is the drone bee whos only job is to mate with the queen. The last bee is called the worker bee. The worker bee undergoes 6 jobs in his life span of about 2 months. First they are a house bee, which cleans and polishes the cells. Next they are a nurse bee. Then they are a wax-making bee,

IN THEIR SHOES

NAME IT	Thinking about information from the perspective of a person or living thing mentioned in your book. What would your experience be?
	Sentence stem: *If I were . . .*
WHY DO IT?	Helps you synthesize information you know so far about a particular person, animal, or living thing through a first-person lens.
MODEL IT	*If I were a worker bee, my favorite job would be when I would get to be a forager bee and go collect pollen and nectar from the different flowers. The hive must get crazy busy. So it must be nice to spend time outside. I mean what a great job to do, to just go from one pretty flower to the next! I would probably want to stay out longer than I should except that, when I get back to the hive, I get to do a cool dance to tell all the other bees where the flowers are.*
	Ask students to name what you would do or think if you were in a worker bee's shoes.
TRY IT	**Turn and talk:** Have students tell a partner what it means to use the "in their shoes" strategy when writing about nonfiction. What words can they use? Follow with a brief, whole-class share.
	Strategy entry: Students turn to the next blank page in their reader's notebooks and write "In Their Shoes" at the top. Have students choose one person, animal or living thing from a particular part of the shared text. For *The Honey Makers*, they can also write about what they would do if they were a bee or they can write from the perspective of one of the people who collect honey. Remind students that they can use the sentence stem *If I were . . .* to think about information from one person's or animal's perspective.
SHARE IT	All students share their entry with a partner. Then two students, previously chosen, read their entries to the class. Classmates comment on where each student used the strategy taught.

THEN AND NOW

NAME IT	Comparing how something is done today versus years ago.
WHY DO IT?	Helps us draw on both our prior knowledge and facts learned from the book to think about how people's knowledge or ways of doing things have evolved.
MODEL IT	*People have gathered honey for thousands of years but how they did it was different. They used to use holes in logs or clay pots because they knew that bees liked dark places. But now they use the "hanging movable frame beehive." These new beehives are different because they have frames with wax cells in the shape of honeycomb so bees will make the honey faster.*
	Ask students to name what has changed about bee collecting from long ago to today.
TRY IT	**Turn and talk:** Have students tell a partner what it means to write using the "then and now" strategy. Follow with a brief, whole-class share.
	Strategy entry: Create a T-chart on the board or on chart paper with one column labeled "Then" and the other column labeled "Now." Ask students to take out their shared text and, on their own, look through the pages to see whether they can find anything that they could make a "then and now" comparison. After a minute have students talk in pairs or small groups about what they found so far.
	For more scaffolding, read aloud a different book that has a clear description of objects, inventions, or knowledge such as *Snowflake Bentley* by Jacqueline Briggs Martin. Biographies and historical fiction or nonfiction work particularly well with this lesson.
SHARE IT	All students share their entry with a partner. Then two students, previously chosen, read their entries to the class. Classmates comment on where each student used the strategy taught.

ON THE OTHER HAND

NAME IT	Thinking about a concept or information from different angles. **Sentence stem:** *On the other hand . . .*
WHY DO IT?	Thinking about information from different perspectives helps you synthesize different facts and points of view you have gathered about a particular topic; encourages readers to revisit the text to confirm information.
MODEL IT	*Collecting honey seems like an easy thing to start doing yourself. You're using a process that is hundreds of years old and really not too much different than how they made honey in the old days. You can even buy hives already made. Plus it is the bees that do all the work! On the other hand, you have to know a lot about bees in order to do a good job as a beekeeper. You also have to have that machine called an extractor, which does not look cheap. Also, when I went back to look at A Beekeeper's Yearbook it mentioned lots of jobs the beekeeper has like inspecting the hive, checking to see how the queen bee is doing, and seeing whether they need to add things called supers, which look like boxes that the frames are kept in.* Ask students to name what opposing ideas you argued using the phrase *On the other hand . . .*
TRY IT	**Turn and talk:** Have students tell a partner what words you can use to analyze information from different angles, followed by a brief, whole-class share. **Strategy entry:** Have students turn to the next blank page in their notebooks and at the top write "On the Other Hand" On the document camera or chart paper, write a general statement or opinion related to the read-aloud, such as *The queen bee is the most important bee in the hive*, which students copy down in their notebook. Tell students to write a strategy entry in which they first write sentences that support the statement. Then they should use the phrase *On the other hand . . .* to shift their point of view and argue against their original idea. Encourage students to use their shared text to look for information that supports both sides. For more scaffolding, have students record the same first sentence. Then create a T-chart on the board with one side labeled "For" and the other side labeled "Against." Ask students to take out their shared text and talk in pairs about facts that support the idea that the queen bee is the most important bee. Have a brief, whole-class share and record two to four ideas in the T-chart. Then have students talk in pairs about the other side of this argument. What information can they give to argue why the queen is *not* the most important bee? Have another whole-class share and record ideas. Then direct students back to their reader's notebooks to write a strategy entry. Remind them to first write in support of the statement they already wrote and then to use the sentence stem *On the other hand . . .* to write from a different point of view.
SHARE IT	All students share their entry with a partner. Then two students, previously chosen, read their entries to the class. Classmates comment on where each student used the strategy taught.

ANALYZING RELATIONSHIPS

NAME IT	Analyzing how different people, animals, or things work together as a system.
WHY DO IT?	Taking a more global, bird's-eye view about a topic helps you synthesize information you have learned about individual people, animals, things, or concepts.
MODEL IT	*All the bees seem to work together like a well-run company. Just about every bee has a job at every time. They also communicate with one another to help out the entire hive. For example, when a forager bee has found new flowers, she'll go back and do a circle dance or a wag-tail dance to explain where the flowers are. And all the other forager bees understand! Another example of how bees work well together is . . .* Ask students to name what you noticed about bees' relationship with one another.
TRY IT	**Turn and talk:** Have students tell a partner what it means to analyze relationships when it comes to nonfiction, followed by a brief, whole-class share. **Strategy entry:** In the strategy section of their reader's notebooks, students write "Analyzing Relationships" at the top of the next blank page. Ask students to talk in pairs or small groups about the relationship between certain people, animals, or objects in the read-aloud. With *The Honey Makers*, you can have students talk about how the beekeepers interact and relate with one another. Encourage students to use their shared text as a resource and gather information they learned from different parts of the book. Then have students write a strategy entry in their notebooks. For more scaffolding you can use a read-aloud about topics, such as the solar system, ecosystems, or politics, which are particularly conducive to using this strategy.
SHARE IT	All students share their entry with a partner. Then two students, previously chosen, read their entries to the class. Classmates comment on where each student used the strategy taught.

Drawing in Notebook Entries

Another way to support synthesizing with nonfiction is to allow students to draw diagrams and pictures in their notebooks (Figure 5.5). Whether copying a diagram of the water cycle from their book or making up their own picture of a grasshopper with its various body parts labeled based on information they've read, drawing factual information gives students an additional way not only to present learned information but also to better process information. Since this kind of drawing is meant to support writing, I give either a number limit (one drawing or diagram per day) or impose a time limit ("You can use the last five minutes to add any diagrams to your writing"). In either case, diagrams or drawing with labels are optional activities except for days I teach them as part of a text feature lesson.

FIGURE 5.5

Diagrams in Nonfiction Entries

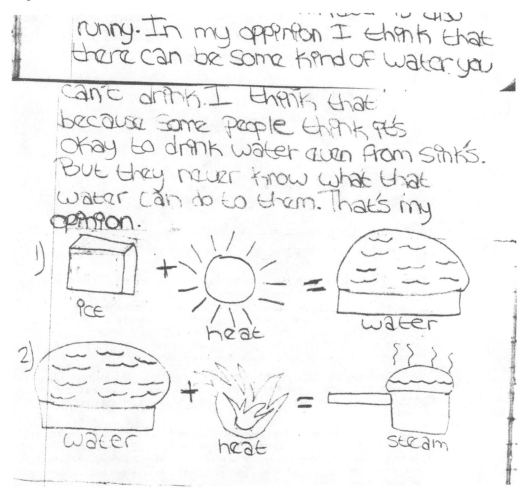

Drawing can also be used as a modification for students who struggle with writing, whether for motivational or academic reasons. Drawing a picture or diagram first is a more accessible first step and a way to generate ideas for sentences to write.

Evaluating

Nonfiction books are particularly suited for evaluating because they tend to have more text features than chapter books and so offer more concrete characteristics to evaluate. Students usually have stronger opinions about the effectiveness or ineffectiveness of how information is represented visually as opposed to how an author writes. In addition, the evaluation of information, as opposed to literature, more closely relates to college and career readiness skills, which involve the ability to "evaluate, synthesize, and report on information and ideas" (National Governors Association Center for Best Practices 2010, 4). Similar to the evaluating lessons in Chapter 3, the following strategy lessons include foundational strategies for noticing text features and author's craft as a way to scaffold subsequent lessons in which students evaluate these same features.

NOTICING AUTHOR'S CRAFT

NAME IT	Noticing how an author writes and the language he or she uses.
	Sentence stem: *I notice how . . .*
WHY DO IT?	Makes us more aware of the way an author writes; creates a reading-writing connection.
MODEL IT	*I notice how Gail Gibbons puts vocabulary words in italics when she writes. There isn't a glossary in the book, but when I come across the italicized words I know that they are specific to the honey-making business. Then I know to look at the pictures if I don't know what the word means...*
	Ask students to name what you noticed about the way Gail Gibbons writes.
TRY IT	**Turn and talk:** Have students tell a partner what it means to notice author's craft, followed by a brief, whole-class share.
	Strategy entry: In the strategy section of their reader's notebooks, students write "Noticing Author's Craft" at the top of the next blank page. On the board, write a list of craft to consider, such as imagery, descriptions, sentence variety, dialogue, and any other aspects of writing the class has recently studied. Have students look through their shared text with a partner and talk about what they notice about the way this author writes, either the language they use or how they visually represent text. Remind students that they can use the sentence stem *I notice how . . .* to start their conversation.
	With *The Honey Makers*, students may notice Gail Gibbons's use of short sentences, how she writes the information as a story, the first two introductory pages that lead up to the title, her use of a "sound lead," or her sentence variety (sentences often begin with different words).
	For additional scaffolding, hand out copies from a nonfiction picture book that has a distinct and noticeable way of writing such as *Martin's Big Words* by Doreen Rappaport. After several minutes, have a brief, whole-class share in which students share what they noticed about this author's way of crafting language. Then direct students back to their reader's notebooks to write a strategy entry.
SHARE IT	All students share their entry with a partner. Then two students, previously chosen, read their entries to the class. Classmates comment on where each student used the strategy taught.

EVALUATING AUTHOR'S CRAFT

NAME IT	Assessing the effectiveness of the way an author writes. **Sentence stems:** *This is effective because . . . ; The author might have considered . . .*
WHY DO IT?	Helps us think more objectively about the impact of an author's decisions, either in the language they use or in the layout of text.
MODEL IT	*Gail Gibbons's use of italics in her writing is effective because she draws attention to certain words. That way, a reader knows which words are special to the topic of bees and honey making. Gail Gibbons also reinforces word meaning because most of the words in italics, like "metamorphosis" and "pupa," are also in a nearby illustration. One thing the author might have considered was including a glossary at the back. This way a reader can review all of the important words, either before or after reading the book.*
TRY IT	**Turn and talk:** Have students tell a partner what the difference is between noticing author's craft and evaluating author's craft, followed by a brief, whole-class share. **Strategy entry:** In the strategy section of their reader's notebooks, students write "Evaluating Author's Craft" at the top of the next blank page. Have students reread their previous entry on "Noticing Author's Craft." Then have them go back to the same pages they looked at before and review them with a more evaluative and critical eye. What is particularly effective about the way this author writes? Are there certain places that are not effective? Are there suggestions you would give this author if they were to write another edition of this book? Remind students that they can use the sentence stems *This is effective because . . .* or *The author might have considered . . .* After several minutes, direct students back to their notebooks and have them write a strategy entry in which they evaluate the way this author writes.
SHARE IT	All students share their entry with a partner. Then two students, previously chosen, read their entries to the class. Classmates comment on where each student used the strategy taught.

NOTICING ILLUSTRATOR'S CRAFT

NAME IT	Noticing an illustrator's craft. **Sentence stem:** *I notice how the illustrator . . .*
WHY DO IT?	Makes us more aware of an illustrator's technique and choices about how he or she represents information.
MODEL IT	*I notice how Gail Gibbons every now and then has a close-up illustration of the bees and labels the parts of the body. I really like this because I can see all the little parts of the bee and know what they are called. The illustrations are also very colorful and fun to look at.* Ask students to name what you liked about the way Gail Gibbons draws her illustrations.
TRY IT	**Turn and talk:** Have students tell a partner what it means to notice an illustrator's craft. What kinds of things might you notice? Follow with a brief, whole-class share. **Strategy entry:** In the strategy section of their reader's notebooks, students write "Noticing Illustrator's Craft" at the top of the next blank page. Have students look through their shared text with a partner and talk about what they notice about the choices this illustrator makes and what they like about it. For more scaffolding, write a list on the board of aspects of illustrations to consider such as medium used, range of color, tone and mood, details, and size of pictures.
SHARE IT	All students share their entry with a partner. Then two students, previously chosen, read their entries to the class. Classmates comment on where each student used the strategy taught.

EVALUATING ILLUSTRATOR'S CRAFT

NAME IT	Evaluating the style and choices of an illustrator. **Sentence stems:** *This is effective because . . . ; The illustrator might have considered . . .*
WHY DO IT?	Helps us think more objectively about the impact of an illustrator's decisions about how to visually represent information that is and is not in the text.
MODEL IT	*Gail Gibbons's decision to include close-up illustrations in her book is very effective because bees are so small in real life that people don't get much of a chance to look really carefully at them. Even if they were bigger, they are moving so fast. Not to mention, people would not want to risk getting stung just to get a closer look! By having a close-up picture, Gail Gibbons also gets the reader to focus on one particular piece of information at a time . . .* Ask students to name what you said was effective about Gail Gibbons's illustrations and why it is effective.
TRY IT	**Turn and talk:** Have students tell a partner what the difference is between noticing illustrator's craft and evaluating illustrator's craft, followed by a brief, whole-class share. **Strategy entry:** In the strategy section of their reader's notebooks, students write "Evaluating Illustrator's Craft" at the top of the next blank page. Ask students to reread their previous entry on "Noticing Illustrator's Craft." Have them go back to their shared text and talk about the same illustrations except now with evaluative and critical eye. Remind students they can use the sentence stems *This is effective because . . .* or *The author might have considered . . .* to start their conversation. After several minutes, direct students back to their notebooks and have them write a strategy entry in which they evaluate the style and choices of the illustrator. For more scaffolding, choose one aspect of the shared text's illustrations to discuss as a whole class. You can also use a T-chart to structure a conversation about what is effective about this particular aspect and what the illustrator might have also considered. Then direct students back to their reader's notebooks to write a strategy entry.
SHARE IT	All students share their entry with a partner. Then two students, previously chosen, read their entries to the class. Classmates comment on where each student used the strategy taught.

FIGURE 5.6
"Evaluating Illustrations" Strategy Entry

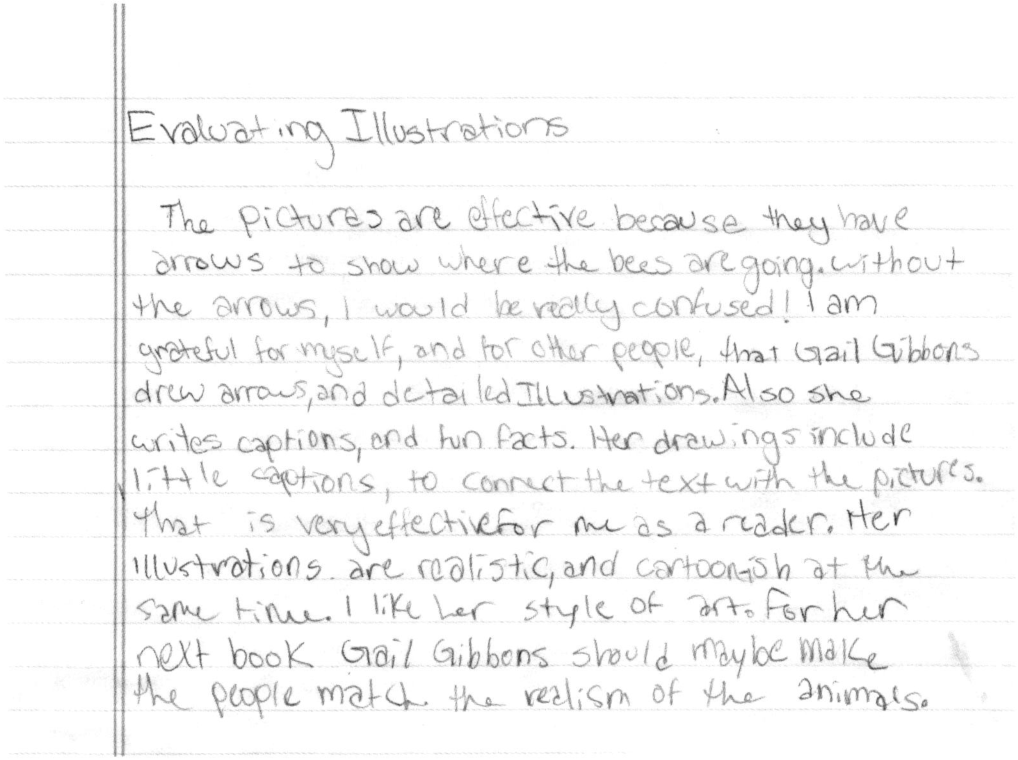

Evaluating Illustrations

The pictures are effective because they have
arrows to show where the bees are going. Without
the arrows, I would be really confused! I am
grateful for myself, and for other people, that Gail Gibbons
drew arrows, and detailed Illustrations. Also she
writes captions, and fun facts. Her drawings include
little captions, to connect the text with the pictures.
That is very effective for me as a reader. Her
illustrations are realistic, and cartoonish at the
same time. I like her style of art. For her
next book Gail Gibbons should maybe make
the people match the realism of the animals.

OPINIONS ABOUT TEXT FEATURES

NAME IT	Noticing text features that do or do not appeal to you.
	Sentence stem: *I like/I don't really like how the author (or illustrator) . . .*
WHY DO IT?	Makes us more aware of authors' and illustrators' choices about how to represent information in different ways; makes us more aware of what appeals to us as readers.
MODEL IT	*I like how Gail Gibbons has "A Beekeeper's Yearbook" in the back of the book. Each month has a paragraph as if it's written by an actual beekeeper. I like it because it kind of reviews all of the information that was in the book but in a different way. And because it's written in diary form, it makes all the information seem so real and part of someone's life. I keep a diary, which is maybe another reason I like it.*
	Ask students to name what text feature you wrote about and what you liked about it.
TRY IT	**Turn and talk:** Have students tell a partner what it means to write about your opinion of a text feature, followed by a brief, whole-class share.
	Strategy entry: In the strategy section of their reader's notebooks, students write "Opinions About Text Features" at the top of the next blank page. Have students skim through all the pages in their shared text with a partner and name the book's different text features. Then have partners choose one or two to talk about in particular. After several minutes, direct students back to their notebooks to write a strategy entry.
SHARE IT	All students share their entry with a partner. Then two students, previously chosen, read their entries to the class. Classmates comment on where each student used the strategy taught.

EVALUATING TEXT FEATURES

NAME IT	Describing the value of certain text features an author chooses to include.
	Sentence stems: *(Text feature) is effective because . . . ; The author might have considered . . .*
WHY DO IT?	Helps us think more objectively about the value of text features rather than just how much certain text features appeal to us personally; by assessing the value of text features, we have to call on our background knowledge of text features from other books.
MODEL IT	*"A Beekeeper's Yearbook" is an effective and clever text feature in* The Honey Makers *for Gail Gibbons to review information from the book. It has some of the same information that is in the book but is written like a diary entry from the point of view of the beekeeper. The facts are much shorter and categorized by month. So this text feature reinforces important facts that Gail Gibbons thinks readers should take away from the book, but in a creative way. One thing she might have considered doing was having a page for each season. The months and pictures of the seasons are all squished together so you can barely tell they are separate seasons.*
	Ask students to describe your evaluation of this text feature. What did you think was effective, and why? What did you think the author might have considered?
TRY IT	**Turn and talk:** Have students tell a partner what the difference is between giving your opinion about a certain text feature and evaluating that text feature.
	Strategy entry: In the strategy section of their reader's notebooks, students write "Evaluating Text Features" at the top of the next blank page. First, have students reread their previous entry on "Noticing Text Features." Then have them go back to the shared text and talk with their partner about the same texture but with a more evaluative and critical eye. What exactly is effective about this text feature? What could be better? Do you have any suggestions? After several minutes, direct students back to their reader's notebooks to write a strategy entry.
SHARE IT	All students share their entry with a partner. Then two students, previously chosen, read their entries to the class. Classmates comment on where each student used the strategy taught.

EVALUATING BOOK COVERS

NAME IT	Assessing how well the cover of a book conveys information, reflects information inside the book, and creates interest. **Sentence stems:** *The cover is effective because . . . ; The author might have considered . . .*
WHY DO IT?	Makes us more aware of how the design of a book cover can stimulate background knowledge and predictions about the book and how it can affect the text selection process.
MODEL IT	This lessons works best if the teacher models with a different cover and students write their strategy entry about a more familiar cover, the current read-aloud, or a shared text. Keep the cover of your book in view as you read your writing out loud. *The cover of* A Drop of Water *by Walker Wick has a close-up picture of a drop of water falling into a glass of water. It's a stop-action photo that shows how a drop makes the water move. This close-up image is very effective because it captures the small behaviors of water that we don't normally see, even if we try. Yet we interact with water all the time. The cover is effective because it gives the reader the idea that inside the book we will get to know lots of cool information about this common topic and probably see more photographs. The subtitle,* A Book of Science and Wonder, *also reflects the idea of the amazing science behind water and how it behaves.*
TRY IT	**Turn and talk:** Have students tell a partner what it means to evaluate the design of a book cover. **Strategy entry:** In the strategy section of their reader's notebooks, students write "Evaluating Book Covers" at the top of the next blank page. Show an image of the cover of students' shared text (unless they have their own color cover page to study). Have students talk in pairs about the cover design. In what ways is the cover design effective? How does it reflect the content of the book? What changes they would suggest for a new edition of this book? Once students have talked, direct them back to their reader's notebooks to write a strategy entry.
SHARE IT	All students share their entry with a partner. Then two students, previously chosen, read their entries to the class. Classmates comment on where each student used the strategy taught.

EVALUATING TOPIC PRESENTATION

NAME IT	Assessing how well a book covers a particular topic and the choices an author made about what information to include. **Sentence stems:** *The author does a good job. . .; The author could have . . .*
WHY DO IT?	Draws on our ability to make value judgments based on what else we know about a topic and about other books on the same topic.
MODEL IT	For this lesson, it is better to model with a different nonfiction book so students can write about the shared text for their strategy entry. *Walter Wick does a good job presenting the topic of water in a different way. Most books on water seem to focus on rivers and oceans or talk about how important water is to our life. A Drop of Water instead sort of goes inside the water! By reading this book we learn about the properties of water and why it behaves the way it does. By capturing water in action through close-up photographs, the author also draws the reader in to wonder with him, more than if it was just information. One thing the author might have considered was to have a glossary of scientific terms. He does do a good job explaining words as he writes, but a glossary would help some kids really understand certain terms . . .* Ask students to name how you think Walter Wick handled the topic of water in *A Drop of Water.*
TRY IT	**Turn and talk:** Have students tell a partner what it means to evaluate an author's topic presentation. **Strategy entry:** In the strategy section of their reader's notebooks, students write "Evaluating Topic Presentation" at the top of the next blank page. Have students take out their shared text and talk in pairs to assess this author's presentation of their topic. Did the author do a good job in how much information he or she decided to present and how it was presented to the reader? What changes would they suggest for a new edition of this book? Remind students that they can use the sentence stems *The author does a good job . . .* or *The author could have . . .* to start their conversation. Then direct students back to their reader's notebooks to write a strategy entry. A more advanced option is to give students a copy of an opinion article about a topic students have some background knowledge about, such as texting or school uniforms. Read the article aloud as students follow along. Then have students talk in pairs about how well this article covered the given topic. What important information did the writer include or exclude? Did the writer cover the topic fairly? Were there points he or she could have added to strengthen the argument? Then direct students back to their reader's notebooks to write a strategy entry.
SHARE IT	All students share their entry with a partner. Then two students, previously chosen, read their entries to the class. Classmates comment on where each student used the strategy taught.

Visualizing and Monitoring Comprehension

The following lessons support the in-the-moment skills used to make sense of text: visualizing and monitoring comprehension. While the concept of visualizing and monitoring is the same whether students are reading narrative or informational text, there are important differences in actual usage. Due to less obvious story structure and content-specific vocabulary, students usually need to call on these skills more often to make sense of informational text. At the same time, using these skills with nonfiction requires more active participation and effort on the part of the reader. Although visualizing and monitoring are skills ideally used *during* the reading process, teachers can use strategy entries to strengthen students' attention to and awareness of using them.

Visualizing

One of the many joys of reading stories is that, as we take in the words on the page, we have a movie in our mind that belongs to us and no one else (Harvey and Goudvis 2007). Part of our job, of course, is to helps students see the parallels between visualizing fiction and nonfiction texts. In a book about the water cycle, for example, we can emphasize the sense of story with the help of well-written text and model picturing the story unfolding in our minds. One challenge about asking students to use the author's words to create a "mind movie" with informational texts is that most nonfiction books made for students these days have wonderful and colorful pictures, photographs, and diagrams. While these improved text features are, of course, a positive change, they can sometimes make an implicit, but erroneous, statement that visualization is not really needed. There is some truth that pictures or photographs *support* visualization. But ideally the reader uses these images as a starting place for their own visualizing. In addition, our role of preparing students for high school and beyond, where there is far less picture support, means we need to help students garner information from the written text as much as possible.

Many teachers are familiar with the importance of modeling visualizing with nonfiction read-alouds and having students turn and talk during read-alouds about what they see in their minds. Even though students are not writing during these turn and talks, I still like to anchor this visualization practice in language by offering them the optional sentence stem "In my mind I see…" This phrase supports the idea that visualizing is a combination of what is provided in the text and your own personal experiences. As long as the images make sense given the words written by the author, there is no exact right or wrong about what they see.

The Five Senses

We can also use read-aloud time to model how using other senses besides sight can enrich the visualizing that we do. At first, my students aren't very aware of sounds, smells, or tastes when I am reading a nonfiction book out loud. But I act as if they do. When I pause during a page about whaling ships, for example, and say, "Okay, tell a partner what sounds were in your mind," students usually think about possible sounds they *could have* heard, even if they weren't really in their minds as I was reading. Then they start talking to each other about the creaking of the board, the sound of waves, and people shouting. Even if students are inferring sounds after the fact, this exercise still has the desired effect, which is to strengthen the reading muscles that bring books to life. And once students get used to this expectation, they are more apt to actually do this type of three-dimensional visualizing as they read.

Soon I turn the visualizing over to the students. Rather than specify certain senses, I give the generic prompt, "Turn to someone next to you and just say what's going on in your minds right now." Because it can be easy for students to slip back into just the visual part of visualization (understandably), I put up a small poster in the rug area that depicts the different senses as a visual reminder.

Although this "catching students in the middle of the reading" is a particularly effective way to support visualization, this work can also be extended into the reader's notebooks. For visualizing strategy lessons, I use language similar to what I use during the read-alouds except I say, "In my mind I saw . . ." rather than "In my mind I see . . . ," which highlights the difference between thinking *while* reading and thinking *about* reading. Because students should practice visualizing using only the author's words, they should not see any illustrations during this lesson. You can read aloud an excerpt from a nonfiction book or, for more scaffolding, hand out copies that contain only the words from a book. Ideally, these lessons use text students have not yet heard or seen so that they are not calling on their memory of any illustrations or photographs.

MY MIND MOVIE

NAME IT	Describing the images you saw in your mind as you were reading.
	Sentence stem: *In my mind I saw . . .*
WHY DO IT?	Makes you more aware of how you visualized what the text was saying to help you better understand what you read.
MODEL IT	*I just read the part that describes the job of the forager bee and how it goes around to different flowers. In my mind I saw a bunch of bees flying near a garden of flowers on a clear, sunny day with just a few clouds. They were diving in and out of the different flowers, which were all sorts of colors like red, pink, and yellow. In my mind, I saw their wings all blurry because they were moving so fast.*
TRY IT	**Turn and talk:** Have students tell a partner why it can be good to write about what you visualized as you read, followed by a brief, whole-class share.
	Strategy entry: In the strategy section of their reader's notebooks, students write "My Mind Movie" at the top of the next blank page. Read several pages of a nonfiction text out loud but at a slower pace than normal. Before reading, remind students to be aware of the movie playing in their minds. After a few pages, ask students to write about what they visualized as you read, reminding them they can use the sentence stem *In my mind I saw . . .*
	For more scaffolding, have students turn and talk about their "mind movie" before starting their strategy entry.
SHARE IT	All students share their entry with a partner. Then two students, previously chosen, read their entries to the class. Classmates comment on where each student used the strategy taught.

ALL MY SENSES

NAME IT	Describing what you could hear, smell, taste, or feel as you were reading.
	Sentence stem: *I could hear (or smell or feel) . . .*
WHY DO IT?	Helps you think about reading as experiencing text in a more three-dimensional way; helps the text come to life.
MODEL IT	*I just read the part that describes the job of the forager bee and how it goes around to different flowers. In my mind, I saw a bunch of bees flying near a garden of flowers on a clear, sunny day. There was a constant hum of buzzing that got louder every time a bee moved from one flower to the next. In my mind, I could feel the warm breeze of summer and could even smell the perfume smell of the flowers.*
TRY IT	**Turn and talk:** Have students tell a partner what other senses we can use besides sight when we are reading, followed by a brief, whole-class share.
	Strategy entry: In the strategy section of their reader's notebooks, students write "All My Senses" at the top of the next blank page. Reread the same pages of a nonfiction book that you used with the "Mind Movie" lesson. Before reading, tell students they will hear the same words, but this time, they will focus on the other senses. What can they hear, smell, or feel (or taste if applicable) as you read? Then have students write a strategy entry about one or two senses that came alive as they read, reminding them that they can use the sentence stem *I could hear (or smell or feel) . . .*
	For more scaffolding, have students turn and talk about their "Five Senses mind movie" before starting their strategy entry.
SHARE IT	All students share their entry with a partner. Then two students, previously chosen, read their entries to the class. Classmates comment on where each student used the strategy taught.

Monitoring Comprehension

Similar to visualizing, monitoring one's comprehension is something that in actuality is done during the reading process, not after. That said, students can write about and reflect on how they used these strategies while reading to support metacognition and continued use of these strategies. Since monitoring text is highly personal and based on each student's background knowledge and vocabulary, many of these lessons use a "strategy practice" in which students process or practice the strategy in some way but do not actually write an entry. We can't assume, for example, that all students will be genuinely confused by a particular word or section of text. Instead, students talk in small groups and then, as a class, we debrief by sharing one or two students' experiences that reflect the strategy being taught.

Many of the monitoring strategy lessons use the phrase "At first" for students to write about challenges they encountered while reading and how they responded. Implicit in this phrase is a cause-and-effect relationship. It's hard to write a sentence that starts with "at first" without presenting what comes next. While no single phrase ensures a paragraph of developed writing, offering this sentence stem can help students get beyond just listing strategies they used or writing sentences with literacy buzzwords such as "I used context clues."

The first lesson teaches the general concept of monitoring of comprehension followed by lessons that demonstrate writing about particular monitoring strategies. The final lesson emphasizes that the attempt and *use* of these strategies is what matters most and not necessarily whether that attempt solves the problem. Using context clues, for example, is an important strategy for students to know and use, but it does not always lead to better understanding of the unfamiliar word. Unless there is direct support later in the sentence as to the meaning of the word, independent reading is not as dependable a resource for instant word learning (Beck, McKeown, and Kucan 2002). In these cases, students can use the sentence stem "I didn't understand . . ." rather than "At first . . ." to write about using monitoring strategies even when they didn't actually help to improve understanding.

"AT FIRST" STORIES

NAME IT	Writing about a strategy you used when you didn't understand something you were reading.
	Sentence stem: *At first I didn't understand . . . but then I . . .*
WHY DO IT?	Makes you realize what monitoring strategies you know and can use to help you figure ideas out when you are confused.
MODEL IT	*At first I didn't understand where the forager bee was coming from. The author didn't really talk about them before so what were they doing in the hive? But then I went back one page and realized they were talking about the same bees but that they just change names whenever it changes jobs.*
	Ask students what "At first" story you described. What confused you and what did you do about it?
TRY IT	**Turn and talk:** Have students tell a partner what it means to write an "At first" story about your reading process, followed by a brief, whole-class share.
	Strategy practice: In the strategy section of their reader's notebooks, students write "'At First' Stories" at the top of the next blank page. Ask students to talk with a partner about strategies readers can use when they are (1) confused about the information they read or (2) when they don't understand a word they read. After several minutes, have students offer suggestions. Write their ideas on chart paper and add any that should be included. Have students copy this T-chart in their notebooks. Tell students you will keep this poster up to remind them of strategies they can use and write about in their reader's notebooks.
SHARE IT	In a whole-class discussion, ask if anyone remembers using any of these strategies in the last few days. Have one or two students share and describe their "At first" story.

SUPPORT FROM TEXT FEATURES

NAME IT	Using text features (i.e., diagrams, pictures, captions, fonts in bold or italics) to clear up confusion or help you better understand what you read. **Sentence stem:** *At first I didn't understand . . . then I looked at the picture of . . .*
WHY DO IT?	Makes you aware of how helpful text features can be and how authors include them to provide supportive or additional information.
MODEL IT	*At first I didn't understand the part about when beekeepers harvested honey. How do they know how much to take? They can't take too much or the bees would go hungry. So I went back to some of the pictures of the beehives and looked more closely at the diagram. The top part was labeled the "Honey Super," which is for the beekeepers, and there is a whole section called the "food chamber," which is just for the bees. So then I realized that the beekeepers only take from that top section.* Ask students to name what you did to help clear up your confusion.
TRY IT	**Turn and talk:** Have students tell a partner why pictures and diagrams can sometimes help you better understand information, followed by a brief, whole-class share. **Strategy practice:** Have students take out their shared text and direct them to two pages that have useful pictures and diagrams. With *The Honey Makers*, for example, you can have students turn to the pages that show the beekeepers harvesting the honeycomb and extracting the honey. Have students talk in pairs about how any of these visuals might help a reader better understand the text.
SHARE IT	After five minutes, have a whole-class conversation in which students share what they discussed in their pairs.

WORD HELP FROM TEXT FEATURES

NAME IT	Using text features of a book (labeled pictures, diagrams, glossary, vocabulary words in a different font) to help you figure out a word in the text **Sentence stem:** *At first I didn't know the word . . . but then . . .*
WHY DO IT?	Makes you aware of how helpful text features can be in figuring out unfamiliar vocabulary; helps you take advantage of the tools an author provides to support understanding.
MODEL IT	*At first I didn't understand the word* metamorphosis. *But then I looked at the pictures of how bees are born and grow. One box showed a pupa that looks like a gray blob and then in the next box it looked more like a bee, and that picture was labeled "metamorphosis." So I am pretty sure it has something to do with it changing its shape.* Ask students what you did to better understand the word *metamorphosis.*
TRY IT	**Turn and talk:** Have students tell a partner what kinds of text features a book might include to help you with new vocabulary. Follow with a brief, whole-class share. **Strategy practice:** Have students look through their shared text with a partner and come up with a few vocabulary words a reader might better understand if they used the text features provided. For additional scaffolding you can tell students to turn to certain pages that are conducive to this strategy. With *The Honey Makers*, for example, you might have students turn to the pages about how a bee collects honey, which has supportive text features for words like *the honey stomach, proboscis, pollen basket,* and *pollination.*
SHARE IT	After five minutes have a whole-class conversation about the words students talked about in their partnerships.

USING WORD PARTS

NAME IT	Using your understanding of word parts to help you figure out a new word.
	Sentence stem: *At first I didn't know the word . . . then I . . .*
	(This particular lesson is a great complement to any work teachers do with Greek and Latin root words, prefixes, and suffixes.)
WHY DO IT?	Helps you use language you already know to make an educated guess about the meaning of a word; creates independence in figuring out unfamiliar words.
MODEL IT	*At first I didn't know the word* metamorphosis. *Then I saw the word* morph *and I remembered that when Ms. Smiley talked about butterflies she said that caterpillars morphed into butterflies, meaning they changed into butterflies. So I was pretty sure* metamorphosis *had something to do with the pupa changing into an actual bee.*
	Ask students how thinking about word parts helped you make a guess at what the word *metamorphosis* means.
TRY IT	**Turn and talk:** Have students tell a partner how looking at words parts can help you better understand some words, followed by a brief, whole-class share.
	Strategy entry: In the strategy section of their reader's notebooks, students write "Using Word Parts" at the top of the next blank page. Give students a short list of words from the shared text that lend themselves to breaking meaning down by prefixes, suffixes, and root words; have them copy them down in their reader's notebooks. Then ask students to work in pairs to make guesses about what the words mean by studying the word parts. Ideally, words reflect a range of difficulty so there is some familiarity but also some challenge. Words you might use from *The Honey Makers* include *proboscis, pollination, evaporate,* and *coveralls.*
	Emphasize that using word parts may not always help you completely figure out the word, but it can sometimes give you a hint, which you can then combine with other word-solving strategies. Although you can use an excerpt from a text, the isolation of words in this exercise is meant to get students to focus on meaning within the words themselves rather than using the context of the sentence.
SHARE IT	In a whole-class share, go down the list of words and ask pairs of students to share ideas about how they tried to guess the meaning of a word by studying its parts.

GIVING IT A TRY

NAME IT	Attempting to figure out unfamiliar vocabulary using a word-solving strategy even if it does not work.
	Sentence stem: *I didn't understand . . .*
WHY DO IT?	Shows awareness of using strategies to help yourself better understand text.
MODEL IT	*I didn't understand the word* metamorphosis *so I tried to break it down into parts. I saw the word* meta *and the word* morph, *but I didn't know what they meant so I just kept reading.*
TRY IT	**Turn and talk:** Have students tell a partner why it can be good to write about how you attempted to figure out a word even though it didn't actually help that time.
	Strategy practice: Have students turn to the entry from the previous strategy lesson on using word parts and to any pages in the shared text you used in a different monitoring strategy lesson. Ask students to talk with their partners about any words or parts of the book they attempted to figure out but still did not understand.
SHARE IT	In a whole-class share, ask several students to talk about which words or ideas they attempted to figure out and how.

Although strategy entries, both narrative and nonfiction, can generate lots of great thinking in writing, they are not the end goal. All this direct and guided instruction is in service of helping students to improve the way they write independently in their reader's notebooks. The next chapter looks at the important transition to supporting students as they move into the second part of the notebook where they write about their own books without any prompt or strategy to try. In these pages, students write entries that are guided by their own unique questions and thoughts while incorporating the strategies they have learned so far, from the other side of their notebook.

CHAPTER 6

Supporting Independence

In the summer of 2012, my son, Dexter Stanton, was born. I knew the first few weeks would be filled with extreme joy, amazement, and exhaustion. What I didn't know is how much advice I would be given about, well, everything! From how to soothe him, keep him awake, and when to feed him, to what I should buy and absolutely had to have. And as a new mom, I welcomed it all.

I learned lots of strategies from family and friends about how to calm Dexter and help him fall asleep. My mom showed me how to hold and rock Dexter near soft music. I watched how my mother-in-law rubbed his back in a circular motion. I read a book about swaddling that my friend Jenna gave me. And my sister-in-law Eva showed me how to use and navigate the new bassinet stroller our family gave us, telling me how much going for a walk soothed her kids when they were babies.

Even with all this great advice and modeling, no one could give me exact directions for which soothing strategy I should use when, once I was on my own. I had to figure that out for myself. An important part of learning to be independent at something—being a mom, learning to play basketball, or writing about reading—is that inevitably there is a certain degree of messiness. This certainly was true in my first month with Dexter. The first time I took him for a stroll on my own I had a tranquil vision of being like all the moms I had seen in the neighborhood, pushing the stroller with one hand and sipping a cup of coffee with the other. But my first experience with the stroller was anything but tranquil. By the time I got the stroller awkwardly down the porch stairs and figured out how to unlock the brakes, my good mood was dissipating. Once we started moving, I remembered that prompt from my elementary school years, "What would you do if you had a third arm?" because I definitely needed one. One hand held a spilling cup of coffee as I tried to navigate the stroller with the other hand, which was also being occasionally tugged by my dog, Dewey, and the leash that was (I had thought, cleverly) around my elbow.

As if this wasn't awkward enough, the sidewalk had these jagged little mounds from tree roots that turned it into a twenty-second obstacle course. Funny how I had never noticed them before. Finally, I shouted, "What am I doing? Forget the coffee!" I dumped the coffee out, put the travel mug in my pocket, and used my two hands to guide the stroller over one more root. But after only a week, I could go out for a stroll with Dexter, Dewey, and a cup of coffee. As any parent will attest, managing a stroller is only one in a long list of things that requires a learning curve. No matter how many baby books we read or advice we get, it just takes time to get the hang of it ourselves.

When students transition to writing independent entries, they rarely produce the perfect entries we envision, particularly if they haven't used reader's notebooks in previous grades. It takes time for students to get used to bringing different types of thinking into their entries on their own and to do so skillfully. Just like my strolls with Dexter, children need time to struggle and experiment with what they have learned. So even if students show proficiency in their strategy entries, expect a period of time where students will use strategies awkwardly or perhaps not at all.

While it may be tempting to suggest what students could write about when they turn to the blank page, this kind of scaffolding can dilute the expectations of independent entries. Too much "help" defeats the purpose of strategy teaching, which is to put the responsibility of thinking and writing on students themselves when they are writing independently (Buckner 2009). Instead, it is best to teach students *how* to be independent and to make the most of strategies they have already learned. As Peter Johnston states: "Teaching strategies results in their knowing strategies, but not necessarily in their acting strategically and having a sense of agency" (2004, 31). If we want our student to feel this sense of agency, then it is important to take the time to teach lessons about writing independent entries.

This chapter presents two complete lessons that support this transition from just writing strategy entries to writing independent entries about their own books. The main tool in these lessons is an anchor chart (see Figure 6.1), which lists the strategy lessons that have been taught so far in your classroom as well as related sentence stems. Once a poster is up, it expands as students learn more strategies. Every time you teach a new strategy lesson, it is added to the poster.

FIGURE 6.1

Strategy Poster

STRATEGY POSTER

In My Reader's Notebook I Can Write About:

- What "I think"

- The Characters
- Analyze a Character
- Analyze Relationship
- My Opinion of a Character
- Character Development

- Big and Small Questions

- Feelings Questions

- My Theories (*Maybe . . .*)

- Arguing My Theories (On the Other Hand . . .)

- Evidence for My Ideas (One Time . . . For Example . . .)

- Points of View

- Prior Knowledge Connections

For nonfiction strategy lessons, you can create a separate poster that is specific to this genre (see Figure 6.2). Another option, whether teaching narrative or nonfiction strategy lessons, is to organize the strategy poster according to comprehension skills (see Figure 6.3).

FIGURE 6.2

Nonfiction Strategy Poster

NONFICTION STRATEGY POSTER

In My Reader's Notebook I Can Write About:

• My Thinking ("I think . . . ")

• MY Questions

  - What I Wonder ("I wonder why . . . ")

  - What Is Confusing ("I don't understand that part when . . . ")

  - Personal Questions

• Book, Movie and World Connections (" . . . reminds me of . . . ")

• My Reactions

• Language Connections ("I have also heard that word used . . . ")

• My Theories (*Maybe* . . .)

• Before and After ("I used to think . . . Now I understand . . .)

• Evaluating Text Features ("This is effective because . . .) ("The author might have considered . . . ")

FIGURE 6.3

Nonfiction Comprehension Strategy Poster

NONFICTION STRATEGY POSTER	
The Different Kinds of Thinking I can do in My Reader's Notebook!	
QUESTIONING	**CONNECTING**
Wonder Questions	Book and Personal Connections
Personal Questions	Knowledge Connections
Confusion Questions	Language Connections
Explain My Questions	
ANALYZING	**SYNTHESIZING**
What "I Think"	Putting It All Together
Describe My Reactions	Before and After
Analyze Relationships	"On the Other Hand"
EVALUATION	**VISUALIZING AND MONITORING**
Noticing Author Craft	My Mind Movie
Evaluating Text Features	"At First" Stories

Regardless of the style, these anchor charts tend to be much more productive than giving students a list of ideas for entries because they reflect instruction in your classroom. Premade lists often include many good suggestions, but they are not always as usable for students as we might hope. Suggestions such as "noting the tone of the text" or "identifying possible imagery," for example, may sound "readerly," and are! But not all students know how to use such suggestions. Some students might have the relevant background knowledge and experience with these types of thinking and can use these lists to their potential, if they are motivated to do so. But other students, who struggle with reading comprehension and who are most in need of support, are less likely to make meaningful connections.

The strategy poster, however, is meaningful and accessible to *all* students. Each strategy listed has been taught and modeled and then practiced by each of your students. Teaching students how to use the strategy poster as a resource does not mean students *have* to use these strategies when writing in their reader's notebooks. After all, students can write reflective and insightful entries that do not contain any language or strategies you have taught. The point of the strategy poster is not to dictate what kinds writing and phrases should be in students' entries but rather to give students a tangible way to include higher-order thinking in their entries so that, regardless of their level, going beyond retell is attainable.

The following lessons on independence have the same components as a typical workshop mini-lesson. Similar to strategy lessons, these also have a try-it in which students process the point of the lesson, in this case, using the strategy poster as a resource. The main difference is that, after the try-it, students open to the independent section of their notebooks and are not given directions about what to write, only for how long.

Independence Lessons
This first lesson introduces students to the strategy poster. The strategy poster is a resource students can use when they are not sure what else to write about their books.

USING THE STRATEGY POSTER

NAME IT	*Now that you've learned several different strategies for writing about reading, it's time to start writing independent entries. Today, you get to write in your independent entry section, and you get to write about your own books.*
	Being an independent writer means that you get to write about whatever you are each thinking about your book! You can write about all sorts of thinking and really focus on parts of your book that you wonder about or the characters and theories that you want to explore. So that means when it's time for independent entries, I am not going to tell what to write. And there is no lesson. I am just going to say, after independent reading time, "Okay, it's time for writing in your reader's notebooks."
	But I also have something in case you get stuck for what to write about. Everyone look up here near the door. This is called our strategy poster. The things written there should look very familiar. Can someone tell me what they are . . . ? Right, they are the strategies you've learned and practiced these last few weeks. So if you are stuck for what to write about next or you think you have written too many sentences just describing what happened in the book, you can look up here for ideas. Remember, your primary job when writing about reading is to explore and show your thinking. You don't have to use the poster. You may have other types of thinking to write about. Or sometimes when you are stuck you just need a minute or so to think. But it's here to use if you are not sure what else to write about.
WHY DO IT?	*Let me ask you a question, why do you think I would want you to write independent entries? We've been learning lots of strategies for writing about reading. Why not just do those every time? Turn to the person next to you and talk about why you think it's important for you to write independent entries in addition to strategy entries?*
	Follow this turn and talk with a brief class share. If needed, mention that the best thinking about books occurs when writing is guided by the reader and that when you are independent you can write about all sorts of thinking, not just one type.
MODEL IT	*So I'm going to start an independent entry up here about our read-aloud* Bud Not Buddy. (I write a few sentences on the document camera.) *Hmmm. I am not sure what else to say . . . What should I do? Should I say, "Ms. Hale, Ms. Hale, help me, I don't know what to write?" What should I do?* (Students say, "Look at the poster!") *Oh! Good idea! Hmmm* (I scan the poster.) *. . . Oh yeah! I could write about my opinion of one of the characters.* (I go back to the document camera and talk out loud as I write.) *I think Mr. Caldwell is a real grouch. Bud is clearly a nice boy and hungry, but this man doesn't seem to care at all. Mr. Caldwell just doesn't seem to get along with kids . . . Hmmm, what else could I say.* (I scan the poster again.) *Oh yeah, I could give examples from the book that make me have that opinion of Mr. Caldwell!* (I continue to write a few more sentences.)
	Turn and talk: *Turn to the person next to you and tell them which ideas I got from the poster when I was stuck for what to write next.* (Call on one person to offer an answer.)
TRY IT	**Turn and talk:** *Now turn to the person next to you and say what you can do if you're writing in your notebook and you get stuck for what else to write about. Should you say, "Ms. Hale! I don't know what to write about"? Tell the person next to you what you can do.*
	Independence practice: Sometimes I complement this turn and talk with a one-minute interactive try-it that supports the kinesthetic memory of what I am teaching. I have students do "pretend writing" with their notebooks open and an invisible pen. Then at the count of three they all pretend to be stuck for what to write and practice turning to look at the poster.
INDEPENDENT WRITING	*Great job, I think you are all ready to be independent writers. So turn to the first page of your independent entries and write today's date. Today you get to decide what YOU want to write about. Remember, the poster is a resource to use if you get stuck for what to write.*
	Students write independent entries about their own books.
SHARE IT	All students share their entry with a partner. Then two students, previously chosen, read their entry to the class. Classmates comment on the types of thinking that they noticed.

As mentioned in previous chapters, the number of minutes students have to write will depend on the age of your students and the time of year. Ideally the time given for independent writing starts off small and increases over the next several weeks, regardless of the grade level. Figure 6.4 shows an excerpt of an independent entry written by a fourth grader. As described in Chapter 4, students also write in the independent section of their reader's notebooks after reading nonfiction books in their Expert Teams, shown in Figure 6.5.

FIGURE 6.4

Independent Entry

Sometimes I feel really bad about Zero. He has been homeless for years and he does not have a mother. He asks Stanley to teach him how to read because he does not know how to. I think that maybe Zero stole the shoes so that he could have something he would care about - something he would never be able to afford. Zero also never speaks but he has found a friend in Stanley and starts to talk to him. There are kids in my neighborhood who do not have parents and speak to only a few people. I hope that I can be like Stanley to someone one day. Kids shouldn't have to live like Zero. He seems like a very nice boy.

FIGURE 6.5

Nonfiction Independent Entry

The book I am reading
is called "The good guys of
Baseball. It is about 17 amazi
true stories about baseball
The story I was reading
was about Mark McGwire
and Sammy Sosa breaking
the single-season home-run
record. I wonder how McGu
and Sosa felt. Maybe they
felt like kids, just like When
they were in little league.
Or maybe they remembere
all there happy moments
in there life (getting married wite havi
a baby etc.) McGwire and Sose
don't hold the record any more
In 2001 Barry Bonds held
the single season record
of home runs with 73. The
book was printed
in 2000. so that's why

In the share that occurs after independent entries, students are not given a direction of a particular strategy to listen for. Instead, students are responsible for noticing and naming any type of thinking they hear. I might ask, for example, "So what kinds of thinking did you notice in Randy's entry?" after he finished reading what he wrote that day. Classmates often identify strategies that have been taught before, but any type of thinking can be named. My criterion for choosing students to share after independent entries is also somewhat different than a strategy lesson since there is no particular strategy that needs to be reinforced. As students are writing, I usually look for entries that show a range of thinking or for students who simply haven't had a turn to share in a while.

STUDENT POSTERS

Students can also keep their own strategy posters in their notebook. The day the poster is introduced, students can write down and color their own "mini-poster" on half a piece of construction paper, which can then be glued in their notebook. Another option is to just have students create a running list of each strategy lesson in the first page of their independent entry section and add to it after each strategy lesson. Either way, these lists need to have room to grow. Every time a new strategy is taught, it should get added to both the classroom poster and to students' personal lists.

Day Two Lesson: Being an Independent Writer

Ideally, I could just teach the preceding independence lesson and students would be completely independent the next day. And when I announce, after independent reading, "Okay, everyone, take out your reader's notebooks. Time for independent entries! Ready? Go ahead . . ." I would only see the tops of my students' heads as they fill line after line in their notebooks. In reality, it just doesn't happen that way. Students are so accustomed to being told what to write that teaching them how to use the poster as a resource, although an important first step, does not necessarily instill the *habits of mind* of independence.

On the second day of independent entries, I teach the following lesson that focuses on being an independent writer. Usually, I don't have independent entries on adjacent days (although you could), but I want to keep the momentum when I am teaching expectations for independent entries. This second lesson also includes an anchor chart, the independence poster, which spells out the three expectations for writing independent entries. This poster (see Figure 6.6) is similar to the poster I use for writing workshop and is usually familiar to students. The only difference is that, with reader's notebooks, step 3 is about starting an idea or a line of thinking rather than a completely new entry.

You can also make a separate independence poster for reader's notebooks, but I like to reinforce that independence expectations are the same for writing about memoir and

FIGURE 6.6
Independence Poster

When You Think You
Finished an Entry . . .

1. Reread what you wrote

2. Can you add more?

3. Begin a New Line of Thinking!

writing about your reading. Some teachers may also want to have students include the title of the book each time students write an entry. This addition can sometimes provide a helpful context for teachers and students during conferences. Since the main content of the reader's notebook is thinking about reading, and not necessarily about "the book," however, I usually don't require that they write the title each time. Students also have a book log for independent reading where they record the name of their book and the pages they read that day. When I am looking at students' independent entries, either in planning for lessons or in a conference, I am looking for types, range, and depth of thinking, which I can do regardless of what book they are writing about.

BEING AN INDEPENDENT WRITER

NAME IT	*Great job yesterday with your first independent entries! When I walked around it was so nice to hear the different kinds of thinking you are all doing about your own books. Today you're going to continue writing in the independent section of your reader's notebooks. But first I want us to talk about what it means to be an independent writer. You are already independent writers in writing workshop so you know a little bit about this. But what does it mean to be an independent writer?* (Have students turn and talk first about what they think it means to be an independent writer. Follow with a brief, whole-class share.) *So after today, we will still have strategy lessons once a week. But now we'll also have two days a week when you will write independent entries in your reader's notebook after independent reading. The only thing I am going to say is, "All right everyone. Take out your reader's notebooks! It's time for independent entries." That's it. No reminders. I'm taking time to teach these independence lessons so you know exactly what to do. If you do need some help, remember that you can use the independence poster, the same one we use for writing workshop.* (Or if this poster is new to students, introduce the poster on this day.) *Let's review the three steps and why they are important for being an independent writer.*
WHY DO IT?	**Number One:** Reread what you wrote. *Rather than tell you why this is important, I want to see what you think. Turn to the person next to you. Why do you think it's so important to reread what you wrote last time before you write some more?* (This brief turn and talk is followed by a quick class share.) **Number Two:** Write the date in the margin. *It's important to write the date because if there are three pages of writing, you should know—and I want to know too—did you write this over two days? Over four days? Writing the date helps you keep track of how much you wrote each time and when you wrote about certain ideas.* **Number Three:** Add more or start a new idea. *So you can either continue with what you were writing about last time or start a new idea in a new paragraph. For example, if Shelbbie was writing about a certain character, she may decide she has some new ideas to add about that character. In fact, she might have even changed her mind about this person. So in this case, Shelbbie would just continue with that paragraph. And when she is done with that idea, she'll start a new entry or a new paragraph. So that's one choice.* *The second choice is to begin that day's entry by starting a completely new paragraph about a different idea. You may have a totally different line of thinking you want to explore. In that case, just skip a line and start a new paragraph.*
MODEL IT	Bring back your independent entry from the previous independence lesson. Reread the entry out loud, write the date in the margin, and do a think-aloud about whether you want to write more about this idea or start a new paragraph. Either add a few more sentences or skip a line to start a new paragraph.
TRY IT	**Turn and talk:** *Turn to the person next to you and name the three things you do when I say "Okay it's time for independent writing?"* (Turn off the document camera or stand in front of poster while students talk.) Follow with a brief class share using the poster as a guide. For each step you can also ask why it is important.
INDEPENDENT WRITING	*Great. All right, so it's time for independence entries. And remember if you are stuck you can use the strategy poster. Okay, go ahead!*
SHARE IT	Have students share their entry in pairs and talk about how they did with the three steps on the independence poster. Then two students, previously chosen, read their entry to the class. Classmates comment on the types of thinking that they noticed. You can also have a whole-class debrief about how writing an independent entry went for everyone.

Scheduling

In these first two lessons, independent writing is embedded in the framework of the mini-lesson. From then on, there is no lesson when students write independent entries. There is just an independent writing session followed by a partner and whole-class share. The main condition for scheduling independent entries is that they follow a time when students are reading independently (see Figure 6.7). In order for students to write, to think, and to wonder about what they read *to their potential*, stories, characters, and information need to be fresh in their minds. Most often I have twenty minutes of independent reading followed by fifteen minutes of independent entries, and then ten minutes for the pair and whole-class share. Implicit in this condition of independent reading is that students are reading books on their own level during independent reading. Only when students can understand text at a literal level are they capable of doing all the higher-order thinking the pages of their reader's notebook encourage.

FIGURE 6.7

Independent Writing Sessions

INDEPENDENT READING	Students should know before they start reading if they will be writing independent entries afterward.
INDEPENDENT ENTRIES	Announce it's time for independent entries and give students a few minutes to transition. Students should know how many minutes they have to write.
THE SHARE	Students share their entries in pairs. Then two students, previously chosen, read their entry to the class. Classmates comment on the types of thinking that they noticed.

Because there is no instruction affiliated with independent entries, this kind of writing can be done at any point during the day. I still teach strategy lessons but now have to balance them, scheduling-wise, with times for independent entries. Most weeks I will teach one or two strategy lessons and then have students write independent entries two or three times throughout the week. How many days you can devote to writing about reading, of course, depends on your schedule and other types of reading instruction that need to be taught.

Management of Independent Writing

The amount of time students have to write independent writing is generally longer than for strategy entries. Since students are not confined to practicing a particular way of writing about reading, they have the freedom to pursue many different thoughts about their reading. The first week of independent entries I start off with the same amount of time given to strategy entries, about five minutes, and then slowly increase it every week or two.

My goal is to build the *quantity* of writing time without losing any of the *quality*. Soon I want to get to a point where I can have one-on-one conferences as the rest of the class is writing. I know, easier said than done! Such a goal relies on a combination of clear instruction and expectations, consistency, and management strategies in addition to having a system that ensures all students are reading and choosing books on their level. While there is no one right way to manage independent writing times, the following section offers suggestions for creating an environment that supports high-quality, focused writing.

Intermission

Just like the intermission during a play or half-time during a soccer game, the reader's notebook intermission is an in-between pause that gives students a mental and physical break from writing. Instead of a twenty-minute block of time for independent writing, for example, you can have two sessions of independent writing, each lasting eight minutes, with a four-minute intermission in between. Giving students two smaller goals of time rather than one big one makes it much easier for them to just get going and stay focused.

In the beginning of the year when I am building up the time for independent writing, the two writing sessions might initially be only four or five minutes each. These might seem like small time frames for writing (and they are), but these very short sessions make it easier for my students to meet expectations of maintaining a high degree of concentration to their notebooks. As students get used to this way of focused thinking and writing, the amount of time allotted for independent entries increases.

When I introduce the intermission, we spend a few minutes practicing the transitions. The first one begins when I say, "All right, time for the intermission. You have about five minutes to just talk to someone about what you are reading." In my classroom, I allow students to stand up and talk but not actually move to another table or part of the room. Then, when time is up, I let students know intermission is over, and then the next session of writing begins.

Most of the time students talk about their books although it's not something I monitor, since the primary reason for having the intermission is how it affects the quality of independent writing. You can also choose to give students a more instruction-related prompt to reinforce other reading comprehension lessons. For example, if you have been working on character analysis or text features you can also have students talk about one of these particular aspects during the intermission.

Build Up Time

The emphasis on quality over quantity in no way suggests that the number of minutes students spend writing is not important. Volume is a critical component of developing ideas and advancing the kinds of thinking one can do through writing. But without putting a priority on the quality of independent writing (or independent reading for that matter), the amount of time we give students to write becomes somewhat irrelevant. The key is to start by giving students short writing times with strict, high expectations of quiet and full attention to thinking and writing, and then slowly increase the amount of time you expect students to write *while keeping those same high expectations.*

To make this goal more explicit, I often teach a management lesson in which I introduce a number line that goes from 1 to 20 at the front of the classroom, above the chalkboard, and has a big, construction paper arrow pointing up to a number. This arrow usually starts out under the "10" for the first week, which represents two five-minute periods of focused writing on either side of the intermission. Each week I move the arrow up one or two minutes, as long as the independent writing sessions were relatively quiet and focused. The objective, of course, is to get to 20, which reflects two ten-minute, focused, quiet writing sessions. The number will also vary according to the age of students you teach and how much time you allow for independent entries.

Once we get the arrow to the twenty-minute mark (or however many minutes you ultimately want your writing time to be), the class can earn a reward, such as a Friday movie or an extra recess or any other incentive that is developmentally appropriate for the age of your students. One of the best aspects of the number line is that, even though there might be an extrinsic reward at the end, the task itself (being focused on ideas for a sustained amount of time) can influence movement toward authentic and intrinsic motivation such that the task itself becomes the reward (Ryan and Deci 2000). Students may not necessarily use the term *reward*, but as they write with more focus, they tend to feel more engaged with thinking and writing, and they write more than they perhaps thought they were capable of, creating more opportunities for positive feedback.

Music

The first time I experienced music during independent reading or writing times was when I was a student teacher in New York City. During any independent work, my cooperating teacher would put on this classical music CD, and I was aware of how the wordless songs positively affected my mood and my demeanor. There was a peaceful calm in the room that seemed to encourage reflection, the very thing we were asking student to do in their notebooks.

As it turns out, studies show that calming background music can positively impact the emotional and cognitive state of children (Hallam, Price, and Katsarou 2002). From a management standpoint, these pleasant sounds also offer a sort of aural substitute for talking. Having the air filled with soft music, as opposed to total silence, seems to invite conversation a little bit less.

The turning on and off of the music can also be a classroom job. Each morning the "music person" can choose which classical music CD is used throughout the day. Then it is his or her responsibility to press play when I announce it is time for independent writing and to stop the music when we are transitioning from independent writing to the share.

Writing Spots

One of my favorite management strategies is "writing spots," which I use during any kind of independent reading or writing. These spots, which I also describe in *Crafting Writers*, are comfortable locations around the room, away from their desks. I've used beach chairs, pillows, the rug area, and even my chair for these spots. They support management in several ways. First, these writing spots create an ideal and comfortable writing environment for a handful of students, and at the same time reduce the number of students who sit near one another while writing (Hale 2008). Second, students know they can only be considered for a writing spot if they are focused and working quietly. So these spots can also serve as an incentive for getting down to writing.

Connections to Book Clubs

The independence poster and the language of strategy lessons can also greatly support the independent talking students do in book clubs. One of the best aspects of implementing these small, student-facilitated book conversations is that they support student engagement and independence (Daniels 2002). While in-the-moment thinking and reactions primarily drive conversations in book clubs, many times students "get stuck" on what to say. So we can teach students that, when this happens, they can look at the strategy poster to kick-start a new line of thinking.

Any strategy, whether or not it uses a sentence stem, can spark discussion just as much as it can spark ideas for writing. Since the writing-about-reading strategies on the poster are not specific to any book or character, and instead are grounded in thinking, they can be used many times over by any member of the group. In fact, using these strategies in more than one context creates a desirable connection between talking and writing about reading and allows for greater variety and depth of thinking. While writing gives students space to form their own ideas, dialogue about ideas provides an immediate pushing and shaping of one's thoughts and a context for learning important discussion skills.

Whether in the context of reading or writing, providing space and support for students to independently use what we teach is a critical part of the gradual release of responsibility (Pearson and Gallagher 1983). Teaching students strategy lessons, like the Dexter lessons I got from my family or the guitar lessons from Sam, allows for heightened attention on one particular strategy at a time. With this kind of isolated teaching and practice, students are more likely to understand, become comfortable with, and take ownership of new ways of thinking. But we also have to let go and give our students space to try out what we teach, using their own initiative, so that what we teach becomes part of their independent skill set.

Independent entries in reader's notebooks also support the important cycle between instruction and independence. Although strategy entries can give us an understanding of students' capabilities, only independent entries can give us a sense of the kinds of thinking they have taken on as their own. The independent entry "gives us a window into students' minds" (Harvey and Goudvis 2007, 39) and so is the greatest resource for instruction. The next chapter looks at how teachers can use reader's notebooks, particularly independent entries, to inform their comprehension teaching in both conferences and planning for whole-class lessons.

CHAPTER 7:

Noticing Comprehension Strategies in Student Writing

When I was a junior in college, I volunteered as a reading tutor at a nearby elementary school in New York City. Every Tuesday morning, I walked to P.S. 165 on 108th Street and read with Jasmine, an eager second grader, who would flash a shy, missing-two-front-teeth smile whenever I appeared at the classroom door. Jasmine and I would carry two little chairs into the hallway and work on her reading for half an hour.

I loved my Tuesday mornings. Looking back, however, I am not sure I was all that helpful. I was not an education major and had no training in reading. Back then, the only way I knew how to "help" Jasmine was to pronounce words for her. When Jasmine would say "Then the little bird w . . . w . . ." I would wait a few seconds, watching her brow scrunch up and her face slowly move forward until her forehead was practically touching the page. When the silence started to feel awkward, I would just blurt out "went!" Jasmine would repeat the word and continue reading until she came to the next word she didn't know, and I would "help" her all over again.

It sounds simple, but the reason I was so limited in my ability to tell Jasmine what she was doing well or what she could work on was because I didn't know what I was looking for! My observations were on a surface level, so I could only judge how she doing overall. Years later I learned about the different cueing systems that support reading acquisition and all the teaching moves that go with them. Now, when I listen to a second grader read in a conference, I can identify when the student uses particular strategies such as going back to the beginning of the sentence, sounding out words in chunks, or looking at the picture for context clues. This means I can go beyond general, surface feedback, such as "good effort," and name a specific strength about the way she or he reads or figures out words.

My knowledge of all these small decoding strategies helps me see not just what students are doing well but also what students might work on next, because I know what it looks like when students are *not* doing them. Knowing what the absence of a decoding strategy looks and sounds like is a key factor in figuring out what you might teach young students in a reading conference. For example, when a student is not chunking words, she is usually trying to figure out a word letter by letter. So noticing a student sound out a longer word letter by letter automatically makes me think of chunking as a possible strategy to teach in that conference.

The same is true when we teach fluency in a conference. Our background knowledge of the smaller skills that go into "reading fluently" is what helps us notice when students use them and when they don't. When a student runs over periods, I see the *absence* of pausing at periods or when a student reads dialogue in a monotone voice, I see the *absence* of making dialogue sound like real people. The absences we "see" then become possible skills to teach.

There are noteworthy differences, of course, between these kinds of reading skills and comprehension strategies. Decoding and fluency skills are much more observable than thinking. When I first tried to teach comprehension skills in a one-on-one conference to my fourth graders, I felt like I was back in that hallway at P.S. 165. I wasn't teaching so much as "helping" students with whatever was in front of them. I would talk with students about their books, ask questions that got them to infer or predict, and then suggest that they "write that down." I didn't know what else to do. Although there is some benefit in supporting students this way, I wasn't really offering them any particular teaching points the way I was in my decoding conferences. I might see improvement on whatever pages we were talking about, but I didn't really see much transfer to students' independent entries. I was helping the writing but not the writer of reading.

A Way In

Once I began teaching strategy lessons, however, I found a way in. It turns out that naming specific types of language and thinking in writing is not just beneficial for teaching practical comprehension mini-lessons, but it also makes conferring about reading comprehension much easier (and more enjoyable). Where previously I might have only noticed when an entry showed "lots of thinking," now I can see and name more specific comprehension strategies. Instead of just telling Angela that her entries show thinking or inferring, for example, I can show her how she is describing how a character feels, a particular type of inferential thinking. Instead of just telling Kevin that he is doing a good job writing about sharks, I can show him how he is synthesizing information when he compares what he used to think about sharks to what he learned from his book.

Similar to decoding or fluency skills, knowing specific ways to write and think about reading can help you not just name what students *are* doing well, but also notice specific possible teaching points. Both kinds of observations can inform teaching in individual conferences and whole-class comprehension lessons. This chapter takes an in-depth look at the internal part of this observation process: noticing strengths and possible teaching points when looking at student writing. The next chapter looks more explicitly at the actual teaching of a conference using reader's notebooks.

Why Research and Teach Strengths?

Whether I am researching reader's notebooks for upcoming conferences or lesson planning, I focus on identifying and teaching strengths first. Noticing strengths and needs can certainly happen simultaneously and in some ways is the most natural way to examine writing. But compartmentalizing our noticing of students' strengths makes researching a little easier, and it ensures that we don't rush this important step so we can hurry up and talk about what students need to do better.

When looking at student writing, a common tendency is to focus on what will help our students move forward, especially those who struggle and are behind grade-level expectations. While such intentions are good, there is a missed opportunity to capitalize on the affective side of learning. Taking the time to teach students their strengths, regardless of their ability level, can affect one of the most influential aspects of learning: student's academic self-perception (Hale 2008).

An additional reason to teach strengths is that it can have a strong effect on how open students are to hearing what they can do to improve. In his book *Choice Words* (2004), Peter Johnston describes how making students aware of their successes affects students' sense of efficacy and agency and creates openness for new learning. The goal is "to confirm what has been successful (so it will be repeated) and simultaneously assert the learner's competence so she will have the confidence to consider new learning" (13).

Researching strengths also makes us more informed teachers because we better understand our students. Knowing what our students cannot yet do or need to work on is important information. But it is only part of the equation. When we can identify the space where ability meets potential ability, then we can offer more targeted instruction. More about teaching strengths in conferences will be discussed in the next chapter. This next section describes the internal process of noticing particular kinds of higher-order thinking in student writing.

Be Specific

Whether you are noticing strengths to teach in conferences or looking at student work with colleagues, the goal is to be as specific as possible when naming the thinking students are doing in their writing. General teaching points in a conference still come across as positive feedback to students (see Figure 7.1). But naming a specific strategy goes beyond a compliment. It teaches students what they are doing well and why it is good.

Numerous studies, from primary classrooms to medical schools to the workplace, show that specific feedback, as opposed to general praise, is critical to whether feedback has a lasting impact. Studies of classroom teaching have found that specific praise has a stronger effect on both on-task behavior and students' academic self-concept (Chalk and Bizo 2004; Dweck 2000; Simonsen, Myers, and DeLuca 2010). As one research team suggests, "When praise is specific it carries with it more information than a purely positive remark, and thus affords pupils more control of their learning" (Chalk and Bizo 2004, 349).

FIGURE 7.1

Specific Versus General Feedback

GENERAL STRENGTH	SPECIFIC TEACHING
You did a great job writing about when Peter finds the hatchet. I really liked that part.	One thing you did well in your entry is the way you write about Peter finding the hatchet. Instead of just describing what happened, you also describe the emotions he was feeling.
What an interesting entry about your book on the Pyramids! Lots of good thinking. It makes me want to read this book myself!	What an interesting entry about your book on the Pyramids. I notice that you are starting to think more critically when you write about nonfiction. Like here, when you describe what the author could have added when he talked about the people who actually built the pyramids. This is evaluating because you are talking about what is or is not effective about a text based on background knowledge you have as a reader. So in this case you are evaluating how the author handles a topic. Very nice.
One thing you do well is you include lots of inferences in your entries.	One thing you do well is that you're including different kinds of inferences in your entries. In particular you are good at inferring about characters' motives, the reasons they do certain things. So, see here, where you are describing how Kendra probably threw away the invitation because she was jealous? You're inferring, based on what you know about Kendra, about why she would throw away the invitation. You're thinking about her motive.

The key to "teaching specific" is to move from noticing good writing or "writing that shows a lot of thinking" to naming a particular way a student is thinking about his or her reading. If you notice a student showing lots of thinking in a paragraph, for example, that's a great place to start, but narrow down your focus to the sentence level. What kind of thinking are they doing? Always try to keep narrowing if you can. For example, if you see a student is writing about characters, are they describing them? Putting themselves in the character's shoes? Reacting to what a character did? Or if they are making many personal connections, how are they different from one another? Is there one in particular that stands out?

To teach strengths to all students, it's important to be familiar with a wide range of specific, academic strategies, from the most basic to the more complex. As mentioned previously, the strategy lessons in this book are meant to offer not just suggestions for whole-class instruction but also a wide range of ideas about what you might see in student writing. Knowing many different nameable and specific strategies means you have more in your noticing "tool belt" to bring to conferences looking at student work sessions.

Noticing Possible Teaching Points

The most commonly asked conferring question is, "When I look at my students' writing, how do I know what to teach?" Conferring is not about magically knowing what to teach; it's about looking for as many specific possible teaching points as you can that might lift up the way a student is thinking and writing about reading and then choosing one (Hale 2008). This may sound a bit more challenging than researching students' strengths. After all, it's a lot easier to notice something that is actually there than something that *could* be there. But, just as we can use our background knowledge of decoding and fluency strategies to see teaching opportunities about students' reading of text, you can also use your knowledge of writing about reading strategies to notice comprehension teaching opportunities.

Although there is no exact science to researching students' writing, I find it much easier to think in terms of categories when looking for possible teaching opportunities. This next section discusses and demonstrates three ways you can get ideas for teaching points when looking at student writing.

- *Absence of a Strategy*

- *Related Strategies*

- *Developing a Strategy*

ABSENCE OF STRATEGY

Noticing the absence of a strategy relies on the experience of having seen (or at least considered) what writing looks like *without* a particular strategy. As described at the start of this chapter, the absence of a strategy comes in the form of an alternative behavior, which is something you can recognize. For example, the absence of "reading dialogue like people" comes in the form of reading text in a monotone voice. The absence of chunking words, breaking words into parts, comes in the form of sounding out words letter by letter or making a guess at a multisyllable word based on the first few letters.

Noticing the absence of a strategy in a reader's notebook is a little less obvious than these examples since *every* strategy comes in the guise of words and sentences. You can still recognize the absence of a comprehension strategy because, once you learn a specific way of writing about reading, you start to recognize what it looks like to *not* do this kind of thinking. Most of the time, the alternative of a comprehension strategy comes in the form of a more average choice (see Figure 7.2).

FIGURE 7.2

Noticing the More Average Choice

COMPREHENSION SKILL	WHAT IT LOOKS LIKE	(A MORE AVERAGE CHOICE) WHAT THE ABSENCE OF THIS SKILL LOOKS LIKE
Asking Big Versus Small Questions	Along with smaller, more immediate questions about what is happening in the book, students are asking overarching, more complex questions.	Students are only asking smaller questions that are easily answered.
Describing How a Character Feels and Why	Students describe how a character feels and offer explanation or analysis about why the character feels that way.	Students describe characters, what they look like or what they do in the book, but never explore the internal story of the character.
Describing Motives Behind a Character's Action	A student analyzes a character's action and offers theories about why he or she does something.	Students describe characters, what they look like, and what they did in the book, but never explore the internal story of the character.

This thinking about the more average choice of a strategy is already part of the design process for strategy lessons. To determine "the why" of each strategy, I often compare it to a more average choice. Initially, I did this comparative kind of thinking to make strategy lessons more meaningful and relevant for my students. When I wanted to figure out and verbalize why a particular way of writing about reading was beneficial, it just helped to juxtapose it in my mind with a more average alternative. As I read students' independent entries, however, I started noticing these more average choices, which would immediately remind me of a particular strategy I could teach.

Figure 7.3 shows this reverse relationship. Compared to Figure 7.2, in which I spotted certain types of questioning and analyzing and then thought about their more average alternatives, in Figure 7.3 I recognize the more average choice in student writing first, which I have already associated with particular questioning and analyzing teaching points.

FIGURE 7.3
Noticing Possible Teaching Points

IF I NOTICE . . .	I COULD TEACH . . .
Students are only asking smaller questions that are easily answered.	Asking big versus small questions
Students describe characters, what they look like, or what they did in the book, but never explore the internal story of the character.	Describing how a character feels and why or Describing motives behind a character's action

RELATED STRATEGIES

Another way to recognize teaching opportunities is to notice thinking that falls within a particular category of writing about reading and then consider a more complex strategy within that category. For example, I might notice that Deborah makes several personal connections in her independent entries using the words "reminds me of," such as "Ms. Honeychurch reminds me of my second-grade teacher because she is really nice." Whether or not I decided to teach a strength related to her personal connections (such as using the word *because* to give evidence), I can consider using the conference to lift up the way she is writing about connections. I can consider other "Making Connections" strategies from Chapter 3 and teach one of the more complex ways of thinking and writing about a connection.

When you notice a basic use of a comprehension strategy in writing, it can make you think of more than one possible teaching point. Figure 7.4 shows how noticing a student's basic use of personal connections can lead to several different possible teaching points. The first related strategy in the "I Could Teach" column helps a student expand the way he or she writes about a personal connection, while the next two nudge the student to try a different type of connection with a character.

FIGURE 7.4

Noticing Related Teaching Points

IF I NOTICE . . .	I COULD TEACH . . .
A student includes personal connections about characters, but she rarely goes beyond "That reminds me of when I . . ."	• Personal connections that describe similarities and differences • Putting yourself in a character's shoes using "If I was . . ." • Personal connections about how a character feels

Related strategies can also go beyond their own category of comprehension skills. For example, there are other strategies not technically in the making connections category but are still ways a student could elevate or expand how he or she thinks and writes about characters (Figure 7.5).

FIGURE 7.5

Noticing Related Teaching Points in a Different Comprehension Category

IF I NOTICE . . .	I COULD TEACH . . .
A student includes personal connections about characters but rarely goes beyond "That reminds me of when I . . ."	• Analyzing a character • Writing your opinion of a character • Analyzing a minor character • Analyzing the relationship between two characters

Deciding which strategy to actually teach is the next step in the conferring process and is discussed in the next chapter. This chapter's intentional and separate focus on the research phase reinforces the important idea that deciding what to teach in a conference rests on first gathering a number of possibilities from which to choose.

DEVELOPING A STRATEGY

Sometimes you might confer with a student who is doing a good job incorporating a variety of thinking in his or her writing but needs support in developing and deepening those ideas. In those cases, you can consider teaching points that help students develop a type of thinking rather than introduce a new writing about reading strategy (Figure 7.6). In both Chapters 3 and 5, these developing strategies are included with the "Analyzing" strategy lessons.

FIGURE 7.6

Noticing Teaching Points for Developing Strategies

IF I NOTICE . . .	I COULD TEACH . . .
A student writes only one sentence for each idea	• Developing your thinking by writing at least two or three sentences for each idea • Explaining your ideas by writing "I think this because . . ."
A student might write a few sentences about his or her thinking but rarely develops ideas	• Giving evidence from the text that supports your thinking using "One time . . ." • Using "for example" to give evidence for your thinking • Writing in paragraphs: "Developing Paragraphs on My Own"

Planning for Whole-Class Lessons

This method of noticing the specifics of thinking in writing can greatly impact your ability to plan whole-class lessons. Years ago, when my colleagues and I would look at any kind of response to literature, we spent most of our energy noting how well students had done the assignment. We would notice when students were showing predicting or "doing lots of inferring" or we could say when students were *not* "doing lots of inferring." So we had a general understanding of how well students were or were not bringing higher-order thinking into their writing. But these observations were often too broad to offer any meaningful contributions to our instruction other than we had to do more work on "inferential thinking."

When you can identify specific kinds of thinking in writing, however, you have a way of seeing beyond the general quality of the entries. You can start to see specific strengths in your students' entries as well as more average choices that can make you think of possible teaching points. With whole-class planning, of course, you are starting with individual noticing but also considering class patterns so that lessons are relevant for most of your students. This kind of noticing can take some practice, although familiarity with this book's range of strategy lessons will make it much easier.

Designing Your Own Strategy Lessons

You can also be on the lookout for new ways of writing about reading. In fact, many ideas for strategy lessons come from reading students' independent entries and trying to name precisely what kind of thinking they were doing. The steps shown in Figure 7.7 illustrate a process for developing strategy lessons by looking at your own students' writing.

FIGURE 7.7

Designing Your Own Strategy Lessons

NOTICE IT	NAME IT	WHY DO IT?	MODEL IT
What sentence or sentences show an interesting kind of thinking?	What is a student doing in these sentences? Is there a name you can give this kind of thinking?	How does this strategy, even if in a small way, help a student with thinking or writing about reading?	Is this strategy transferable and doable? If you had to model with a read-aloud, what might it look like?

Designing lessons from your own students' writing is a powerful practice because you can, with a student's permission, use his or her writing as an additional model in your lesson. In this case, I usually show the student's entry on the document camera after I model the strategy myself, and even share that I got the idea for this lesson from him or her.

You can also get ideas for whole-class lessons by noticing patterns of need. You might, for example, notice many students not offering any evidence for ideas, writing run-on sentences that do not allow them to carefully develop ideas, or letting personal connections turn into memoir stories. Other times, noticing patterns is not so much about concerns but noticing where many students are stagnant and would benefit from a strategy that would lift up the way they write about reading.

Especially if this way of studying reader's notebooks is new, it is best accomplished with a colleague or within a grade team meeting. Talking out what you can see in students' independent entries with colleagues, whether it is thinking that reflects strategy lessons in this book or thinking you work together to name, helps you get used to noticing the smaller parts of thinking in writing. This kind of collaborative practice not only supports responsive lesson planning but also makes for great conferring practice, which is less about preparing to confer with a particular student than it is about strengthening your conferring muscles.

Oftentimes, it is not feasible to read all students' entries during a grade team meeting. In this case, you can, on your own, look at the last few independent entries of all or most of your students and come to the meeting with a sample of notebooks. This way you can spend valuable meeting time more wisely, sharing patterns you notice and then discussing what kind of lesson you might teach in response.

Book Clubs and Researching Student Talk

As mentioned in Chapter 4, the comprehension strategies you can notice in students' writing can also be applied when students are talking about reading in pairs or in book clubs. This research, of course, entails hearing language rather than seeing it. There are many ways to respond to the talk you notice in book clubs. Some groups of students may benefit from a nudge, a whispered suggestion, or the teacher joining the group to lift up the level of conversation (Serravallo and Goldberg 2007; Calkins 2000). You can also use the knowledge of the strategy lessons in Chapters 3 and 5 to offer a more direct type of differentiated instruction in the form of a book club conference.

Figure 7.8 illustrates how strategy lessons can translate into noticing specific strengths and possible teaching points when researching book clubs. Since both are teaching points, I often use the term *next step* to distinguish the teaching point that is meant to lift up the way a student is thinking and writing about reading.

FIGURE 7.8

Researching Comprehension Teaching Points with Book Clubs

Comprehension Teaching Point	TEACH AS A STRENGTH IF YOU NOTICE . . .	TEACH AS A NEXT STEP IF YOU NOTICE . . .
Asking Questions	Students asking their group thoughtful, open-ended questions.	Students discussing ideas about the book but rarely posing questions to one another.
Comparing Similarities and Differences	Students discussing differences as well as similarities when making connections.	Students talking about only similarities whenever they make a connection.
Small Questions Versus Big Questions	Students asking global questions that span the book.	Students primarily asking questions that relate to the plot of the book.
Analyzing a Character	Students talk about different aspects of a character in trying to understand who they are.	Students talk about only one dimension of a character, such as what they look like or how they are mean.
Analyzing the Relationship Between Characters	Students sometimes discuss the relationship between two characters.	Students discuss only one character at a time but never explore the relationship between two characters.
Using Evidence to Back Up Ideas	When students offer theories they often describe examples from the book.	Students offer theories but rarely give examples to back up their thinking.

Conversation Teaching Points

One of the greatest benefits of book club conversations is that they offer a dynamic, multilayered, and interactive context in which to explore ideas. So how students talk to one another in book clubs is as important as what they talk about. Not all students come to our classrooms adept at having sustained literary conversations that require expressing ideas and listening, negotiating air space, and developing lines of thinking. So in addition to noticing comprehension teaching opportunities when researching the strengths and needs of a book club, you can also notice teaching points that relate to conversational skills (Figure 7.9).

FIGURE 7.9

Researching Conversation Teaching Points with Book Clubs

CONVERSATION TEACHING POINT	TEACH AS A STRENGTH IF YOU NOTICE . . .	TEACH AS A NEXT STEP IF YOU NOTICE . . .
Building a line of thinking	Students spend time developing ideas about one idea before moving on to another topic.	Students take turns offering different ideas but don't spend time developing any one particular idea.
Including voices **Sentence stem:** *What do you think?*	Students are aware of group members who have not spoken much and encourage them to offer ideas by saying, for example, "Celia, what do you think?"	Some students dominate the conversation and are unaware of students who have not said anything.
Asking clarifying questions **Sentence stems:** *Can you explain what you mean by that?* *Can you give an example?*	Students ask one another questions to get clarification or to get another person to explain their idea more fully.	Students do not ask for clarification when they don't understand what someone else is saying.
Using the book as a resource	Students suggest looking back in the book when they disagree or have a question about something.	Students can't recall a character's name or disagree about what happened but are not going back in the book to resolve questions.
Disagreeing respectfully **Sentence stems:** *I disagree with that because . . .* *I see what you mean but . . .*	Students show autonomy in disagreeing respectfully, using language such as "I see what you mean, but . . ."	Students disagree about ideas but get defensive or focus on one person being right.

When it comes to the actual conference, whether it is with reader's notebooks or book clubs, students play an important role. Conferring is meant to be a partnership between the student and teacher in which both have a voice that impacts the teaching. While conversation with students can contribute to the direction of a conference, teaching tends to be both difficult and less productive if this is the *only* source of information we rely on. We certainly want students to be self-aware and verbalize the work they do as readers. But we are also their teachers and have a responsibility to come to the table prepared to help all levels and types of readers move forward in their ability to use writing and talking to think critically. This preparation begins with an ability to notice what children can do and what is possible in their writing. The next chapter builds on this skill of researching student writing and focuses on structures and strategies for using the notebook to teach comprehension in a reading conference.

CHAPTER 8:

Conferring with Reader's Notebooks

How we teach our students in a conference matters just as much as *what* we teach. While the previous chapter focused on the internal process of recognizing possible comprehension teaching points when looking at student writing, this chapter describes how to incorporate those noticing skills within the larger structure of a conference.

Teachers can confer with students in numerous ways. In some conferences, the teacher may act more as a facilitator or thinking partner rather than as a teacher. Still others may not use the reader's notebook at all to teach comprehension. The conferences presented in this chapter build on the idea that, when teachers know many specific ways of thinking in writing, they can offer their students tangible and attainable teaching points that support higher-order thinking.

Even though student contributions play an important role, the kind of conferring described here is more teacher-directed than other types of conferring. Some students, but not all, are capable of directing their own teaching so that the conference is a valuable use of time. The more options we have in how to help students become critical thinkers of reading, the more we can meet the range of abilities and personalities that fill our classrooms.

Research Before the Conference

I used to read students' writing during my conferences, but now I do this as part of the research before I meet with students. Reading notebook entries without a student next to me allows my conferences to be more productive and efficient. I am able to be a much better, more thoughtful researcher of student writing when I am not trying to juggle this reflective practice with my responsibilities to a classroom of students. I still wait until the actual conference, when I can talk with the student, to decide what to teach. But by reviewing independent entries beforehand, I come to the conference with an idea of strategies I might teach.

When I research a student's writing, I start by reading the last three or four entries and noticing as many strengths as I can. I jot notes about what I notice in my conference notebook as I go. Then I reread the same entries, except this time with a more focused eye on *next steps*, a teaching point that might lift up the way this student thinks and writes about reading. I reread the list of strengths and possible teaching points, and then I make a checkmark next to the ones that I think are good possibilities to bring with me to the conference the following day.

Out-of-conference research can be especially good for teachers who are new to conferring. With space for reflection, teachers can use this book as a resource for specific teaching points for a conference just as when planning for whole-class lessons. For instance, if you notice a student is only writing surface personal connections, the personal connections lessons—which are listed in developmental order—can offer some ideas for teaching points that would help the student write about connections in a more complex way.

Research During the Conference

Figure 8.1 lists some of the other research tools you can use to observe the presence or absence of reading skills that impact comprehension. Although reading text out loud is an important source of information for students who still need support with decoding and fluency, this chapter focuses exclusively on comprehension teaching.

FIGURE 8.1

Research Tools

RESEARCH TOOLS	RELATED READING SKILLS
Reader's Notebook	Comprehension of text
	Higher-order thinking with text
Conversation with Students	Student's experiences, intentions, or challenges
Book Log	Genre choices

Student Observations	Reading stamina and effort

Conversation with Students

Most conferences begin with an opportunity for students to talk about their reading. The most valuable aspect of this initial conversation, from an academic standpoint, is that it offers insight into students' experiences and intentions that may not be visible from simply listening to them read or reading their notebooks. In addition, it makes a statement that students have a role in their own learning and that teaching and learning is a partnership. Sometimes these conversations, on their own or in tandem with other research, can offer valuable information and influence the direction of the conference.

Conferences can begin with a general question, such as "How has your reading been going?" which allows students to be forthcoming with their own thoughts about the books they've read and the work they've been doing in their notebooks. During this time, I try to keep my research questions in reaction to what students say. You might hear me say, "What do you mean by that?," "Show me how you did that," or "Tell me more about that." These questions or comments are meant solely to better understand what they are telling me. If I have questions about students' independent entries, based on my "before the conference" research, I bring them up at this point. You can also ask more probing questions, by asking students to describe a type of writing or thinking they tried or about the decisions behind their writing (Anderson 2000).

During this initial research phase, I do *not* ask students the kinds of questions that push their thinking, such as "So what do you think will happen next?" or "What do you think about the main character?" These questions can be productive, but they come into play later in the conference if I am having a hard time deciding what to teach. Early on, I want to hear about the thinking students offer on their own so I can base my teaching on where my students are independently. I also want my conferring to match my expectations: I should find their thoughts about their books in the pages of their notebooks.

Because these initial conversations in conferences are authentic and as unique as the students we are meeting with, they do not always stay on a straight path. A student may start a conference by talking about the new *Wimpy Kid* book he received as a birthday gift, he may tell you he doesn't like his literature circle, or he may say for the third time that week, "There's no books I like in the library!" Such statements are legitimate reading experiences, and our job is to react as fellow human beings, not only as academic teachers (Calkins 2000).

While conferences should be flexible in making space for students' voices and conversations, we also have to balance the human aspect of conferring with keeping our teaching efficient. It's not easy. Even with a predictable structure, some conferences go on too long. There is no formula for a perfect conference. What matters is that you are simply aware of balancing the personal and academic aspects of conferring.

Supporting Student Talk

Many years ago when I was working with Michelle Gulla, a fourth-grade teacher at the Tobin School in Boston, we both noticed our reading conferences seemed more like fishing expeditions than conversations:

"How's your reading going?"

"Good."

"Why is it good?"

"I don't know… I like my book."

At some point, we realized that, although we had high expectations that students could contribute to the conversation, we weren't supporting them in doing so. As a result, we kept feeling responsible for nudging the conversation along. So we came up with the following poster (Figure 8.2):

FIGURE 8.2

Reading Conference Poster

IN A READING CONFERENCE YOU CAN TALK ABOUT . . .
* How you went about writing your current entry
* Any challenges or frustrations you had when writing
* A writing about reading strategy you tried
* Goals you have for your writing
* Parts of your entries you like
* Parts of your entries you are not happy with
* What you like or dislike about your book
* Challenges or success with reading at home

We taught a mini-lesson explaining how to use this anchor chart and why we made it, explicitly sharing what we had noticed in our conferences. Michelle also made small paper copies of this chart so students could keep them in their reading folders. After our lesson, students knew that, at the start of a reading conference, they could take out these mini-anchor charts to help them think of what to say. When we asked, "So how is your reading going?" students were much more self-sufficient in offering information, even if it meant skimming the list before answering. Then, as the suggestions on the list became more intrinsic, students gradually stopped needing the scaffolding.

Book Log

After our conversation, I ask students to show me their book log, where they keep track of the books they read and the number of pages they read each day. Having a predictable structure helps the teacher to cover each source of information, while students are more apt to give their full attention to the discussion and content of the conference when they can predict how the conference will be organized each time (Serravallo and Goldberg 2007; Calkins 2000).

Sometimes I have a few questions about their book logs, but usually I check quickly for anything particularly positive or concerning about their book choices, their volume of reading, or how they fill out the log. I also look at book logs at the start of a conference as a matter of accountability. If I have an expectation that students are filling out these book logs every day, but I never have a predictable time to look at them, students' loyalty to this expectation naturally wanes. I find that looking at book logs in a conference, rather than going around once a week to make sure they are being filled out, brings a more authentic purpose in what might otherwise seem like busywork.

Student Observations

During the research phase, I also consider recent observations of students' reading habits. Usually, these observations impact what I teach in a conference when a reading behavior has been something I have noticed recently, either for positive or negative reasons. For example, if I noticed Shane helping another student choose books in the library or I notice he has recently made a lot of improvement in bringing in his reading homework, I will keep these in mind as possible strengths to teach. However, if I have noticed Shane procrastinating during independent reading, I may ask him about it during our initial conversations, which could influence what I decide to teach.

Reader's Notebooks

As mentioned in the previous chapter, I come to conferences having already researched students' writing as a way to save time and to have more space to be reflective about possible teaching points. Since the goal is to teach the reader, and not to help them "fix up" a particular entry, it's important to read two or three of the most recent independent entries, not just the one they are currently writing. I might also look at their strategy entries, but the independent entries offer the most information about the active thinking and reflection students are doing on their own. Even though we might come to the conference with an idea of what we might teach, based on prior reading of notebooks, it is important to not make any decisions until the actual conference when we can incorporate what we learn from talking to the student and the other sources of information.

Deciding What Strengths to Teach

Since teaching strengths is about naming and reinforcing something students are already doing, I sometimes choose two strengths to teach in a conference. Several factors can influence which strengths to choose. The first is your record of the previous conference with this student. If a strategy that was taught in a previous conference is now visible in their writing, this would definitely be a strength to consider teaching.

Another factor that should influence your decision is your understanding of which skills are standard for this student and which skills he or she is just beginning to do. For example, I may notice that Nora is making personal connections or quoting dialogue in her independent entries. If these are skills she has been demonstrating for a while, it's not as valuable to spend time on them compared to other ways of writing about reading that show growth. A third factor for deciding what to teach would be recent strategy lesson instruction. Although conferring is meant to be tailor-made and is not a time to "make sure they are doing the mini-lessons," we still want to see a connection between recent instruction and what students do in their independent entries.

Are there ever times when I am conferring and can't find a strength that seems new or shows growth? Absolutely! In fact, that happens a lot, in part because, well, students are human and don't always grow in perfectly incremental ways between conferences. And I'm human too. When that happens, I simply choose *any* strength I notice, no matter how small. Any area of reading can be a source for reading strengths. I might choose, for example, to talk about the way a student keeps her book log organized or the comments she made during a read-aloud the day before. These skills are perhaps not out of the ordinary, but they are still academic and support the work a reader does, even if in a very small way. As demonstrated later in this chapter, any strength you choose, no matter how basic or small, is talked about with the same respect and attention during the teaching phase.

Deciding What Next Step to Teach

Deciding what to teach rests squarely on the shoulders of the research stage, when you gather as many strengths or next steps as you can notice. Deciding, then, is simply a matter of making an educated guess about which one to choose (Hale 2008). This is the reason a whole chapter was dedicated to noticing possible teaching points. Trying to decide what to teach in a conference without having a list of specific choices is like trying to decide what to order at a restaurant without a menu. So the more specific choices you can gather during the different kinds of research, the more options you have from which to make a wise choice.

As I research, I am mentally ranking which teaching point might be best to make public for this conference, based on what I see, hear, and know about the student in addition to the possible teaching points I have already considered based on my observations of their reader's notebooks. Sometimes you will see more than one possible teaching point. To help narrow down the possibilities, you can ask yourself the following questions.

- *What teaching point is most attainable and realistic for this student?*
- *What teaching point fits best with the entry the student is currently writing?*
- *What teaching point connects most with what the student talked about in our conversation?*
- *What teaching points have already been taught in whole-class strategy lessons?*

You can also make space on your conferring sheet to jot down notes about teaching points you did not choose this time, that you might consider next time.

ADDITIONAL RESEARCH

Sometimes, even with all this research, it may be difficult to figure out what to teach in a conference. Keep in mind that there is no perfect teaching point; however, there is additional research you can do to generate more ideas about what to teach students. Sometimes, it helps to ask more questions about their independent entries or to ask whether there are areas the student wants to improve in writing about their books. You can also use one of the following strategies for additional research.

One option for additional research is to continue talking with students about their reading but ask leading comprehension questions—the kind I held off asking at the start of the conference. Previously, I wanted to hear students' ideas without any prompting from me. When I'm not sure what to teach, I use prompting questions with the goal of getting students to verbalize thinking that is not in their writing (but that they are capable of doing) and then use their responses as a vehicle for teaching.

Questions can be specific such as "What did you think about the text features in your book?" or "Show me which text feature you thought was particularly effective." You can also ask more open-ended questions with the purpose of letting students' responses guide the teaching. For example, asking a student "So what were you thinking about these characters?" can spark different types of thinking for different students. Whatever their response, you can use the thinking they show through talking as a basis for what they could include in their writing.

Another option for additional research is to use students' strategy entries as a resource. You can look at the most recent strategy entries and see whether there is one strategy the student tried out with more proficiency than others. I know students have background knowledge of these strategies, and there is an added benefit of using a student's *own writing* as a model for what they can do in their independent entries. Since students will be trying out the teaching point in their independent entry, a move described later in this chapter, you can also consider which strategy would be most appropriate for the independent entry they are working on at that time.

Teaching the Conference

Like many teachers, my conferences follow the general research-decide-teach model but with an explicit, symmetrical focus on both strengths and next steps (Figure 8.3).

FIGURE 8.3
Research-Decide-Teach Model

RESEARCH	
DECIDE what strengths to teach	**DECIDE what next step to teach**
TEACH the strength	**TEACH the next step**
Name the strength	Name the teaching point
Explain why it's good	Explain why it's good
	Teach Forward

Record Conference

Strategies for Teaching Strengths

I use the language "teach strengths" rather than "point out strengths" or "give a compliment" because I want students to not just feel positive about the work they do as a reader but also understand precisely what they do well and why it is good. Students might know what words they wrote on paper, but they aren't always aware of the kind of thinking that language represents. Similar to strategy lessons, the more specifically you can name what a student is doing well, the more influential your teaching.

Some researchers caution against only using academic praise as opposed to praise that focuses on students' effort. They explain that students who have been exposed to process-praise are more likely to incur a growth mind-set and view intelligence and learning, not as fixed entities, but as characteristics that can be influenced by hard work and effort (Mueller and Dweck 1998). Praising effort is important but only positive *academic* feedback can impact students' *academic* self-concept while general positive feedback does not (Chen et al. 2011).

The practice of teaching academic strengths in conferences rests on the concept of redefining what "academic" means. Rather than see academic praise as conditional, that is, something reserved for performance or ability that is at or above grade level, it can refer to any academic strength. The ability to see small, specific strengths within writing (or any reading behavior for that matter) makes it possible to value academic strengths for all levels of students because it allows you to assess thinking without a comparative lens.

The strengths I teach in a conference may sometimes be small, and not in the state standards, but they are always genuine. For example, the phrase "Harriet was mad" is not what one would see as an exemplar of fifth- or even fourth-grade writing in response to literature. But "Harriet was mad" *does* show inferential thinking. Not to mention, some students, even if they are adept at analyzing and synthesizing ideas at a high level, don't stop to think about how characters feel. So if "Harriet was mad" is the most thinking students show in their entries, then this strength gets just as much value from me as any other strength I teach in a conference, both in the time I take to teach it and the tone with which I describe what they do as readers.

Regardless of what strength you decide to teach, you can use one of the phrases in Figure 8.4 to heighten student understanding of their academic ability. Each of these teaching moves helps students understand what they did well by giving them a hypothetical "poorer" or more average choice, which makes the strength more pronounced to the student.

FIGURE 8.4 Teaching Strengths Language Examples

TEACHING PHRASE	IF I WERE TEACHING	HOW IT MIGHT SOUND
Some Kids . . .	Using characters' names	*So one strength I see in your notebook entries is that you use characters' names. See here where you wrote Amanda and then Mr. and Mrs. Beale?* **Some kids** *just write the name of the main character and then for other characters just write "his friend" or "her parents."*
Most Kids . . .	Describing how a character changes	**Most kids** *just write about the parts of the book they read that day, which makes sense. But one thing a thoughtful reader does is think about how the parts they read today connect with other parts of the book, which you do here when you write about how Gilly has changed since the beginning of the book . . .*
You Don't Just . . .	Describing your personal opinion of a character	*One thing I notice you did in your independent entries several times is you describe your personal opinion about a character. Here when you talk about Cassie and then in this entry when you talk about Little Man. You really describe what you, Sasha, think of this person.* **You don't just** *give a description of them: you offer a more personal reaction. Do you see how you did that?*

As illustrated in the last example in Figure 8.4, I also sometimes use the question "Do you see how you did that?" I didn't have any specific intention to say this. As a third grader who swore out loud during math in Ms. Cooper's class once declared, "It just came out my mouth!" Once I thought about this phrase, however, I realized that it invites students to participate in the noticing with me and, even if it's just a head nod with a shy smile, it gets students to participate in the acknowledgment of their strength.

These teaching phrases can be used with all levels of students, as illustrated above, but they are particularly effective when conferring with below-grade-level students because they give an extremely powerful message, which is that *you are doing something that other students aren't* (Hale 2008). Students who are not as successful as their peers in school are often used to being on only one end of the academic spectrum, whether it is about how state assessments see them, their peers see them, or how they see themselves. By teaching students the small things they do well in their independent entries and comparing them to "other kids," they are taking a turn on the other end of the spectrum.

After naming the strength and describing it, comes "the why." The following phrases can be helpful in making clear to students you are shifting from naming the strategy to giving "the why."

"That's important because …"

"That's good because …"

"Including (name of skill) in your writing deepens your thinking because … "

Figure 8.5 offers examples of what teaching strengths might sound like with students of three differing ability levels: Karina, Marvin, and Risa. While each conference is unique, you can detect the same structure running underneath: naming the strength and saying why it is good. Keep in mind that these conference excerpts reflect only the teacher's voice and do not include any responses or questions from students. We will return to these same students throughout the chapter as each step of conferring is discussed.

FIGURE 8.5

Examples of Teaching Strengths

KARINA	
	Strength: Using Characters' Names Reading: *Freckle Juice* by Judy Blume
Naming the Strategy and the Why	So, Karina, one strength I notice in your entries is that you use characters' names. See here where you write Sharon and then Mr. and Mrs. Marcus? Some kids might write the name of the main character and then just write "his friend" or "her parents" for other characters. But you're including the names of different characters. And that's important because, first of all, it helps keep your ideas about people organized, for yourself and for the reader. I know who you're talking about. But it also means you are aware of who the different characters are as you read. So keep doing that in all your entries. Great job.

MARVIN	
	Strength: Describing How a Character Feels and Giving Evidence with *One Time* Reading: *Roll of Thunder, Hear My Cry* by Mildred Taylor
Naming the Strategy and the Why	Marvin, one thing you do well in your independent entries is that you sometimes describe how a character is feeling, like here when you wrote about how annoyed Stacy must get at his little brother T.J. You didn't just explain what was happening. You talked about how a character feels. I've noticed you do this in other entries too, which is good because it helps you think of the inside story of a character.
Naming the Strategy and the Why	Another great thing you've done in your entries is you give evidence for your opinion about characters by giving an example from the story. See, here you say, "One time . . ." and then say how his brother tried to cheat on his test. That's great because you are grounding your ideas and inferences in specific events in the book. Sometimes kids will describe a character but then never really explain why they think that.
	So today there are two strengths I am going to write down on my conference sheet. First, that you are writing about how characters feel and, second, that you give evidence for your thinking using "One time . . ."

RISA	
	Strength: Evaluating Illustrations Reading: *Space Travelers* by Simon Seymour
Naming the Strategy and the Why	Risa, this is great how you describe how the author uses real photographs in the book. You are actually evaluating this author's use of illustrations. It's not something I see often unless I have taught it in a mini-lesson. Most students stick to just talking about how much they like the pictures. But here, where you explain why the photographs are effective, this is more complex than that. You are not just thinking about whether you, Risa, like it or not. You are thinking critically about what these real photographs do for the reader, how it affects the reading process of this book. Do you see the difference? That's really great. And being evaluative of the books you read, whether it's about the way an author writes or the text features, is something I hope you continue to do in your independent entries.

After I teach strengths, I sometimes have students say back to me what they are doing well. Most often, however, I save this "say it back to me" move until the very end of the conference and move on to teaching next steps.

Teaching Next Steps

To make an explicit shift to the next part of the conference, I say one of the following introductions:

"One thing that you can work on is …"

"One thing I think you're ready for is …"

Notice that the language in both examples is targeted at the student and not at the notebook entry. This language reinforces the concept that conferring is meant to teach the writer, not the writing. Using the phrase "one thing" reinforces the idea that there is never just one way to get better at writing about reading. I am simply offering them one small strategy that can lift up the way they write and think about reading.

Next I name and describe the strategy I am teaching along with an explanation of "the why." Since this part of the conference is about helping students incorporate a certain way of thinking they are *not yet doing*, at least in writing, there is an additional section in which students practice the teaching point.

Teaching Forward

This next part of the conference I call "teaching forward" because it reflects the forward movement in how students process the teaching point. Rather than have students fix sentences they've already written (or squeeze sentences into what they've already written) students practice the teaching point by moving forward in their entry. We do want students to be critical and reflective editors of their work, and there may be some students who would benefit from a teaching point about rereading and editing their work more carefully. But editing and writing are different processes.

The main purpose of these comprehension conferences is to help students become thoughtful, reflective thinkers *as* they write, when thoughts, ideas, and questions are still forming in their minds and before their pencils hit the paper. With teaching forward, students use the strategy being taught, but they have to decide how they will *incorporate* the strategy within a short amount of time. This kind of practice more directly supports student ownership because it emulates the true act of writing, when students have blank lines ahead of them and have to make decisions about what to think about and how to say it.

Teaching forward begins with bringing the students' attention back to the independent entry they are currently working on and asking their intentions for what they might write next. Then ask students to keep going with their entry and try to, in the next few minutes, use the strategy just discussed. The teaching point does not always fit perfectly with where students are in their entry. But because independent entries are about exploring thinking, as opposed to telling a narrative that has a certain sequence, there is quite a bit of room for moving around to different ideas.

Before students start writing, I always ask, "So, can you say back to me what you're about to do?" This small question is a critical factor in my ability to momentarily leave the conference. I learned years ago that this kind of question is a very different one than, "So do you understand what you're going to do?" to which I usually get a head nod. Having students verbalize what they are going to do solidifies their understanding, creates a public accountability, and shows me they are clear on what they are about to do. If a student ever has a hard time saying what they are going to do, then I just condense the directions by saying, "That's okay, you're going to …" Then I have them say it back to me again.

Figure 8.6 shows examples of how teaching next steps, including teaching forward, might sound. These are continuations of the conferences (again reflecting only the teacher's voice) with Karina, Marvin, and Risa.

FIGURE 8.6

Examples of Teaching Next Steps

KARINA	
	Teaching Point: Using "I think"
Naming the Strategy and the Why	*So one thing you can work on is to bring more thinking into your independent entries. I noticed that you have a lot of writing for each entry but most of it is explaining what happened in the book. It's okay to sometimes write about what is happening in the book but the main purpose of keeping a reader's notebook is to write about your thinking. When I read these independent entries, I want to hear what Karina thinks about* Freckle Juice, *what Karina thinks about all the things that Nick is doing.*
Teaching Forward	*One thing you can do to get better at this is to start some sentences with "I think." Remember we had a lesson on that a few weeks ago? This phrase helps you get more thinking in your writing (or I could ask Karina what she remembers about this lesson). There are lots of ways to include thinking in your independent entries but this is one easy way. And "I think" can lead to all different kinds of thinking.*
	Okay, let's see, right now you're talking about how Sharon is about to give a recipe to Nick for Freckle Juice. I can't wait to hear what you think about that part! So keep writing for a few minutes and see if one or two times you can use the phrase "I think" to bring some of your own thoughts into your writing. Before I go, can you say back to me, in your own words, what you are you going to do in the next few minutes?

MARVIN

	Teaching Point: Analyzing the Relationship Between Two Characters
Naming the Strategy and the Why	*Marvin, you are starting to give evidence for your ideas, but now I think you are ready to start developing the way you write about characters. And one way you can do that is by writing about the relationship between that character and another person in the book. Because who you are with a certain person says a lot about one part of who you are. So for me, who I am with my friend Jeanne Marie is different than how I am with my mom.*
	The same is true for characters. So whenever you are writing about a particular character, one thing you can do is analyze the relationship between that person and another character. Remember how we talked about analyzing a character? Well this is similar except you are analyzing the relationship between two characters. You think about the different ways these two characters act with each other, which can change depending on where they are, what is happening in the book, or even who else is around.
Teaching Forward	*Let's see, tell me what you are writing about right now. Okay, you're writing about Cassie. Great. So keep writing about her, but in the next few sentences, I want you to try this strategy of exploring a character by writing about their relationship with someone else. So you can write about the relationship between Cassie and any of the other characters. I'll be back in a couple of minutes, okay? First, can you tell me what you're about to do? What are you going to write about?*

RISA

	Teaching Point: Explaining Your Questions
Naming the Strategy and the Why	*One thing I think will be great to work on today is the way you are writing about questions. I notice that when you are writing about a story you will let a question lead to lots of thinking. But when you write about a nonfiction book you don't ask that many questions. And when you do, they just kind of stop. You ask it and then move on to something else. Did you notice that? Any thoughts why? I actually have seen this with other students since nonfiction questions seem so unanswerable. Like there is one right answer. But remember the point of asking questions in your reader's notebook is to explore your ideas and thoughts about that question, which you can do with any genre, including nonfiction.*
	So here, when you asked a question about where space begins and then where does it end. That's a fantastic question! I wonder that too. But see how in the next sentence you just start writing about something else? So one thing you can work on in your independent entries is to, whenever you ask a question, explain your question a little bit more. Just spend a few sentences describing your question. Especially with information, writing more about the question can help you narrow down what you understand and what exactly is confusing. Then you can have a better foundation when you go on to offer a theory about that question.
Teaching Forward	*Since you have such a good question, why don't we use that as a place to start. Can you copy that question you have about space on the next page? This is such a great question. I want you to write for a few minutes while I check in with a few other students. And what are you going to try today that we just talked about? Right, you're going to explain that question before you move on to any other ideas. Why do you wonder this? What exactly doesn't make sense? I can't wait to read about it when I get back.*

Notice in the conference excerpts above I do not ask Karina, Marvin, or Risa to talk out what they were going to write. Instead, I get their *thinking process* ready for writing. While both types of support can be helpful and involve the student, the latter offers students a more autonomous role and is more supportive of student ownership. Of course, there are some students who may need the scaffolding of talking out sentences to generate writing. My only suggestion is, except for cases where accommodations are clearly needed, to not immediately assume a student needs this to be successful.

Once the student starts writing I leave the conference to check in with the rest of the class for about three or four minutes. The main reason I leave the conference is because it heightens students' independence. They also seem more engaged when working alone, perhaps because there is a demeanor of trust and belief that they don't need me, in addition to the fact that their time to produce something is quite short. The other reason I leave the conference has to do with classroom management, which, as any teacher who confers knows, can be one of the challenges of this type of instruction. These few minutes give me time to check in with the other twenty-four or so students who are writing independently. Walking around, peeking over shoulders, and offering small nudges or positive feedback help students to feel my presence and also help me get a sense of how they are doing.

Once I get back to the conference, I ask the student how he or she is doing and if I can read what he or she wrote. Sometimes I let students read their writing out loud, but not the entire entry, only the portion they just wrote. Because there is up-front investment in giving students attainable and clear teaching points and getting their thinking ready before writing, students are almost always successful with this step. Another benefit of the heightened student independence is that, when I read what they wrote, I am reacting to sentences they composed independently as opposed to sentences I fished out of them or said out loud and then got my "So why don't you write that down" approval. Any positive feedback tends to be more meaningful to students.

Connecting to Other Writing

Since conferences are meant to "teach the writer" and not just help with an entry, it helps to end the conference by making a connection between what the student just did in their entry and writing about reading in general. As shown in some of the examples that follow (Figure 8.7), you can use the phrase "So whenever you are writing about . . . " when wrapping up the conference to reinforce the fact that this strategy is now something they own and can use whenever they are writing in their reader's notebook.

FIGURE 8.7

Examples of Wrapping Up the Conference

KARINA

	Teaching Point: Using "I think" in Writing
Positive Feedback	*Look at that. You didn't just use "I think" once. You used it twice! And see how they are different types of thoughts? That is the beauty of this phrase—it can lead to so many different types of thinking.*
Connecting to Other Writing	*So whenever you are writing independent entries and you realize "Whoa, I guess I have just been writing about what happened in the book!" what phrase can you use? Right, "I think", just like you did in this entry.*
Say It Back to Me	*Can you say back to me in your own words, what are the two things I suld that you were good at in terms of writing about reading? Right, using characters names. And do you remember why I said that is good? Great.*
	And what are you are getting better at with independent entries? What did you work on today? Right, using "I think." So next time I read your reader's notebook I want to read a lot about Karina's thinking. I am looking forward to it! Okay so just write your teaching points in your student conference sheet, and you're all set.

MARVIN

	Teaching Point: Analyzing the Relationship Between Two Characters
Positive Feedback	*Okay, can I read what you wrote? Hey, you did it! Terrific. You wrote a few more sentences about Cassie, and then you wrote about the relationship between her and Uncle Hammer. Very nice. Now I get to see a side of Cassie I didn't see before.*
Connecting to Other Writing	*Remember, analyzing a relationship between two characters is something you can do whenever you are writing about characters in your reader's notebook. And if you want to, you could write about the relationship between Cassie and someone else in her family or someone at the store, because each relationship is unique.*
Say It Back to Me	*All right. So can you say back to me what strengths you show in your writing? There were two we talked about today. Can you tell me the first one? Great! And what about the second strength? That's okay. It has something to do with this word, "because." Right, giving evidence for your ideas.*
	And what is your next step? What did you do just now that will help you develop your thinking? Yes, analyzing relationships. You did a great job with that today. So just copy those teaching points in your student conference sheet, and we're done.

RISA

	Teaching Point: Explaining Your Questions
Positive Feedback	*Very nice! You really thought about this question. Notice how in trying to explain why you wondered about the idea of space beginning and ending so much great thinking surfaced! This is a terrific example of explaining your questions with informational texts. Could I maybe make a copy of this? Because I think this would be a great strategy lesson to teach the class, and I would love to use this as an example of "Explaining Your Question."*
Connecting to Other Writing	*So there are lots of ways to let questions lead to thinking. But whenever you are writing in your notebook, especially with nonfiction, explaining your question is now one strategy you know you can use.*
Say It Back to Me	*All right. Can you first say back to me one thing I said you were good at in terms of the way you are writing about reading? Well, more than just writing about illustrations. You are evaluating them, you are describing what is effective about them, which requires critical thinking, not just saying that you like them. So can you say back to me—what is the difference between just writing about illustrations and evaluating them? Great. And like I said, I have not seen students evaluating books in their reader's notebook much, so good for you.*
	And what is your next step from this conference? What did you just work on? Right, explaining questions. So I hope to see more of this in your entries. You can go ahead and write these in your student conference sheet.

Say It Back

One of the last things I do when wrapping up a conference is ask students to say the teaching points back to me, both the strength and the main teaching point, which has less to do with checking for understanding (although it does that) and more to do with supporting accountability throughout the conference. When students know they will have to say their teaching points at the end of every conference, they are more likely to listen carefully.

Having students verbalize their strengths has a particularly strong effect on struggling readers and writers, who may not be accustomed to acknowledging what they do well. This small teaching move has become one of my favorite parts of conferring, with students of all ability levels, because I often see slightly stifled smiles as they recognize a type of academic thinking that I named. And I know how important self-perception is to how they experience learning in general and writing about their reading in particular.

Asking students to verbalize the teaching points also helps students to remember what they learned. As a result, they are more likely to incorporate it when they are writing on their own. Sometimes students have a hard time verbalizing their strength or next step, not because they were not listening, but because they aren't sure of how to sum it up. In that case, I just give students a hint or ask them to explain what they remember and then show them how I phrased it in my conference sheet.

Recording Conferences

Some teachers have told me, "I do confer, I just don't write things down." While this is certainly possible to do, there are important reasons to record conferences. Keeping track of individual conferences first supports an equitable system to make sure you are checking in with all of your students. Writing down teaching points also supports student accountability and shows evidence of differentiated instruction (Serravallo and Goldberg 2007).

The good news is that recording conferences does not require a lot of time or writing. If effective teaching is specific, then describing the teaching point should only take few words or a phrase. Some teachers find it helpful to make notes about all the things they notice when reading student writing or during the conference. I would argue that this kind of documentation is most helpful in the research stage, similar to the way a running record keeps track of observations that support our teaching and holistic understanding of students but does not reflect what we actually teach.

After students say their teaching points back to me, they also record them in their student conference sheets (see excerpts in Figure 8.8), which are kept in the back of the reader's notebook. Although you can dedicate a few blank pages for recording conference teaching points, these formal pages keep conference notes more organized, and their official look heightens the appeal.

FIGURE 8.8

Examples of Recording Conferences

Reading Conference Sheet

Name _Karina_

Date	Reading	Strengths ☺	Next Steps ⇨
11/2	Freckle Juice	Using characters' names	Include Your Thinking (I think)

Reading Conference Sheet

Name _Marvin_

Date	Reading	Strengths ☺	Next Steps ⇨
11/5	Roll of Thunder Hear My Cry	• Describing how characters feel • Giving Evidence (one time)	Analyzing Relationships between 2 characters

Reading Conference Sheet

Name _RISA_

Date	Reading	Strengths ☺	Next Steps ⇨
11/6	Space Travelers (NF)	Evaluating Illustrations in NF	Explaining Your Questions more

Beyond the Conference

One way to reinforce the teaching we do in conferences, or to lessen the demands of time that individual conferences require, is to have group conferences. If you walked into my classroom during a group conference, you might think I was doing guided reading or writing. But group conferences have a different purpose and structure. Groups are determined solely on a reading challenge a few students have in common, and they typically meet only once or twice. I primarily use group conferences with students who need extra support in word-solving strategies or fluency or students who are leaning on retelling in their reader's notebooks. I don't teach strengths during these conferences because of the group nature and because their purpose is to target needed support.

For conferences to make a more lasting impact, it is helpful to allow time for students to review and reflect on their strengths and next steps as readers, whether this is done individually, with a partner, or both. In *Conferring with Readers* (2007), Serravallo and Goldberg suggest having follow-up conferences with students. These types of conferences take less time because not as much research is needed, and they serve a valuable purpose of accountability and reinforcement. This kind of teaching also acknowledges that the goal of conferring is not about students getting to meet with the teacher but incorporating new skills into their independent work.

Another way to reinforce instruction from conferences is to ask students to turn to a peer and talk about one or two things they are good at in reading and something they are trying to improve on in reading. Students might turn to the page where they recorded their teaching points from recent conferences. But they can talk about *any* reading skills they think they are good at or need to work on since conferences can only capture one aspect of who they are as readers. This brief activity, which takes only three or four minutes, reaffirms the expectation that "of course you're aware of what you are good at and what you need to work on." After all, like any skill you are trying to improve, whether it is pottery or playing basketball or knitting, how can you get better if you aren't aware of what you already do well and what you need to work on next? By naming students' unique strengths and giving them short-term, attainable comprehension goals, we can create conditions of self-awareness that can get students invested in their own learning.

Assessment and Final Thoughts

In the summer of 2012 my mom decided it was time to clean out the attic. So one weekend my sister and I went to our parents' house and went through all the boxes we had stored there. What at first seemed to be a chore quickly turned into an enjoyable visit through the decades of our lives. In one cardboard box, among letters from my camp friends and my old Girl Scout sash, was a folder full of schoolwork from elementary school. In it was a book report from Mrs. Matthews's class about *Tales of a Fourth Grade Nothing*. I smiled at my loopy handwriting and what a big deal it was to be writing in cursive. Reading about these books in my eight-year-old voice made me nostalgic for my elementary school and all the simplicity that went with that age—and, of course, all those Book Bucks.

Rereading those old book reports reminded me just how much retelling was the norm for writing about reading back then. There had certainly been no mention of or expectation for me to include thinking, wondering, or analyzing about Peter and his little brother's antics. Reading it with my teacher's lens, I thought about it as an assessment and how little it offered teachers, either then or now, in terms of planning for reading instruction.

My next thought, as I sat among those cardboard boxes, was "Well, what instruction was it supposed to impact?" Like most elementary classrooms of the 1970s, reading com-

CHAPTER 9:

Assessment and Final Thoughts

n the summer of 2012 my mom decided it was time to clean out the attic. So one weekend my sister and I went to our parents' house and went through all the boxes we had stored there. What at first seemed to be a chore quickly turned into an enjoyable visit through the decades of our lives. In one cardboard box, among letters from my camp friends and my old Girl Scout sash, was a folder full of schoolwork from elementary school. In it was a book report from Mrs. Matthews's class about *Tales of a Fourth Grade Nothing.* I smiled at my loopy handwriting and what a big deal it was to be writing in cursive. Reading about these books in my eight-year-old voice made me nostalgic for my elementary school and all the simplicity that went with that age—and, of course, all those Book Bucks.

Rereading those old book reports reminded me just how much retelling was the norm for writing about reading back then. There had certainly been no mention of or expectation for me to include thinking, wondering, or analyzing about Peter and his little brother's antics. Reading it with my teacher's lens, I thought about it as an assessment and how little it offered teachers, either then or now, in terms of planning for reading instruction.

My next thought, as I sat among those cardboard boxes, was "Well, what instruction was it supposed to impact?" Like most elementary classrooms of the 1970s, reading comprehension instruction was not really about teaching. It was about assigning a worksheet that we completed or reading excerpts out loud. The closest thing to reading comprehension instruction was when the teacher asked a question, often one that required mostly recall, and students provided an answer (Durkin 1978). All those book reports basically matched the classroom instruction.

With the shift to *teaching* reading comprehension, changes have occurred in how we assess reading. Unlike the book reports from my elementary school days, today's assessments are not so straightforward and simple. Comprehension is a complex, multifaceted process that incorporates numerous skills and interactions of different types of knowledge. It only makes sense, then, that reading comprehension is not accurately captured with any single assessment (Lesaux and Marietta 2012). A complete picture of children's comprehension, in regard to both individual progress and grade-level expectations, requires meaningful evaluation of numerous skills, including students' listening comprehension, their linguistic and vocabulary resources, their motivation, and their self-concept as readers (Snow 2002).

One of the best aspects of reader's notebooks is that they are, at the same time, an instructional tool and an assessment tool. The strategy section allows students to process and try out what we teach, while the independent entries offer information about the kinds of thinking students are doing independently and about the unique strategies they have developed on their own. Both kinds of writing also give us immediate feedback on how students receive and process instruction so that we can more wisely plan subsequent teaching.

In addition to using students' entries as formative assessment, we can use assessments to reinforce expectations and learning related to reader's notebooks. This chapter describes two types of assessments that can support the work of the reader's notebook: strategy homework and notebook rubrics. Together they reinforce comprehension instruction, strengthen and measure student accountability, and provide information about student learning. Also discussed in this chapter is assessment related to Expert Team reading. Like many formative assessments, each way of evaluating serves the purpose of not only informing teachers about student learning but also creating opportunities for learning (Dodge 2009).

Strategy Homework

Figures 9.1 and 9.2 show examples of pages from a homework notebook, a small, easily transportable (and not too expensive) notebook where students can write strategy entries. Each time this notebook goes home, about once or twice a week, there is a prompt for students to respond to in writing. Each prompt is similar to a strategy entry in that the

FIGURE 8.8

Examples of Recording Conferences

Reading Conference Sheet

Name _Karina_

Date	Reading	Strengths ☺	Next Steps ⇨
11/2	Freckle Juice	Using characters' names	Include your Thinking (I think)

Reading Conference Sheet

Name _Marvin_

Date	Reading	Strengths ☺	Next Steps ⇨
11/5	Roll of Thunder Hear My Cry	• Describing how characters feel • Giving Evidence (one time)	Analyzing Relationships between 2 characters

Reading Conference Sheet

Name _RISA_

Date	Reading	Strengths ☺	Next Steps ⇨
11/6	Space Travelers (NF)	Evaluating Illustrations in NF	Explaining your Questions more

Beyond the Conference

One way to reinforce the teaching we do in conferences, or to lessen the demands of time that individual conferences require, is to have group conferences. If you walked into my classroom during a group conference, you might think I was doing guided reading or writing. But group conferences have a different purpose and structure. Groups are determined solely on a reading challenge a few students have in common, and they typically meet only once or twice. I primarily use group conferences with students who need extra support in word-solving strategies or fluency or students who are leaning on retelling in their reader's notebooks. I don't teach strengths during these conferences because of the group nature and because their purpose is to target needed support.

For conferences to make a more lasting impact, it is helpful to allow time for students to review and reflect on their strengths and next steps as readers, whether this is done individually, with a partner, or both. In *Conferring with Readers* (2007), Serravallo and Goldberg suggest having follow-up conferences with students. These types of conferences take less time because not as much research is needed, and they serve a valuable purpose of accountability and reinforcement. This kind of teaching also acknowledges that the goal of conferring is not about students getting to meet with the teacher but incorporating new skills into their independent work.

Another way to reinforce instruction from conferences is to ask students to turn to a peer and talk about one or two things they are good at in reading and something they are trying to improve on in reading. Students might turn to the page where they recorded their teaching points from recent conferences. But they can talk about *any* reading skills they think they are good at or need to work on since conferences can only capture one aspect of who they are as readers. This brief activity, which takes only three or four minutes, reaffirms the expectation that "of course you're aware of what you are good at and what you need to work on." After all, like any skill you are trying to improve, whether it is pottery or playing basketball or knitting, how can you get better if you aren't aware of what you already do well and what you need to work on next? By naming students' unique strengths and giving them short-term, attainable comprehension goals, we can create conditions of self-awareness that can get students invested in their own learning.

FIGURE 9.1

Homework Notebook Example

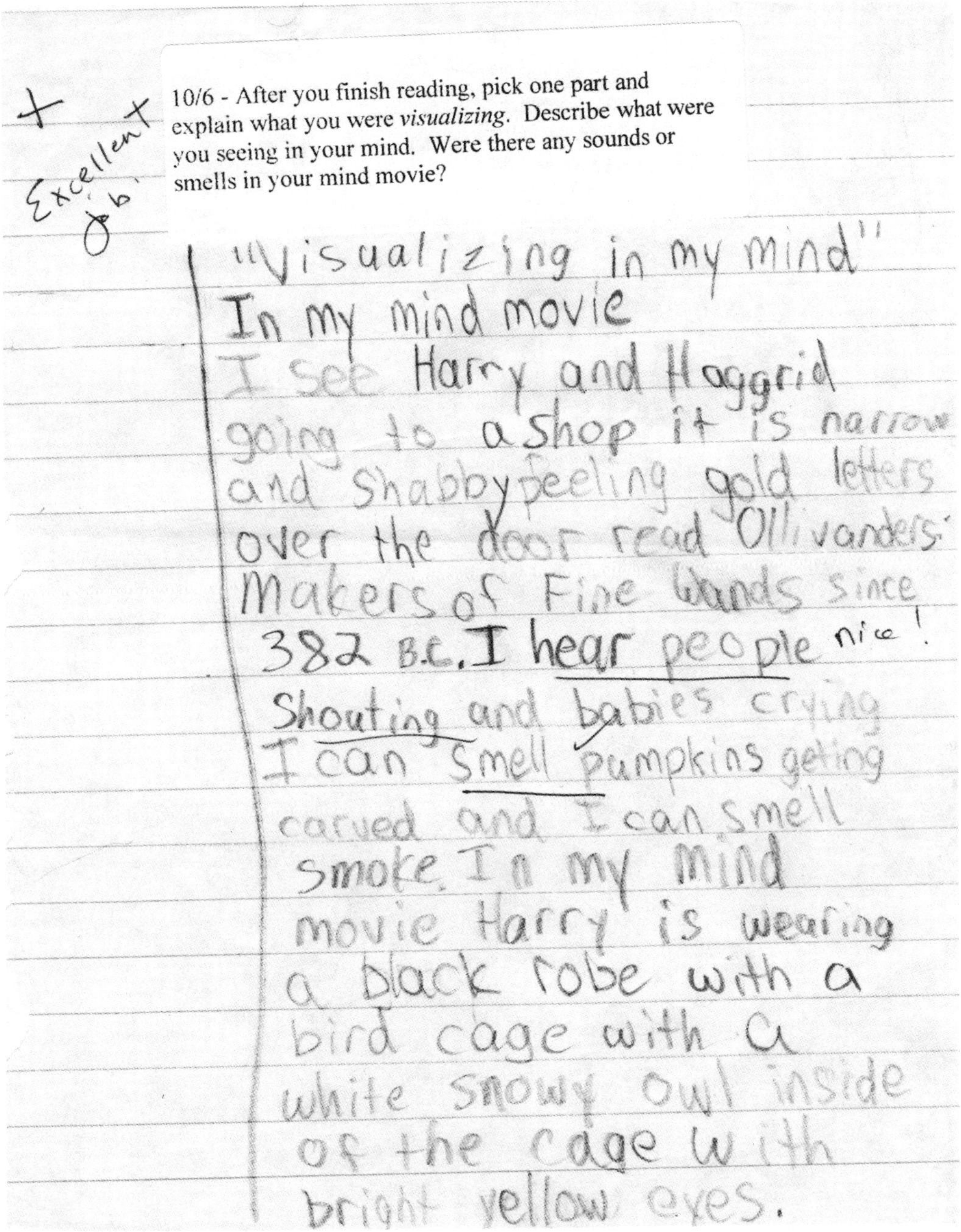

X

Excellent
Job!

10/6 - After you finish reading, pick one part and explain what you were *visualizing*. Describe what were you seeing in your mind. Were there any sounds or smells in your mind movie?

"Visualizing in my mind"
In my mind movie
I see Harry and Haggrid
going to a shop it is narrow
and shabby feeling gold letters
over the door read Ollivanders:
Makers of Fine Wands since
382 B.C. I hear people nice!
Shouting and babies crying
I can smell pumpkins geting
carved and I can smell
smoke. In my mind
movie Harry is wearing
a black robe with a
bird cage with a
white snowy owl inside
of the cage with
bright yellow eyes.

FIGURE 9.2

Homework Notebook Example

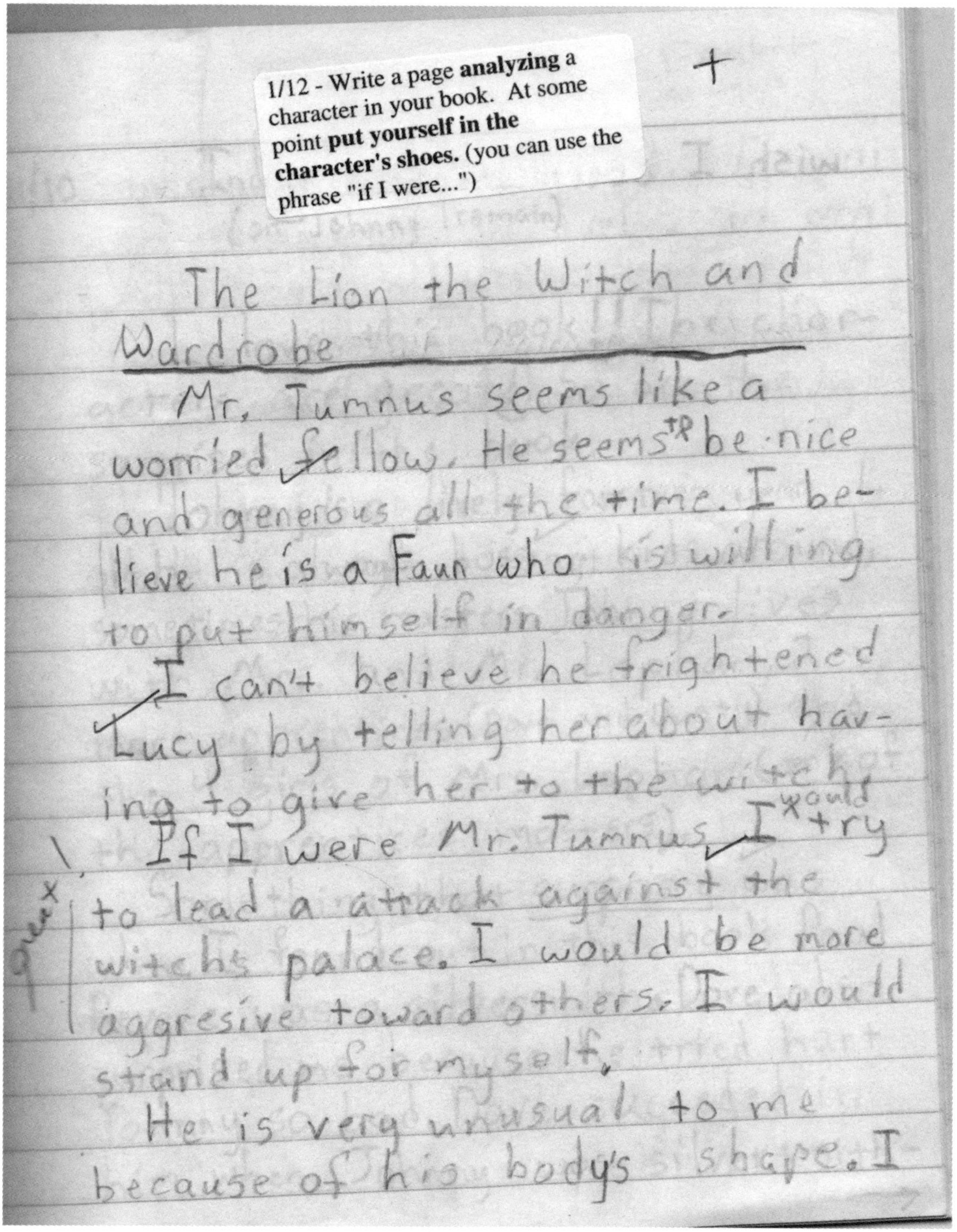

1/12 - Write a page **analyzing** a character in your book. At some point **put yourself in the character's shoes.** (you can use the phrase "if I were...")

The Lion the Witch and Wardrobe

Mr. Tumnus seems like a worried fellow. He seems to be nice and generous all the time. I believe he is a Faun who is willing to put himself in danger.

I can't believe he frightened Lucy by telling her about having to give her to the witch.

If I were Mr. Tumnus, I would try to lead a attack against the witch's palace. I would be more aggresive toward others. I would stand up for myself.

He is very unusual to me because of his body's shape. I

content of the prompt is about strategy use, not a particular text. Unlike a strategy lesson, students' responses are based on their own books, not on a class text.

As you might notice from the examples, these homework prompts require students to use two or more different strategies. Any strategy mentioned in these prompts has already been taught in a whole-class strategy lesson. Students have already practiced each prompt in isolation; so asking them to use two (or even three) at the same time is a fair but slightly more challenging task. Asking students to use more than one strategy is also a bit closer to their independent writing, when they are ideally incorporating different kinds of thinking within one entry. Because these homework assignments are meant to reinforce in-school instruction, I intentionally wait several days after teaching a strategy lesson before including it in a homework prompt, when the strategy is not so fresh in their minds.

Using the "labels" feature on your computer, you can create a document to fit any size Avery label. Type a brief prompt in the box and—presto!—it appears thirty times. Then, all you have to do is print out the one page on label paper and stick the label on the next blank page of students' homework notebooks. Using the labels not only saves time, as opposed to students copying a prompt from the board, but also keeps notebooks neater, and the "officialness" of the sticker makes the homework notebooks more appealing to students.

I usually begin these homework notebooks in late October, once classroom routines have been established and I have taught at least three or four strategy lessons. You can start off with shorter-volume expectations and then increase them as the year progresses. Grades for strategy homework are based on two criteria: (1) whether the student used the strategies requested in the prompt and (2) whether they wrote the expected amount, which should be doable for all students regardless of reading ability. Unlike with the reader's notebooks, I write comments and a grade on the pages. You can also assign independent entries for homework. Grades for independent entries are primarily based on whether students included a variety of thinking in their entry and whether they wrote the requested amount.

Assessing the Reader's Notebook

I aim to assess students' notebooks about once a month, which supports individual assessment and also gives me a better sense of where my students are as a class and what lessons I might want to teach in upcoming weeks. Figure 9.3 shows a notebook rubric that aligns with my expectations for reader's notebooks. These criteria are not usually found in any grade's standards. Like many classroom practices, an indirect link exists between some things I assess in my classroom and larger goals stated in the standards.

FIGURE 9.3

Reader's Notebook Rubric Example

READER'S NOTEBOOK RUBRIC

Name _____

		Score	Comments	Date
STRATEGY ENTRIES	-Strategy entries are labeled -You used the "writing about reading" strategy			
INDEPENDENT ENTRIES	-Entries show different kinds of thinking - Thinking is developed in paragraphs - Volume of writing reflects time given for independent writing			
ORGANIZATION	- Notebook is in good condition - Entries are dated - Handwriting is legible			
WRITING EXPECTATIONS	-Most sentences are complete (no run-ons) -Correct capitals and punctuation -Best effort at spelling			

One part of the rubric worth noting is the section that assesses students' spelling and punctuation. Like many workshop teachers, I don't make corrections in the actual notebook. If we want students to use their notebooks to take risks with their ideas, questions, and wonderings, and to write for long periods, then how we assess their writing matters (Calkins 1994). If struggling readers and writers are penalized for misspelled words, they will quickly learn to play it safe, writing very little and using vocabulary they know how to spell.

That said, we still want students to feel accountable for using correct spelling and punctuation *to their potential* when they write in their reader's notebooks. Our charge then is to find a balance between honoring the impact of feedback and instilling in students both a curiosity and respect for language conventions (Calkins 1994). Finding this balance begins in September when we have class conversations about differences between formal and informal writing assignments, including differences in audience, purpose, and editing expectations.

With the introduction of reader's notebooks, I explain to students that, even though they fall under the more informal type of writing, it doesn't mean attention to what you write and how you write it, does not matter. I compare the importance of checking one's writing to the way people quickly reread an e-mail (or should) to make sure it says what you mean it to say, free of confusing or distracting errors.

To support this habit of checking one's writing, I devote the last two or three minutes of independent writing time to students rereading what they wrote that day. They are encouraged to fix any mistakes they see, although rereading is also meant to heighten their attention to writing as they write. So when I assess notebooks using the rubric, I am grading this attention to text. I do not know exactly which words each student is capable of spelling correctly, but I can usually tell when a student is not attending to what they write, especially when I see missing words and punctuation or many run-on sentences.

As with any formative assessment, take time to introduce students to the rubric, before it is first used, to discuss what each part means. Students can also keep small versions of these rubrics in their notebooks or reading folders. Every now and then, they can use these rubrics to talk with a partner about how they are progressing with each section of the rubric. Another option is to create sample versions of notebook entries, reflecting different strengths and weaknesses, and have students work in pairs to assess them using the rubric. Not only do students enjoy being in the assessor's seat, but these experiences also allow them to "examine writing from a reader's point of view" (Spandel 2006, 19).

Nonfiction Homework

The following nonfiction homework supports the reading strategies presented in Chapter 4, which center on students' ability to actively process informational text to their potential. Similar to strategy homework, nonfiction homework assignments play a dual role in that they act as both a *reinforcement* of classroom instruction and as an *assessment* of strategy use.

This homework includes excerpts of nonfiction text, either from articles or nonfiction books. I try to find a balance between texts that align with content my students are learning in science or social studies and other high-interest topics. Since all students need to be able to comprehend assigned reading homework, I choose two or three different levels of text about the same topic, a differentiation that has usually led me to knock on the second-grade teacher's door before school. Now there are also websites that allow teachers to access and print different levels of text on the same topic.

Once text excerpts are chosen, you can create several pages of questions. Although this homework definitely takes more time and effort than a typical assignment (and so goes home only once a week), it does allow you to pick and choose the reading skills and comprehension you want students to practice. For me, the first part of the homework always supports students' literal comprehension and attention to text using a read-and-pause structure similar to Expert Team reading. Sometimes this scaffolding is done through visualizing questions (see Figure 9.4). At other times, I include questions that ask students to summarize information by stating the main idea for different lengths of text, from a paragraph to an entire article (see Figure 9.5).

The summarizing skills reflected in this homework are taught and practiced apart from reader's notebooks. The ability to paraphrase significant facts is important and creates a foundation for higher-order thinking, such as synthesizing information (Harvey and Goudvis 2007); however, summarizing information is not as conducive to authentic writing and talking about texts. Writing about what you learned, for example, is a different, albeit related, skill than summarizing or giving the main idea of what you read.

The second part of the homework supports inferential thinking with informational text. Questions are tailored for each reading and are meant to reinforce strategy lessons and any other recent comprehension instruction. This nonfiction homework can offer information about which strategies students are comfortable using and which ones still might need some reinforcement. The bigger benefit, however, lies in grounding comprehension instruction in content and reinforcing the important habits of mind of reading informational text with a high degree of attention.

FIGURE 9.4

Nonfiction Homework (Visualizing)

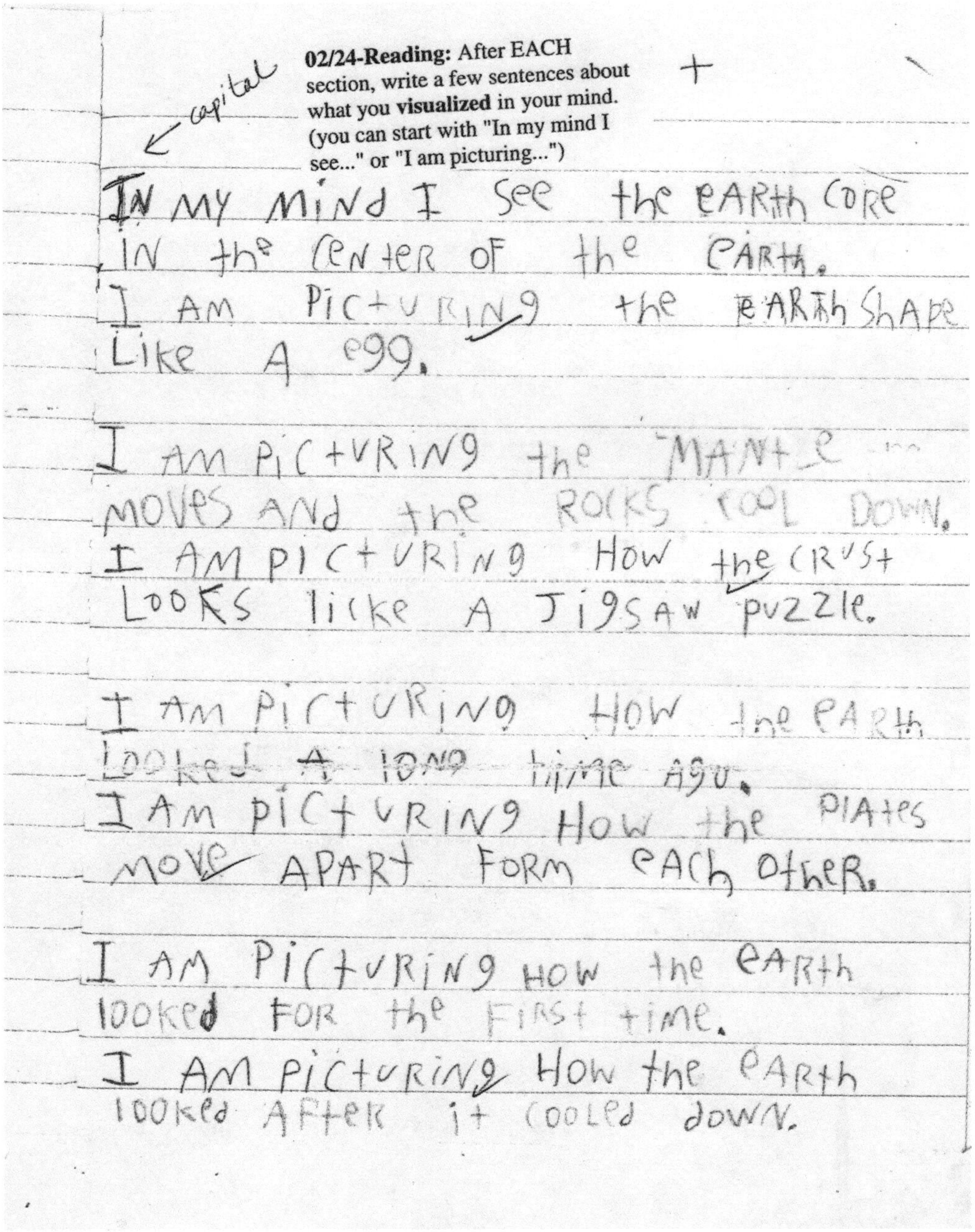

capital →

02/24-Reading: After EACH
section, write a few sentences about
what you **visualized** in your mind.
(you can start with "In my mind I
see..." or "I am picturing...")

+

In my mind I see the EARth CoRe
in the CeNteR of the eARth.
I AM PicturiNg the eARth Shape
Like A egg.

I AM PicturiNg the MANtle
MoVes ANd the RoCKs CooL DowN.
I AM picturiNg How the CRuSt
LooKs liiKe A JigsAw puzzle.

I AM PictURiNg How the eARth
looked A long time Ago.
I AM PicturiNg How the PlAtes
move APARt FoRM eACh otheR.

I AM PicturiNg How the eARth
looked FoR the FiRst time.
I AM picturiNg How the eARth
looked AfteR it CooLed dowN.

FIGURE 9.5

Nonfiction Homework (Summarizing)

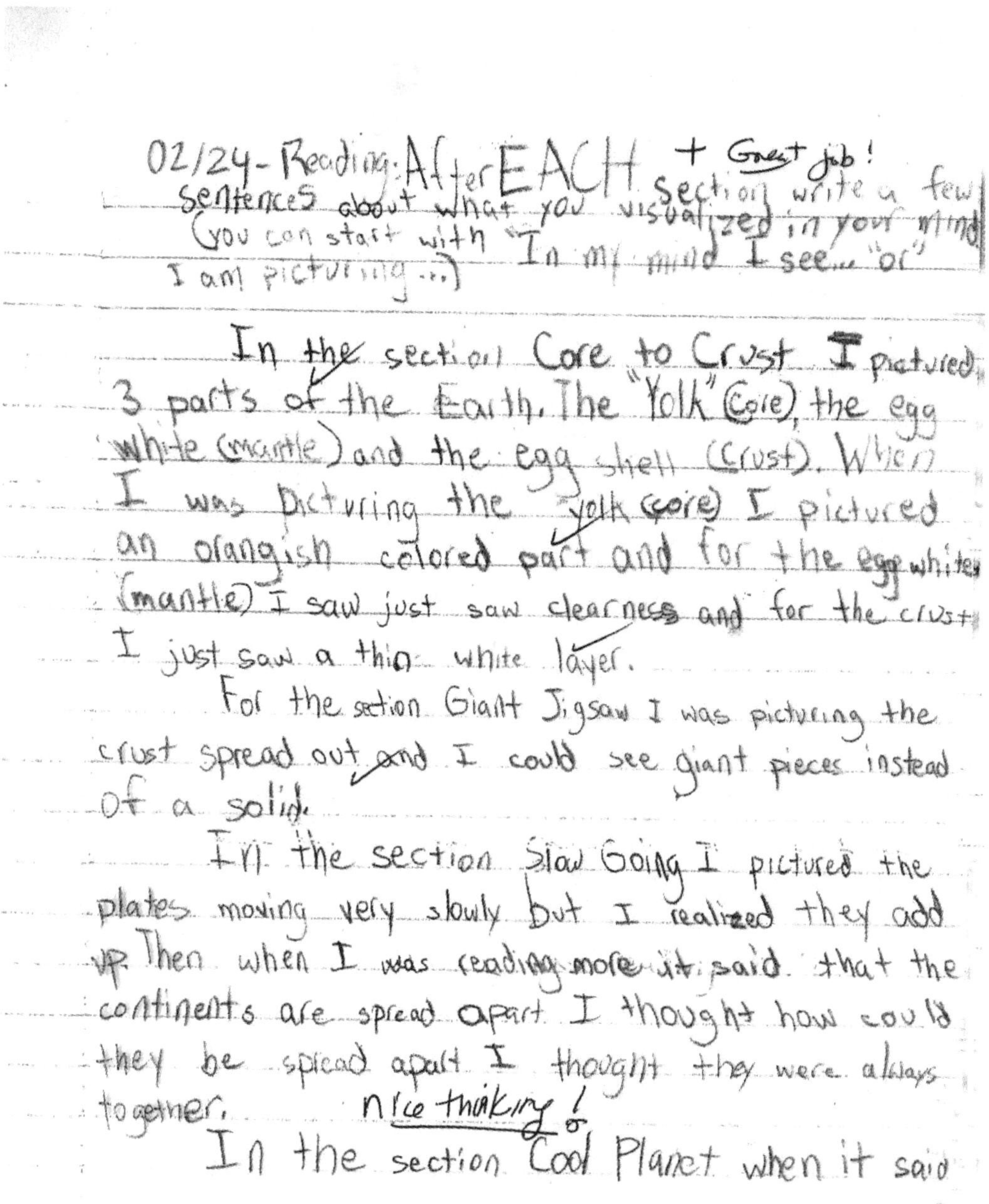

02/24 - Reading. After EACH + Great job! section write a few sentences about what you visualized in your mind (you can start with "In my mind I see... "or" I am picturing...")

In the section Core to Crust I pictured 3 parts of the Earth. The "Yolk" (core), the egg white (mantle) and the egg shell (Crust). When I was picturing the yolk (core) I pictured an orangish colored part and for the egg white (mantle) I saw just saw clearness and for the crust I just saw a thin white layer.

For the section Giant Jigsaw I was picturing the crust spread out and I could see giant pieces instead of a solid.

In the section Slow Going I pictured the plates moving very slowly but I realized they add up. Then when I was reading more it said that the continents are spread apart I thought how could they be spread apart I thought they were always together. *nice thinking!*

In the section Cool Planet when it said

Connections to State Assessments

Although reader's notebooks may not be a type of summative assessment, they play a role in preparing students for district and state standardized assessments. With the implementation of the Common Core State Standards have come calls for assessments that match the complexity of skills listed in the standards. In the domain of English language arts, for example, revisions in assessment design have stressed the need for more test items that evaluate higher-level cognitive skills, such as one's ability to compare, evaluate, hypothesize, analyze, and synthesize ideas and information as well as the capacity to write clearly with reference to evidence (Darling-Hammond et al. 2013). In a standardized test format, writing is the only practical way to assess individual knowledge and thinking. Impending social studies and science assessments in grades six to twelve are also likely to have fewer multiple-choice questions and more items that require students to analyze sources, to evaluate information, and to argue positions in writing (Breakstone, Smith, and Wineburg 2013).

Although reader's notebooks, as described in this book, do not use prompts to generate writing, they provide a critical foundation for the thinking that students need to do in these increasingly high-level, comprehension-driven assessments. With strategy lessons, students learn how to develop ideas independently, to present evidence for their opinions, to evaluate texts, and to synthesize understanding. The ongoing nature of reader's notebooks also means that students work up a comfort level, both mentally and physically, with expressing, explaining, and developing ideas through writing.

Final Thoughts

If there is one thing a teacher never has enough of, it's time. When planning instruction, all teachers, from elementary to high school, have to constantly make decisions about how to best use their time so that they attend to both academic development and student engagement. We know that it takes more—much more—than covering the standards to be a good teacher. How our students experience and perceive the learning and work they do in school matters greatly.

Perhaps that is why I am so drawn to the notebook as a vehicle for learning—because it supports both the academic and affective side of learning. Writing about reading helps to achieve many goals of reading comprehension standards in just about any grade. When students write about literature and the world of information, they are developing not only critical thinking but also content vocabulary, academic language, and background knowledge, all of which further strengthen a student's fluency, word-reading ability, and comprehension of text (Graham and Hebert 2011). By simply making choices about language and how to communicate ideas, students' writing skills also benefit.

At the same time, the reader's notebook cultivates many conditions considered essential for the affective side of learning to reach its potential: self-expression, motivation, self-efficacy, and risk taking. The reader's notebook is also a place where children grow, not just as students but as people. In between and beneath all the comprehension skills we can name are the kinds of life thinking we want our students to bring with them into the world: the ability to be reflective, to see situations from different perspectives, to evaluate information they are given, to question, to wonder. Through the act of writing and the personal space of a notebook, we can help our students become curious, thoughtful readers and thinkers, one strategy at a time.

Appendix A: Book Suggestions for Narrative Lessons

This appendix offers a list of books you may want to consider as read-alouds to support strategy lessons. Just about any read-aloud, especially chapter books, can be used with the lessons presented in this book. The purpose of these charts is to illustrate how a variety of books, presented in order of text complexity, align with the five categories of strategy lessons. Suggestions for each category are meant to offer ideas for strategy lessons as well as prompts for the "Try It." These are also characteristics of the book students might connect with on their own when writing their strategy entry. Three books, *The Bracelet*, *The Other Side*, and *The Watsons Go to Birmingham,* are considered historical fiction since they are about specific periods in American history and, therefore, could also be used with some of the informational strategy lessons in Chapter 5.

Thank You, Mr. Falker

Written and Illustrated by Patricia Polacco

Genre: *Memoir*

In this memoir, author Patricia Polacco recounts her personal and academic struggles as a child with dyslexia. She does not understand why she cannot read like everyone else. But when she meets her new teacher, Mr. Falker, he changes the way she sees letters on the page and how she sees herself.

QUESTIONING	• The different reactions to Patricia's disability give rise to questions about characters' motives.
	• Patricia's ability to hide her challenges could lead to different types of wondering about how it went unnoticed and whether it would be different today.
CONNECTING	• Many children can relate to both the experiences and feelings in this story of fear, intimidation, embarrassment, relief, and joy. They or their friends may also have dyslexia and can connect with her specific experience.
	• Patricia Polacco has written numerous memoir and fiction picture books that provide opportunities for many author and book connections.
ANALYZING	• There are several well-developed and contrasting characters to analyze, such as Mr. Falker, Eric the bully, and Patricia's grandmother, in addition to the main character.
	• Relationships between Patricia and the other characters vary greatly, providing students with significant opportunities to analyze how people affect one another.
SYNTHESIZING	• The story provides opportunities for students to integrate background knowledge about reading disabilities with new information about dyslexia.
	• The story has marked character development and underlying themes, making these types of thinking accessible for students.
EVALUATING	• The author uses noticeable craft techniques such as movement of time and flashbacks, use of font and italics, and effective description and dialogue.
	• Patricia Polacco's dual talents in writing and drawing offer students opportunities to notice how the two forms of craft complement and impact one another.

Readers Writing: Lessons for Responding to Narrative and Informational Text by Elizabeth Hale. Copyright © 2014. Stenhouse Publishers.

The Bracelet

Written by Yoshiko Uchida, Illustrated by Joanna Yardley

Genre: *Historical Fiction*

Emi, a young Japanese American girl, and her family are forced to leave their house and move into internment camps, which were created for Japanese Americans during World War II. Her best friend gives Emi a bracelet as a going-away present and reminder of their friendship.

QUESTIONING	• The perplexing concept of imprisoning Americans in their own country gives rise to many different questions about why and how this could happen.
	• Emi's personal story could inspire many wondering questions and theories about what she and her family could or might do.
CONNECTING	• The main character, Emi, goes through a range of emotions that give different students many opportunities to connect with emotionally and to consider how they would feel in this situation.
	• The story explores assumptions and prejudice regarding race and culture, which can encourage personal, book, movie, or world connections.
ANALYZING	• The divisive act of Japanese American internment camps can elicit strong reactions from readers and analysis about the human condition, including what ties us together and drives us apart.
	• Strong elements of symbolism in the story allow students to access this more complex type of thinking.
SYNTHESIZING	• Readers gather understanding of this period along with Emi and can think about how their understanding changes throughout the book.
	• The story offers a complex scenario in which to analyze different points of view and to consider why humans act the way they do.
EVALUATING	• The telling of this period in American history through Emi's voice allows students to evaluate the author's use of genre.
	• Uchida's use of detailed description and dialogue create opportunities to notice and assess effectiveness of author's craft.

The Other Side

Written by Jacqueline Woodson, Illustrated by E. B. Lewis

Genre: *Historical Fiction*

This powerful, symbolic story is written from the perspective of Clover, a young African American girl who is warned not to go to the other side of the wooden fence that runs behind her house and divides her segregated town. Clover becomes curious about the white girl her age who plays on the other side of the fence. The two girls gradually begin a friendship, eventually ignoring, temporarily, the boundary of the fence.

QUESTIONING	• This story of two girls in a racially divided world encourages global questions about race, prejudice, and society. • Students may wonder about the reactions of other children and adults in the story as well as what happens after the last page.
CONNECTING	• The girls' personal decisions create opportunities for students to consider what they would do in the characters' situation. • Some universal and familiar topics, such as including people in games, being told how to behave by adults, and being brave, run underneath the story and allow for many types of personal connections.
ANALYZING	• The story encourages analysis of global concepts such as societal rules, using one's judgment, and risk taking. • The strong symbolism in the divisive fence allows students to access this complex type of thinking.
SYNTHESIZING	• The gradual interaction between the two main characters offers opportunities for students to consider character and relationship development as the story progresses. • The fence creates a tangible image of division for students to consider different points of view.
EVALUATING	• Many sentences have more than one meaning, which allows opportunities to evaluate how the author uses the craft of writing both to describe and to include commentary on themes in the book. • The author's use of a simple story to portray the issues of race, both from a historical and social perspective, gives students opportunities to assess author decisions about craft and topic presentation.

The Watsons Go to Birmingham–1963

Written by Christopher Paul Curtis

Genre: *Historical Fiction*

An African American family full of personalities takes a car ride from their hometown of Flint, Michigan, to Birmingham, Alabama, in 1963. The story is told from the point of view of Kenny, a young boy with a charming sense of humor. Their visit to the South brings new experiences with racism, fear, and bravery. This family's story intersects with the true events of the 1963 Birmingham church bombing that killed four girls, adding fuel to the already growing civil rights movement.

QUESTIONING	• This book, which describes the humorous antics of Kenny and his family, becomes increasingly heavy with the issue of racism and lends itself to all sorts of questions, from small to universal. • Several dramatic experiences involving Kenny make him question his own understanding of events and could spark different types of wondering by the reader.
CONNECTING	• The Watson family offers students different types of personalities with which to make personal connections with people, family experiences, and family dynamics. • The fear and guilt that Kenny experiences after the church bombing are powerful emotions with which some students may connect.
ANALYZING	• The Watson family gives students a variety of character types and family dynamics to analyze. • The story contains numerous underlying themes, such as racism, injustice, growing up, family, and control.
SYNTHESIZING	• Since historical events are told through Kenny's voice, readers often go through different stages of realization about this family's connection to the event in Alabama. • The traumatic events in the book cause significant changes in several characters, which supports thinking about character development.
EVALUATING	• Christopher Paul Curtis writes through the unique and endearing voice of Kenny, who has distinctive ways to describe what he sees and thinks. Students may also think about how the author's use of the first-person voice affects the reader's experience. • The book includes several unique text features to notice such as the "in memory" page, use of black and white photographs on the cover, humorous chapter titles in handwritten font, and an epilogue.

Stargirl
Written by Jerry Spinelli

Genre: *Fiction*

Stargirl Carraway, a new student at Mica High School, stands out with her unique looks and behavior. She creates a lot of talk and reaction from her peers, especially from Leo, who starts to admire her individualistic spirit and way of seeing the world. As Leo adopts some of her odd behaviors, Stargirl tries to conform to society's standards and the two begin a relationship. But when Stargirl returns to her true self, Leo is caught between his feelings for her and other people's opinion of him.

QUESTIONING	• Stargirl is mysterious to characters in the story and sometimes to the reader, which can spark a variety of questions. • The actions of characters, highly influenced by others, are conducive to wondering about character motives.
CONNECTING	• Characters' experiences with peer pressure and the influence of popularity in a school setting can encourage strong personal connections for many students. • Students are likely to make connections with other media such as movies and television shows that touch on similar topics of friendship and societal influences at school.
ANALYZING	• The very real and personal topics of popularity and outsiders encourage analysis of teenage behavior. • Strong themes of society versus self, and the psychological play between the two, offers substantial material for analyzing human behavior.
SYNTHESIZING	• The many types of characters and interactions offer a wonderful context in which to consider the dynamics of school. • The emotional changes in Leo's perception of Stargirl supports thinking about character development.
EVALUATING	• This story touches on topics with which students are familiar so they can draw on background knowledge to assess the validity of descriptions of school life and the way the author portrays topics such as popularity and peer pressure. • The author's unique writing style and descriptions offer terrific material for students to evaluate author craft.

Appendix B: Book Suggestions for Nonfiction Lessons

This appendix offers a list of books you may want to consider as read-alouds to support nonfiction strategy lessons. Many different nonfiction picture books can be used with lessons in Chapter 5. The purpose of these charts is to illustrate how a variety of books, presented in order of text complexity, align with the five categories of strategy lessons. Suggestions for each category are meant to offer ideas for strategy lessons as well as prompts for the "Try It." These are also characteristics of the book students might connect with on their own when writing their strategy entry. Two books, *Snowflake Bentley* and *Pink and Say*, are written in story form and so can also be used with narrative strategy lessons in Chapter 3.

Pink and Say

Written by Patricia Polacco

Genre: *Historical Narrative*

A tender and true story about two boys in the Civil War, one white, one black, both fighting for the Confederate Army. This memoir is a story of friendship passed down to the following generations as much as it is a personal account of the deadly war between Americans.

QUESTIONING	• The developed characters of Pinkus, Sheldon, and Pinkus's mother, Moe Moe Bay, as well as the strong actions they take, provide opportunities to wonder and think about character motives.
	• The small story within the larger story of the Civil War provides opportunities for students to think about what they don't understand or wonder about this particular war.
CONNECTING	• The topic of war creates opportunities for world connections, including how other wars are similar and different from the Civil War.
	• Patricia Polacco has written numerous books, both fiction and historical fiction, creating many opportunities for author and book connections.
ANALYZING	• Characters' strong decisions and emotions lend themselves to analysis of characters and relationships between different characters.
	• The powerful themes of bravery, friendship, society, and oral history that underlie this story connect with universal concepts for students to examine.
SYNTHESIZING	• Story development around the handshake creates different layers of understanding throughout the book with its significance revealed at the end.
	• Students can merge background knowledge about the Civil War with information learned from this personal story about two soldiers.
EVALUATING	• The historical account told as a memoir provides opportunities for students to reflect about how genre affects tone, reader reaction, and learning information.
	• The variety of dialogue and vernacular speech as well as strong descriptions of emotion give students aspects of author craft to notice and evaluate.
	• Students can evaluate how the author's illustrations add to the understanding of the story, on both a literal and emotional level.

Readers Writing: Lessons for Responding to Narrative and Informational Text by Elizabeth Hale. Copyright © 2014. Stenhouse Publishers.

Martin's Big Words: The Life of Dr. Martin Luther King, Jr.

Written by Doreen Rappaport, Illustrated by Bryan Collier

Genre: *Biography*

This visually stunning book about Martin Luther King Jr. highlights the mission and voice of this important American civil rights leader. By incorporating parts of his "I Have a Dream" speech with informational text, the author and illustrator convey, in tandem with Martin's own words, his important messages about equality, nonviolence, and the power of language.

QUESTIONING	• Both the story of Martin Luther King Jr. and his untimely death may give rise to different types of questions about his life, our country's history, and the role of individuals in shaping society. • The global themes of hope, inequality, justice, and peace encourage universal questions about humanity.
CONNECTING	• There are many published picture books about Martin Luther King Jr. that provide opportunities for book connections. • Many students may make world, and possibly personal, connections to the struggles of a particular population of people or to King's emphasis on nonviolence.
ANALYZING	• The incorporation of Martin Luther King Jr.'s own words along with the author's offers terrific ground for analyzing the use of language and comparing and contrasting how word choice affects tone. • By learning of King's personal experiences, such as encountering the "White Only" signs, students have opportunities for analyzing his reactions, motives, and feelings as well as considering how they would act in his situation.
SYNTHESIZING	• Many students are familiar with Martin Luther King Jr. from a factual level. Throughout this book and after, students can synthesize how their perception of King has changed and how this portrayal affects their understanding of why he is such an important part of our country's history. • Students can make connections between aspects of King's message they already know with new information from this book.
EVALUATING	• The unique use of font and powerful images created by collage encourage evaluation of visual presentation and how an author's and illustrator's craft affect the reader's experience. • Students can evaluate how personal information provided in the author's and illustrator's notes at the start of the book can affect how a reader experiences the book.

From Seed to Plant

Written and Illustrated by Gail Gibbons

Genre: *Informational Nonfiction*

This colorful nonfiction book shows how a plant develops from a small seed. Readers learn about the interdependence of bees, plants, and weather; vivid illustrations include helpful labels and captions.

QUESTIONING	• Detailed descriptions of the life cycle and parts of a plant make room for many small questions, while the interdependence between bees and weather make room for more global questions about nature and ecosystems.
CONNECTING	• The familiar topic of plants and, for some students, gardening and growing seeds, presents opportunities for personal and knowledge connections. • Gail Gibbons has written numerous nonfiction books that offer many opportunities for author connections, particularly with *The Honey Makers*, since the overlapping of content encourages comparing and contrasting.
ANALYZING	• Students have opportunities to analyze the details of how a small seed becomes a plant and to infer criteria that impact growth and development. • Information about the life cycle of plants can encourage students to think about implications for global concepts, such as weather and environmental issues.
SYNTHESIZING	• Students can reflect on how their understanding of plants and the life cycles of a plant changes and develops throughout the book. • The intricate interdependence of birds, flowers, bees, and weather offer a great context for students to analyze relationships between living things and how a system works as a whole.
EVALUATING	• The use of labeling and varying sizes and perspectives of drawings to show information give students opportunities to evaluate illustrator craft. • The author's inclusion of a step-by-step guide for growing bean sprouts and a page of facts support observation and evaluation of text features.

Snowflake Bentley

Written by Jaqueline Briggs Martin, Illustrated by Mary Azarian

Genre: *Biography*

This uniquely illustrated picture book recounts the life of Wilson Bentley, whose hard work and passion greatly contributed to our current understanding of snowflakes. Each page includes sidebars of factual information related to snow and the development of the camera.

QUESTIONING	• Despite what we understand now about snowflakes and snow, there is still a mystery about their creation and uniqueness that encourages wondering. • Bentley's unusual dedication and work ethic may spark personal questions about his drive and motivation.
CONNECTING	• The familiar topic of snow, particularly for students who have played in snow, can lead to strong personal and knowledge connections. • Students may also make personal connections to photography and using a camera to see the world differently.
ANALYZING	• Readers see many sides of the main character, Snowflake Bentley, as they follow his life throughout the book. • Wilson Bentley's story touches on universal themes of perseverance, personal struggle, success and failure, and passion.
SYNTHESIZING	• Students can merge their background knowledge of snow with new information they learn about snowflakes and weather and reflect on how their understanding has changed. • The development of the camera plays an important role in Bentley's understanding of snowflakes throughout the book, which supports thinking about how this tool has changed from the start of Bentley's career to the present day.
EVALUATING	• The use of both narrative and informational text on each page offers terrific material for thinking about how an author's genre choices affect the reader in different ways. • The inclusion of an epilogue, a quote by Wilson Bentley, and photographs of Bentley and his snowflakes support observation and evaluation of text features and their influence on one's reading of the biography.

A Drop of Water: A Book of Science and Wonder

Written and Illustrated by Walter Wick

Genre: *Informational Nonfiction*

This book offers fascinating information about the many different states of water. Photographs capture the beauty of water in action, which is usually difficult to see in our everyday lives.

QUESTIONING	• Information about the journey of a drop of water touches on other topics, such as molecular makeup, motion, gravity, and light, making room for different kinds of information and knowledge questions. • The fascinating photographs of water in different shapes and contexts illicit many questions not brought up in the text.
CONNECTING	• The familiar topic of water and the different ways in which water is shown could inspire numerous personal, knowledge, and world connections. • Sections of the book that show water in relation to weather and the water cycle offer opportunities for students to make text connections and to consider how other books present the same information.
ANALYZING	• The written and visual descriptions of the various states of water with different materials are a great resource for analyzing interactions between water and other objects. • The close-up examination of water can evoke wondering and theories related to their own everyday experiences with water.
SYNTHESIZING	• Students can consider how their understanding of water, light, and the three states of matter evolves as they learn detailed information about these topics. • Using cues from section headings such as "How Clouds Form," "Soap Bubbles," and "Snowflakes," they can synthesize their understanding of how water behaves in general, regardless of context, state of matter, or shape.
EVALUATING	• The amazing photographs in this book offer opportunities to evaluate the use of photography in nonfiction, such as the author's use of multiple images to show change and perspective. • Students can consider how text features such as a summary page of all the topics, the use of quotations to start and end the book, and the author's biographical information contribute to the reader's experience.

Readers Writing: Lessons for Responding to Narrative and Informational Text by Elizabeth Hale. Copyright © 2014. Stenhouse Publishers.

Appendix C: Common Core Alignment: Narrative Lessons

The following charts illustrate alignment between narrative strategy lessons (and their page numbers in this book) and certain Reading Anchor Standards for Literature in the Common Core State Standards. Some lessons directly reflect stated standards, while others, just as important, support the quality of this type of thinking.

KEY IDEAS AND DETAILS

ANCHOR STANDARD	STRATEGY LESSONS	SUPPORTIVE STRATEGY LESSONS
CCRA.R.1 Read closely to determine what the text says explicitly and to make logical inferences from it; cite specific textual evidence when writing or speaking to support conclusions drawn from the text.	• Writing About Your Thinking . . . 35 • *Maybe* Theories . . . . 35 • Making a Theory . . . . 37 • I Think This Because . . . . 47 • For Example . . . . 48 • One Time . . . . 48 • Quoting Dialogue 49	• Wonder Questions . . . . 23 • Prediction Questions . . . . 24 • Small Questions . . . . 25 • Explaining Your Questions . . . . 37 • Wondering Without Questions 24
CCRA.R.2 Determine central ideas or themes of a text and analyze their development; summarize the key supporting details and ideas.	• Big Questions . . . . 25 • World Connections . . . . 33 • Theme Connections . . . . 33 • Analyzing Objects . . . . 43 • Symbolism in Objects . . . . 44 • Symbolism in Characters . . . . . . 46 • Book Themes 54	
CCRA.R.3 Analyze how and why individuals, events, or ideas develop and interact over the course of a text.	• Questioning a Character's Motive . . . 26 • Analyzing a Character . . . . 38 • How a Character Feels . . . . 40 • Analyzing Relationships . . . . . . 40 • Analyzing a Minor Character . . . 42 • Analyzing Minor Relationships . . 42 • Character Development . . . . 52 • Points of View 50	• Personal Connections . . . . 27 • Opinions of Characters . . . . 38 • Character Differences . . . . 30 • Feelings Connections . . . . 29 • Connections Without "Reminds me of . . . " 31

CRAFT AND STRUCTURE

ANCHOR STANDARD	STRATEGY LESSONS	SUPPORTIVE STRATEGY LESSONS
CCRA.R.4 Interpret words and phrases as they are used in a text, including determining technical, connotative, and figurative meanings, and analyze how specific word choices shape meaning or tone.	• Evaluating Author's Craft...... 60 • Evaluating Word Choice 61	• Noticing Author's Craft 60
CCRA.R.5 Analyze the structure of texts, including how specific sentences, paragraphs, and larger portions of the text (e.g., a section, a chapter, a scene, or a stanza) relate to one another and the whole.	• Evaluating Text Features.......58 • Evaluating Word Choice 61	• Noticing Big Text Features......57 • Noticing Small Text Features ...58 • Analyzing Scenes..............44
CCRA.R.6 Assess how point of view or purpose shapes the content and style of a text.	• Prior Knowledge Connections ..50 • Points of View 50	• In a Character's Shoes..........32

INTEGRATION OF KNOWLEDGE AND IDEAS

ANCHOR STANDARD	STRATEGY LESSONS	SUPPORTIVE STRATEGY LESSONS
CCRA.R.7 Integrate and evaluate content presented in diverse media and formats, including visually and quantitatively, as well as in words.	• Movie Connections 31	• Similar and Different 29
CCRA.R.8 Delineate and evaluate the argument and specific claims in a text, including the validity of the reasoning as well as the relevance and sufficiency of the evidence.	• Arguing Your Own Theory ..... 51 • Evaluating Topic Presentation...62	• Evaluating Character Development ....63 • Prior Knowledge Connections ..50
CCRA.R.9 Analyze how two or more texts address similar themes or topics to build knowledge or to compare the approaches the authors take.	• Book Connections............30	• Similar and Different ....29 • Back to the Book.............28

Readers Writing: Lessons for Responding to Narrative and Informational Text by Elizabeth Hale. Copyright © 2014. Stenhouse Publishers.

Appendix D: Common Core Alignment: Nonfiction Lessons

The following charts illustrate alignment between nonfiction strategy lessons (and their page numbers in this book) and certain Reading Anchor Standards for Informational Text in the Common Core State Standards. Some lessons directly reflect stated standards, while others, just as important, support the quality of this type of thinking.

KEY IDEAS AND DETAILS

ANCHOR STANDARD	NONFICTION STRATEGY LESSONS	SUPPORTIVE STRATEGY LESSONS
CCRA.R.1 Read closely to determine what the text says explicitly and to make logical inferences from it; cite specific textual evidence when writing or speaking to support conclusions drawn from the text.	• Confusion Questions . . . . .78 • Explaining Your Questions . . . . .89 • *Maybe* Theories. . . . . .89 • I Think This Because . . . . .92 • For Example 92	• Wonder Questions . . . . .77 • Small Questions . . . . .78 • Writing About Your Thinking . . .88 • Describing Your Reactions . . . . . 91 • "At First" Stories. . . . . 112 • My Mind Movie . . . . 110 • All My Senses. 111
CCRA.R.2 Determine central ideas or themes of a text and analyze their development; summarize the key supporting details and ideas.	• Big Questions. . . . . .79 • World Connections . . . . .84 • Before and After 96	• Then and Now 98
CCRA.R.3 Analyze how and why individuals, events, or ideas develop and interact over the course of a text.	• Personal Questions. . . . . 80 • Analyzing Feelings. . . . . 90 • Analyzing Relationships. 100	• Personal Connections. . . . . 81 • Similar and Different . . . . .85 • In Their Shoes. 98

CRAFT AND STRUCTURE

ANCHOR STANDARD	NONFICTION STRATEGY LESSONS	SUPPORTIVE STRATEGY LESSONS
CCRA.R.4 Interpret words and phrases as they are used in a text, including determining technical, connotative, and figurative meanings, and analyze how specific word choices shape meaning or tone.	• Language Connections. . . . . . . .87 • Noticing Author's Craft . . . . . . .102 • Vocabulary Connections 86	• Using Word Parts. . . . . 114 • "At First" Stories. . . . . 112 • Support from Text Features . . . .113 • Word Help from Text Features. .113 • Giving It a Try. 114
CCRA.R.5 Analyze the structure of texts, including how specific sentences, paragraphs, and larger portions of the text (e.g., a section, a chapter, a scene, or a stanza) relate to one another and the whole.	• Evaluating Author's Craft. 103	• Noticing Author's Craft 102
CCRA.R.6 Assess how point of view or purpose shapes the content and style of a text.	• Evaluating Topic Presentation . .108	• Evaluating Author's Craft. 103

Readers Writing: Lessons for Responding to Narrative and Informational Text by Elizabeth Hale. Copyright © 2014. Stenhouse Publishers.

INTEGRATION OF KNOWLEDGE AND IDEAS

ANCHOR STANDARD	NONFICTION STRATEGY LESSONS	SUPPORTIVE STRATEGY LESSONS
CCRA.R.7 Integrate and evaluate content presented in diverse media and formats, including visually and quantitatively, as well as in words.	• Knowledge Questions . . . . 80 • Movie Connections . . . . .83 • Putting It All Together . . . . .95 • Evaluating Illustrator's Craft . . .104 • Evaluating Text Features. . . . . . .106 • Evaluating Book Covers 107	• Before and After . . . . .96 • Opinions About Text Features . .106 • Noticing Illustrator's Craft. . . . .104 • Similar and Different 85
CCRA.R.8 Delineate and evaluate the argument and specific claims in a text, including the validity of the reasoning as well as the relevance and sufficiency of the evidence.	• On the Other Hand . . . . .99 • Evaluating Topic Presentation .108	
CCRA.R.9 Analyze how two or more texts address similar themes or topics in order to build knowledge or to compare the approaches the authors take.	• Book Connections. . . . . .82 • Author Connections. 84	• Similar and Different 85

Appendix E: Common Core Alignment: Writing and Speaking & Listening

The following charts illustrate how strategy lessons for both narrative and informational text, including the use of the partner share and whole-class share, support some of the key Anchor Standards for Writing and Speaking & Listening in grades 3–8 (NGA/CCSSO 2010).

ALIGNMENT WITH WRITING STANDARDS FOR GRADES 3–5

CCRA.W.1	Write opinion pieces on topics or texts, supporting a point of view with reasons and information.
CCRA.W.2	Write informative/explanatory texts to examine a topic and convey ideas and information clearly.
CCRA.W.9	Draw evidence from literary or informational texts to support analysis, reflection, and research.
CCRA.W.10	Write routinely over extended time frames (time for research, reflection, and revision) and shorter time frames (a single sitting or a day or two) for a range of discipline-specific tasks, purposes, and audiences.

ALIGNMENT WITH SPEAKING & LISTENING STANDARDS FOR GRADES 3–5

CCRA.SL.1	Engage effectively in a range of collaborative discussions (one-on-one, in groups, and teacher-led) with diverse partners on grade-level topics and texts, building on others' ideas and expressing their own clearly.
CCRA.SL.2	Paraphrase portions of a text read aloud or information presented in diverse media and formats, including visually, quantitatively, and orally.
CCRA.SL.3	Ask and answer questions about information from a speaker, offering appropriate elaboration and detail.
CCRA.SL.6	Differentiate between context that call for formal English (e.g., presenting ideas) and situations where informal discourse is appropriate (e.g., small-group discussion).

ALIGNMENT WITH WRITING STANDARDS FOR GRADES 6–8

CCRA.W.1	Write arguments to support claims with clear reasons and relevant evidence.
CCRA.W.2	Write informative/explanatory texts to examine a topic and convey ideas, concepts, and information through the selection, organization, and analysis of relevant content.
CCRA.W.9	Draw evidence from literary or informational texts to support analysis, reflection, and research.

ALIGNMENT WITH SPEAKING & LISTENING STANDARDS FOR GRADES 6–8

CCRA.SL.1	Engage effectively in a range of collaborative discussions (one-on-one, in groups, and teacher-led) with diverse partners on grade topics, texts, and issues, building on others' ideas and expressing their own clearly.
CCRA.SL.2	Analyze the main ideas and supporting details presented in diverse media and formats (e.g., visually, quantitatively, orally) and explain how the ideas clarify a topic, text, or issue under study.
CCRA.SL.3	Delineate a speaker's argument and specific claims, evaluating the soundness of the reasoning and the relevance and sufficiency of the evidence.
CCRA.SL.4	Present claims and findings, sequencing ideas logically and using pertinent descriptions, facts, details, and examples to accentuate the main ideas or themes; use appropriate eye contact, adequate volume, and clear pronunciation.
CCRA.SL.5	Write routinely over extended time frames (time for research, reflection, and revision) and shorter time frames (a single sitting or a day or two) for a range of discipline-specific tasks, purposes, and audiences.

Bibliography

Allen, J. 2008. *More Tools for Teaching Content Literacy*. Portland, ME: Stenhouse.

Anderson, C. 2000. *How's It Going? A Practical Guide to Conferring with Student Writers*. Portsmouth, NH: Heinemann.

Anderson, L. W., and D. R. Krathwohl, eds. 2001. *A Taxonomy for Learning, Teaching, and Assessing: A Revision of Bloom's Taxonomy of Educational Objectives*. Boston: Allyn and Bacon.

Angelillo, J. 2003. *Writing About Reading: From Book Talk to Literary Essays, Grades 3–8*. Portsmouth, NH: Heinemann.

Beck, I., and M. McKeown. 2001. "Inviting Students into the Pursuit of Meaning." *Educational Psychology Review* 13 (3): 225–241.

Beck, I., M. McKeown, and L. Kucan. 2002. *Bringing Words to Life: Robust Vocabulary Instruction*. Portland, ME: Stenhouse.

Bloom, B. S., ed. 1956. *Taxonomy of Educational Objectives: The Classification of Educational Goals*. Book 1, *Cognitive Domain*. New York: David McKay.

Blume, J. 1978. *Freckle Juice*. New York: Yearling.

Breakstone, J., M. Smith, and S. Wineburg. 2013. "Beyond the Bubble in History/Social Studies Assessments." *Phi Delta Kappan* 94 (5): 53–57.

Buckner, A. 2009. *Notebook Connections: Strategies for the Reader's Notebook*. Portland, ME: Stenhouse.

Calkins, L. 1994. *The Art of Teaching Writing*. Portsmouth, NH: Heinemann.

————. 2000. *The Art of Teaching Reading*. Portsmouth, NH: Heinemann.

Calkins, L., M. Ehrenworth, and C. Lehman. 2012. *Pathways to the Common Core: Accelerating Achievement*. Portsmouth, NH: Heinemann.

Cappellini, M. 2005. *Balancing Reading and Language Learning*. Portland, ME: Stenhouse.

Cazden, C. 2001. *Classroom Discourse: The Language of Teaching and Learning*. Portsmouth, NH: Heinemann.

Chalk, K., and L. A. Bizo. 2004. "Specific Praise Improves On-Task Behaviour and Numeracy Enjoyment: A Study of Year Four Pupils Engaged in the Numeracy Hour." *Educational Psychology in Practice* 20 (4): 335–51.

Chen, Y., M. Thompson, J. Kromrey, and G. Chang. 2011. "Relations of Student Perceptions of Teacher Oral Feedback with Teacher Expectancies and Student Self-Concept." *Journal of Experimental Education* 79: 452–77.

Curtis, C. P. 1995. *The Watsons Go to Birmingham—1963*. New York: Random House.

Daniels, H. 2002. *Literature Circles: Voice and Choice in Book Clubs & Reading Groups*. Portland, ME: Stenhouse.

Darling-Hammond, L., J. Herman, J. Pellegrino, J. Abedi, J. L. Aber, E. Baker, R. Bennett et al. 2013. *Criteria for High-Quality Assessment*. Stanford, CA: Stanford Center for Opportunity Policy in Education.

Dodge, J. 2009. *25 Quick Formative Assessments for a Differentiated Classroom: Easy, Low-Prep Assessments That Help You Pinpoint Students' Needs and Reach All Learners*. New York: Scholastic.

Duke, N. K., and P. Pearson. 2002. "Effective Practices for Developing Reading Comprehension." In *What Research Has to Say About Reading Instruction*. 3rd ed., ed. A. E. Farstrup and S. Samuels, 205–42. Newark, DE: International Reading Association.

Durkin, D. 1978. "What Classroom Observations Reveal About Reading Comprehension Instruction." *Reading Research Quarterly* 14 (4): 481–533.

Dweck, C.S. 2000. *Self-Theories: Their Role in Motivation, Personality and Development.* Philadelphia: Psychology Press.

Eccles, J., C. Midgley, A. Wigfield, C. Buchanan, D. Reumen, C. Flanagan, and D. Iver. 1993. "Development During Adolescence: The Impact of Stage-Environment Fit on Young Adolescents' Experiences in Schools and Families." *American Psychologist* 48 (2): 90–191.

Fisher, D., D. Ross, and M. Grant. 2010. "Building Background Knowledge: Improving Student Achievement Through Wide Reading." *The Science Teacher* 77 (1): 23–26.

Fountas, I., and G. S. Pinnell. 2000. *Guiding Readers and Writers (Grades 3–6): Teaching Comprehension, Genre, and Content Literacy.* Portsmouth, NH: Heinemann.

Fountas, I., and G. S. Pinnell. 2001. *Guiding Readers and Writers: Teaching, Comprehension, Genre, and Content Literacy.* Portsmouth, NH: Heinemann.

Gibbons, G. 1993. *From Seed to Plant.* New York: Holiday House.

———. 2000. *The Honey Makers.* New York: HarperCollins.

Graesser, A., M. Singer, and T. Trabasso. 1994. "Constructing Inferences During Narrative Text Comprehension." *Psychological Review* 101 (3): 371–395.

Graham, S., and M. Hebert. 2011. "Writing to Read: A Meta-analysis of the Impact of Writing and Writing Instruction on Reading." *Harvard Educational Review* 81 (4): 710–744.

Hale, E. 2008. *Crafting Writers, K–6.* Portland, ME: Stenhouse.

Hallam, S., J. Price, and G. Katsarou. 2002. "The Effects of Background Music on Primary School Pupils' Task Performance." *Educational Studies* 28 (2): 111–122.

Harvey, S., and A. Goudvis. 2007. *Strategies That Work: Teaching Comprehension for Understanding and Engagement.* Portland, ME: Stenhouse.

Johnston, P. 2004. *Choice Words: How Our Language Affects Children's Learning.* Portland, ME: Stenhouse.

Lesaux, N., and M. Kieffer. 2010. "Exploring Sources of Reading Comprehension Difficulties Among Language Minority Learners and Their Classmates in Early Adolescence." *American Education Research Journal* 47(3): 596–632.

Lesaux, N., M. Kieffer, S. E. Faller, and J. Kelley. 2010. "The Effectiveness and Ease of Implementation of an Academic Vocabulary Intervention for Linguistically Diverse Students in Urban Middle Schools." *Reading Research Quarterly* 45 (2): 196–228.

Lesaux, N., and S. Marietta. 2012. *Making Assessment Matter: Using Test Results to Differentiate Reading Instruction.* New York: Guilford.

Lord, C. 2008. *Rules.* New York: Scholastic.

Martin, J. B. 1998. *Snowflake Bentley.* Boston: Houghton Mifflin.

McKeown, M., I. Beck, R. Omanson, and M. Pople. 1985. "Some Effects of the Nature and Frequency of Vocabulary Instruction on the Knowledge and Use of Words." *Reading Research Quarterly* 20: 522–535.

Mueller, C., and C. Dweck. 1998. "Praise for Intelligence Can Undermine Children's Motivation and Performance." *American Psychological Association* 75 (1): 33–52.

National Governors Association Center for Best Practices, Council of Chief State School

Officers (NGA/CCSSO). 2010. *Common Core State Standards.* Washington, DC: National Governors Association Center for Best Practices, Council of Chief State School Officers.

Neuman, S. B. 2006. "The Knowledge Gap: Implications for Early Education." *Handbook of Early Literacy Research* 2: 29–40.

Ortiz-Marrero, F., and K. Sumaryono. 2010. "Success with ELLs." *English Journal* 99 (6): 93–96.

Pearson, P. D., and M. C. Gallagher. 1983. "The Instruction of Reading Comprehension." *Contemporary Educational Psychology* 8: 317–344.

Pinnell, G. S., and P. Scharer. 2003. *Teaching for Comprehension in Reading, Grade K–2: Strategies for Helping Children Read with Ease, Confidence, and Understanding.* New York: Scholastic.

Polacco, P. 1994. *Pink and Say.* New York: Philomel Books.

———. 1997. *Thunder Cake.* New York: Puffin.

———. 1998. *Thank You, Mr. Falker.* New York: Philomel Books.

Rappaport, D. 2007. *Martin's Big Words: The Life of Dr. Martin Luther King, Jr.* New York: Hyperion.

Ruddell, R. B., and N. J. Unrau. 2004. "Reading as a Meaning-Construction Process: The Reader, the Text, and the Teacher." In *Theoretical Models and Processes of Reading.* 5th ed., ed. R. B. Ruddell and N. J. Unrau, 1462–1521. Newark, DE: International Reading Association.

Ryan, R., and E. Deci. 2000. "Self-Determination Theory and the Facilitation of Intrinsic Motivation, Social Development, and Well Being." *American Psychologist* 55 (1): 68–78.

Serravallo, J., and G. Goldberg. 2007. *Conferring with Readers: Supporting Each Student's Growth and Independence.* Portsmouth, NH: Heinemann.

Simon, S. 2004. *Space Travelers.* San Francisco: Chronicle Books.

Simonsen, B., D. Myers, and C. DeLuca. 2010. "Teaching Teachers to Use Prompts, Opportunities to Respond, and Specific Praise." *Teacher Education and Special Education: The Journal of the Teacher Education Division of the Council for Exceptional Children* 33 (4): 300–318.

Snow, C. 2002. *Reading for Understanding: Toward an R&D Program in Reading Comprehension.* Santa Monica, CA: RAND.

Spandel, V. 2006. "In Defense of Rubrics." *English Journal* 96 (1): 19–22.

Spinelli, J. 2002. *Stargirl.* New York: Random House.

Stead, T. 2002. *Is That a Fact? Teaching Nonfiction Writing K–3.* Portland, ME: Stenhouse.

———. 2006. *Reality Checks: Teaching Reading Comprehension with Nonfiction.* Portland, ME: Stenhouse.

Taylor, M. 1991. *Roll of Thunder, Hear My Cry.* New York: Puffin.

Uchida, Y. 1996. *The Bracelet.* New York: Puffin.

Vasilyeva, M., and H. Waterfall. 2011. "Variability in Language Development: Relation to Socioeconomic Status and Environmental Input." In *Handbook of Early Literacy Research.* Vol. 3, ed. S. Neuman and D. Dickinson, 36–48. New York: Guilford.

Wick, W. 1997. *A Drop of Water: A Book of Science and Wonder.* New York: Scholastic.

Woodson, J. 2001. *The Other Side.* New York: Putman Juvenile.

Zinsser, W. 1998. *On Writing Well.* 6th ed. New York: HarperCollins.